P9-DEE-732

THE OGALLALA ROAD

A Memoir of Love and Reckoning

JULENE BAIR

VIKING

VIKING
Published by the Penguin Group
Penguin Group (USA) LLC
375 Hudson Street
New York, New York 10014

USA | Canada | UK | Ireland | Australia | New Zealand | India | South Africa | China
penguin.com
A Penguin Random House Company

First published by Viking Penguin, a member of Penguin Group (USA) LLC, 2014

LIBRARY OF CONGRESS CATALOGING-IN-PUBLICATION DATA
Bair, Julene, author.
The Ogallala road : a memoir of love and reckoning / Julene Bair.
pages cm
ISBN 978-0-670-78604-6
1. Agriculture—Environmental aspects—Kansas. 2. Family farms—Kansas.
3. Farm life—Kansas. 4. Kansas—Social life and customs. 5. Bair, Julene—Homes
and haunts—Kansas. 6. Agricultural conservation—Kansas. 7. Ogallala Aquifer.
I. Title.
S589.757.K2B35 2014
636'.0109781—dc23
2013036969

Printed in the United States of America
1 3 5 7 9 10 8 6 4 2

Set in New Caledonia LT Std
Designed by BTDNYC

Penguin is committed to publishing works of quality and integrity.
In that spirit, we are proud to offer this book to our readers;
however, the story, the experiences, and the words
are the author's alone.

FOR

Jake, Abby, Josh, Indy,
Jessamin, Jovanni, and Avery

The highest good is like water.
Water gives life to the
ten thousand things and does not
strive.

—LAO TZU, *Tao Te Ching*

Contents

1
A RARE FIND

Falling in love is like reading a novel, it's an act of imagination, a suspension of disbelief.

—MARY ALLEN, *Rooms of Heaven*

1

THESE WERE CALLED THE HIGH PLAINS BECAUSE THEY WERE FOUR THOUSAND FEET ABOVE SEA LEVEL. I could feel the altitude in the way the sun sheeted my skin. It was like standing too close to a fire with no means of escaping, unless I dashed back to the car and switched on the air conditioner. Instead, I trudged through wheat stubble that used to be the south end of our pasture, my shoes filling with powdery dirt and my socks with stickers.

This western Kansas land had belonged to the Carlsons, my mother's side of the family. When I was sixteen, my parents traded their share in it for land elsewhere in the county. Like many other successful farmers, they built a new house in town. More than three decades had passed since then. Although I knew there wouldn't be water in the creek here, I wanted to walk down its dry bed as I had in childhood, picking up every shiny piece of agate I saw, hoping to discover an arrowhead.

In the dry places, men begin to dream, wrote Wright Morris, who grew up north of here, in Nebraska. *Where rivers run sand, something in man begins to flow.* I thought I knew exactly what he meant. The sandy beds of dry creeks unfurl evocatively into the beckoning distance, inscribing their faint script over the land. They entice the exploring spirit.

But when I arrived at the Little Beaver, I discovered that the creek was now nothing more than a depression. Runoff from all the newly farmed pastureland had filled it with silt. Weeds grew where there had once been smooth sand, vacant and pinkish tan. In my childhood, the sand had poured sensuously through my hands, each granule having its own color, shape, size, sheen.

Our sense of beauty is a survival instinct, telling us that a place can sustain us for generations to come. I'd always known this in my bones, but it wasn't until many years after I left Kansas and discovered my passion for wilderness that the intuition became conscious. This creek was now ugly. That didn't bode well for the underlying aquifer's ability to support life in the future. Rain and snowmelt couldn't filter into the ground as efficiently through dirt as it could through sand. And sandy creek bottoms were critical to the meager half inch of recharge that the aquifer received each year. It needed all it could get because irrigation farmers were allowed to pump forty times that amount.

At least the north end of the pasture remained in grass. Standing here as a child, I often pretended that this was the original Kansas, "pre-us." The low-growing grass stitched itself over the ground like a wooly tapestry, accented, especially in the spring, by other pastels. Blue grama grass. Apricot mallow. The yellow and cream waxen blooms of cactus and yucca. Prairie dogs chirped alarms from mounds of whitish clay, and meadowlarks sang from their perches on yucca spires, their notes climbing and dipping like winding ribbons. Instead of cows, I imagined buffalo grazing the hills. The grass had been named after the buffalo because millions of them once thrived on it.

We'd called this our canyon pasture because the creek had carved some cliffs into the otherwise smooth terrain. The canyon was really no more than an "interruption in the earth," as my mother called it. But it was the wildest topography in this part of the county.

The one-room school that she'd attended—and that my brothers and I also went to, before the farm schools were closed and we started riding the bus to town—used to hold field trips here. The boys would try to throw rocks across the canyon, and in its shadowy ruts and ravines, we caught orange-speckled lizards as they dashed beneath the bayonet-shaped leaves of yucca. I remembered my brother Clark's hand on my arm, cautioning me to look closely before grabbing. Once, we heard a buzzing sound and jumped back from the bush I'd been about to reach beneath. A tongue-flicking, tail-rattling snake lay coiled at our feet. Its vibrant, diamond-shaped head bobbed in the air, mouth open, fangs bared.

"Why is it wiggling its tongue at us?" I asked.

"That's how it smells you," said Bruce. Also my elder, but closer to my age than Clark, he loved nothing more than goading me.

"It can't strike this far though," Clark said. "We're safe."

The Little Beaver made a horseshoe turn here. Our old windmill stood on the spit of land formed by the bend. When I paid visits to the canyon as a child, my father's ewes and their lambs would be drinking out of the low troughs. They would scatter as I approached, their hooves sounding like water riffling over rock. But today only a few cattle grazed the hill above the canyon, moving in and out of the shadows of cumulus clouds.

I used to climb the windmill and sit up there for what seemed like hours, transfixed by the shadows. They might have been cast by lily pads or boats on the bottom of a lake. From that height, I could also see our big house's red roof rising above a shelterbelt of elms. But if I climbed the windmill's narrow ladder today, I knew too well that I would not see our roof or even the trees.

My grandfather Carlson had built the house high on a knoll. With stately trees and a huge red barn beside it, it had been a landmark, visible for miles around. Now it was as if all evidence of our existence had been erased by the wandlike arm of the center-pivot irrigation sprinkler I'd parked beside. Like all the sprinklers that circled these plains, this one was made from an eighth mile of pipe strung between steel towers. Along the pipe's length, hoses hung down with spigots on the ends, spraying a uniform mist over a 130-acre circle of six-foot-tall, fully tasseled corn.

I could hear the pump engine's growl, pulsating on the morning's mounting heat. It hadn't been like this in the midsixties, when we left this place. It had been quiet then. But now in this second year of the new millennium, you couldn't escape that sound on the High Plains. Our current farm, only about ten miles from here as the crow flew, was no exception. We had five irrigation wells, some of which ran all day and all night during the growing season.

We drew the water from the most plentiful source of groundwater in the country. The Ogallala Aquifer was the hope and promise at the center of the nation, the source of life that had made habitation possible for millions of years before the words "United States," or any words, for that matter, had been coined. On geologists' maps, it was roughly the shape of a tornado, wide at the top where it lay under parts of South Dakota, Wyoming, and Nebraska, and narrowing to a funnel in Texas, where farmers had been irrigating longest. The maps indicated depletion rates in colors ranging from blue, in much of Nebraska where water was still plentiful, to brown and almost black in some parts of Kansas and north Texas. Meaning gone. Pumped dry, or at least to below usable levels. Those dark freckles of high decline were spreading like cancers, gradually enlarging and taking over hundreds of square miles.

The windmill's fan whirred and the well rods creaked up and down, making a tinny, lonely sound. Water spurted from the pipe into a tank. These, not the growl of irrigation engines, were the sounds I equated with water while growing up. The rhythm was systolic, soothing. I washed my arms and face in the transparent rope, which fattened and thinned as the windmill breathed. I drank. "The best water in the world," Mom used to say. She was right. Going down my throat, it felt as cold and bright as the sunlight was hot and bright.

"Cussed wind!" she also used to say, almost every time she stepped out of the house. But Kansas settlers must have been grateful for the wind. Every drink it pumped must have felt like an answered prayer, relief from the surface realities. Digging a good well would have been like tapping unexpected kindness in a mail-order spouse. Having what you were stuck with turn out to be all right after all.

I removed my cap and put my head under the pipe. When I stood up, ice-cold rivulets ran down my back. I took in the vista, looking north into the neighbor's pasture, at unmarred distance. Too steep to plow, the hills above the Little Beaver were still simple beauty. Grass and sky. Minimalism at its best. I imagined that the green rolled over the valley's rim and continued unfenced until it disappeared around the curve of the earth.

BACK ON THE GRAVEL ROAD, I MADE my way northeast, stopping each time I came to a bridge over the Little Beaver and walking along the bed. After crossing the county line, the land grew craggy with continuous canyons and ravines that were far deeper than our little "interruption in the earth." This was such classic Indian terrain that the county had been named after the Cheyenne, the last tribe that had hunted and camped here. It was too rugged to farm, and without dirt eroding from plowed fields, the bed of the Little Beaver was again the familiar sand of childhood, large grained with many pink and yellow quartzite beads.

The banks became steeper, and standing in the cool shade on the south side of the bed, I thought I could smell moisture. This, I realized, was what excited my dryland spirit most about rivers that ran sand—the possibility that farther on, if I followed their sinewy curves long enough, I would come to a place where they ran water.

I hoped to discover one of the springs that the Indians and pioneers traveling west to the Denver goldfields had camped beside, and that the county's first settlers had built beside. Last year, my family had pumped two hundred million gallons out of the Ogallala Aquifer. That was not an unusual amount for an irrigated farm. But there were thousands of irrigators, and all that pumping drew the water table down and robbed what little surface water there once was. I knew that whatever I did or didn't find would be commentary on my family, an indicator of the price the land had paid for our comfort.

"Please let me find you," I prayed. "Let you still be here."

Pulling to a stop at yet another bridge over the dry creek bed, I saw the dark green shimmer of a lone cottonwood tree far down the bank. A cottonwood sighting means not only welcome shade but also the possibility of water. I smeared on another coat of sunscreen and retied my shoes. Thinking, Snake, Snake, stay away from me, oh Snake, I stepped gingerly through sunflowers and other thick weeds, spread two loose strands of barbed wire, and crawled between them into the pasture.

Part of the creek bank had caved in, leaving at shoulder level an overhang of buffalo grass sod. On the underside, thick masses of roots hung all the way to my feet. I breathed in the musty, earthen smell, lifted the tresses, let them fall. The creek bottom seemed darker here. Leaning down, I pressed my knuckles into the sand and discovered it was damp!

I FOUND THE POND LYING STILL AND innocent, a receptive, vulnerable reflection of the sky. This wasn't rainwater. It hadn't rained in weeks. My brother Bruce had been managing our farm since our father died— four years ago now, in 1997. He had told me he was worried that the ground would be too parched to plant dryland winter wheat this September. No. This pond was what the pioneers and early settlers had called live water. It had found the surface by itself without the aid of rain, or today, a rancher's pump. It came from the aquifer, exhaling into the bed of the Little Beaver.

I dragged a stick, clearing algae away, and laid my palm on the sun-warmed surface. The water wasn't beautiful or bracing or clear like in a mountain lake. But it inspired tenderness in me because it was in danger. How large had the pond been forty years ago, before we started irrigating? Had the creek run all the way from here to the Republican River, a distance of about thirty miles?

A puff of breeze rippled through the cottonwood's upper branches. The leaves sparkled and fluttered, making the sound of rushing water. Thousands of thirsty plainspeople, be they Indians or pioneers, had probably taken heart as I had today, seeing the shimmer of those leaves in the distance, then hearing that sound while drawing near. This place ought to have a tall fence around it, I thought. A monument should be erected. Here was a destination that truly did warrant school field trips.

But I couldn't stand there and worship the water any longer. The sun was bearing down on me from overhead, and a hundred yards beyond the pool, several pairs of large brown eyes in broad white faces looked warily in my direction. The cottonwood beckoned from the bank. To make way for the cows, I climbed out of the creek.

SQUATTING IN THE SHADE, I TOOK SUCH liberal gulps from my father's jug that dribbles ran down my chin. Mom had filled it with iced tea for me that morning, the way she used to do for Dad. It tasted of chlorine, terrible compared with the water I'd drunk a couple of hours ago directly out of the ground in our old canyon pasture.

This is who I am, I thought. It had been too long since I'd last done this type of solitary exploring. Motherhood, for one thing, had prevented it. I felt my pocket for my cell phone, to call my son, Jake. If he didn't answer, it would mean he'd made it to work that morning. I knew that he'd gotten home before ten last night, as I'd instructed, because I'd had a friend check on him. "You're treating me like a kindergartner," Jake had complained.

No answer. Good. As I was preparing to leave a message, I heard a familiar clanging noise. I looked up to see a white pickup coming down the hill pulling an empty metal stock trailer behind it. Great! I thought. Now I've got to deal with some yokel out here in the middle of nowhere.

I tried to warn you, my mother said in my head, where she'd resided for as long as I could remember. "Be careful gallivantin' out there all by yourself," she'd cautioned me that morning as I left her house in town. "I've been gallivantin' my whole life," I'd told her. I could change a tire if I had to. I saw from the way her lips pressed together what she was thinking. She could change a tire too. That had not been what she meant.

Although I doubted that the man in the pickup would rape me, neither was it likely he would appreciate my being on his property. I wanted to vanish, but it would have been ridiculous to be seen hopping into the ravine. So I stood up.

My sudden appearance spooked the blue heeler who rode on the pickup's flat bed. He barked frantically until the truck drew to a stop beside me and his owner shouted, "Can it, Spider!"

"Hello," I said. The dog was keeping me pinned in the gaze of one blue and one brown eye. His lip edged up over canines as he emitted a low growl. "I don't mean to trespass," I said. "I was just looking for springs."

The man got out of his pickup. A half foot taller than I, broad shouldered and large boned, he had the dry, dusty look I expected in plainsmen, his skin sun darkened, his blond mustache sun streaked. He pointed toward the creek. "I guess you found this one."

"Yes. It's so hot out, though. The shade looked inviting."

He extended a hand. "Ward Allbright."

"Julene Bair. I grew up not far from here."

It surprised me that he didn't seem to recognize my surname. There weren't many people in those two counties, Cheyenne and Sherman, who hadn't heard of my father, Harold Bair. He'd been well known for his large herd of sheep. This was mainly cattle country. Ward clasped my hand hard enough to register respect anyway, maybe for my freedom to wander wherever I chose. "Don't worry," he said. "I don't think Conway would care. I came up to collect these horses I loaned his daughter." He raised his chin toward the hill above us where two bays—a mare and a half yearling—grazed. "For a 4-H project."

"This is the first time I ever saw a spring in the Little Beaver. Can you believe that?"

He nodded. "There're plenty of them, but when you're a kid, you don't know anything other than what's out your back door."

"Used to be plenty of them," I said. "I've read that more than seven hundred miles of Kansas creeks and rivers no longer flow."

"Is that a fact?"

"It's a shame what we're doing to the water."

He looked perplexed. Oh boy, I thought. Was I about to have a political argument with one of those fanatics who thinks that owning land gives him the right to abuse whatever was on or under it? Then I reminded myself that here in Kansas it was I who would be considered the fanatic. I probably sounded like one now.

Ward said, "Hey, didn't you write that book? I recognize you from the picture on the back of it."

This was surprising, to say the least. Besides my mother, the only locals I knew who'd read my essay collection had been one fourth-grade and one high school English teacher.

"I liked that book so much," Ward said, pausing to reminisce. "It had this melancholy quality about it that reminded me of *The Last Picture Show*. Larry McMurtry. I'm sure you know his work."

"Not as well as I should." In fact, I hadn't gotten around to Mc-Murtry.

"I even considered writing to you. I figured your publisher would forward the letter."

"You wanted to write to me?" I asked. "Why didn't you?"

"Oh sure, now. You would have thought I was some kind of nut case."

"No, I would have been flattered." I looked up into the shadow his hat cast. For the first time, I noticed his eyes—an arresting Caribbean sea green.

I lowered my gaze. Dark circles stained the underarms of his T-shirt, a light-gray color that a man would grab on a routine morning when he didn't expect anything new to happen. And nothing new was going to happen. After all, this guy wore a silver belt buckle. Burnished by years of wear, it featured your standard calf roper. Jake's dad had cured me of my cowboy fascination.

I could imagine how I looked. After dousing my head at the windmill, I'd just jammed my cap back on. It had the word "Vedauwoo" embroidered on it below a silhouette of that granite mountain range—one of my favorite haunts near Laramie, Wyoming, the town where I lived.

Ward's cap also bore a Wyoming emblem. King Ropes, a famous saddler.

"Do you read much?" I asked.

"Winters get long when you live in the country, and I always liked a good book." Taking a blue kerchief from his hip pocket, he removed his hat, revealing a high forehead. No ring, I couldn't help but notice as he wiped his brow. But ranch and farm types didn't always wear rings. Dad hadn't.

"Could use a little of that winter weather now," Ward said. "My favorite author is Cormac McCarthy."

Were we really standing in a Kansas pasture? Louis L'Amour I might have expected, or Zane Gray. "I like the way he drops into Spanish," I said. "'*Soy yo que traigo las yeguas de las montañas.*'"

"You memorized that," Ward said. "What does it mean?"

"'Tis I who brings the mares from the mountains," I declaimed. "When I taught at the University of Wyoming several years ago, I always assigned *All the Pretty Horses*. Even though I think McCarthy was intentionally overromantic in that book. He was playing with the cowboy myth."

"I don't know about that," Ward said. His tone made me wonder if he'd ever heard the two words "myth" and "cowboy" together before. "I'll admit McCarthy did get some of the details wrong," he continued. "Did you notice that whenever those two boys went into a saloon, they would take their cigarettes out of their shirt pockets and put 'em on the bar top? Now a cowboy just wouldn't do that."

"What would a cowboy do?"

"He'd leave 'em in his pocket, take 'em out when he wanted one, then put 'em back."

This had to be the most ridiculous cowboy rule I'd ever heard, and I'd heard a lot of them. I glanced at Ward's roughout leather boots and his jeans, bunched at the ankle. Jake's dad used to stand before the mirror making sure his pant legs bunched exactly like that. He'd explained that a cowboy wore his pants long so they wouldn't appear too short when he straddled a horse. He had a whole list. Cowboys didn't wear sunglasses or feathers on their hats. They wouldn't wear a buckle like Ward's unless they'd won it. They wouldn't be caught dead in shorts. They called women "ladies," and to him, he said, that's what I would always be. I'd learned the hard way how false such chivalry was.

Ward was tall and formidable looking, but his belly bulged somewhat over his fancy buckle. I was eager to work my way farther down the Little Beaver to see what other water awaited my discovery. But standing opposite me beneath the cottonwood tree, he gave no more sign of leaving than did his dog, which lay curled at his feet, snapping at flies. Finally, he broke the silence, nodding toward the bays. "That mare'll get here soon. She knows there's oats in the deal."

"My dad said a horse'll sell its soul for a bag of oats."

Ward laughed. "They will, too."

"Look at how the heat makes their legs waver," I said, "like a mirage."

"Isn't that somethin'? I can see how the Spaniards confused the buffalo with trees."

"Pedro de Castañeda!" I said.

Ward nodded. "You a history buff too?"

"I've been reading all I can get my hands on that might mention historical springs, for an essay I'm working on about the Ogallala Aquifer and irrigation on the Great Plains. I read Castañeda's journals just last week. From a distance, they could see the sky through the legs of the buffalo and thought they were pine trees." Admittedly, Ward had a nice smile. Slightly crooked, its startling whiteness was set off by a dark face.

Castañeda had been one of Coronado's men. They'd come north searching for the Seven Golden Cities of Cibola, which of course didn't exist. They wound up in what, three hundred years later, would become Kansas. I said, "Can you imagine the Spaniards trying to figure this place out?"

Ward shook his head and continued to smile appreciatively at me. Was he also remarking the coincidences in our meeting? A meadowlark sang from a fence post, its intricate notes running up and down the scale. "It amazed me to find this water," I said.

He drew a quick breath. "I know just what you mean. I've got two sections of grass on the Smoky Hill River. Water changes everything."

"You live on the Smoky?" The Smoky Valley was a paradise of unfarmed hills sloping down into cottonwood groves along the river. As a kid I'd dreamed of marrying Roy Rogers and owning a Smoky

Valley ranch with him. I said, "One of my father's old sheep buddies lives there. He told me that the ponds are mostly gone."

"The river still runs on my place," Ward said, "but it's no bigger than a crick now."

"If I'd come out here looking for springs twenty, even ten years ago, I probably would have found water closer to home."

"Prob-a-*blee*," Ward said. "Water always runs downhill." He was referring to the way the plains slanted downward from the Rockies. Irrigation pumping had naturally dried out the westernmost springs first. "And it is a shame," he added. "I always considered myself lucky I didn't have to farm anything, or dig one of those expensive wells."

The horses had nibbled their way to the pickup and were stretching their necks over the bed, trying to reach a bucket that sat there. "Let me give you a ride to your car. I can load these nags up in no time."

"No thanks. It's not far."

"If I run across any news stories on the Ogallala, I could send them to you."

A flash must have passed from my eyes, because his eyes signaled back, one quick flash.

He found a pen and piece of paper in his truck and wrote down my address. I extended my hand, and he held it for an extra beat. "Say hello to your son for me. Was it . . . Jake?"

This took me aback. "Good memory."

"He must be a teenager now."

"Yes." Did reading my book give him the right to ask about Jake? I wasn't sure. "He's sixteen."

He walked with me to the bank. "Let me give you a hand."

"It's not steep here." Unsteadily I slalomed down into the creek bed I'd climbed out of on my hands and knees. I could feel his eyes following me as I walked away. He had truly unusual eyes. Kaleidoscopic, as if filled with sunlit green stones.

2

IN LARAMIE, JAKE AND I LIVED IN A BIG OLD HOUSE THAT I'D BOUGHT THE WEEK OF MY JOB INTERVIEW IN THE EARLY NINETIES. With only a few days in town, I asked the hiring committee at the university to let me know their decision right away. There hadn't been many houses on the market at the time, but driving around on the last day, I found an old two-story on the west side that I couldn't believe the real estate agent hadn't bothered to show me. It had everything I wanted—a wide front porch facing the Snowy Range Mountains, varnished woodwork, high ceilings.

Back in Iowa that summer, I could barely wait to move. I'd just completed a graduate writing program, and through all the years I'd been studying, I dreamed of living in the West again. Having returned to school in my late thirties, I'd been what they called a nontraditional student. And now I was eager to settle down with my nontraditional family of two in a home that had at least the trappings of tradition. More important, there would be mountains nearby. Jake would learn to love the wilderness as much as I did. And instead of driving eight hundred miles from Iowa to Kansas to see my parents, we could now make the trip in a half day.

When I pulled up to the curb in the Ryder truck two months later, I had to put on my best mommy face. Had I really poured the student loan money I'd managed to save into this brown-and-yellow fixer-upper? The exterior was so badly chapped I would have to sand every board before I could replace the ugly colors. Inside, now that no furniture or curtains hid damage, I saw that the varnished woodwork was scarred. Every room needed new carpeting and paint. But with its graceful turn-of-the-century detail, my house had incredible potential. I knew that I could make it beautiful again. "I'm going to live in this house for the rest of my life," I told my parents when they drove up for a visit.

"Oh, you'll get out of here," Dad said.

I hadn't really expected him to like my house. After all, here was the man who'd moved us out of the grand house that my grandfather Carlson had built on the farm—with high ceilings and varnished-pine woodwork and bay windows and beveled glass in French doors—and built instead a nondescript ranch style in town. I understood what had motivated him. After my grandmother Carlson passed away, my parents traded their share of her land for land closer to my father's other holdings. Although there was an old house on the new land, Dad didn't think that one suitable for Mom. He'd been raised in a sod house and hated remembering his mother bringing up seven children in that "rat hole." *Dirt falling off the ceiling,* he often recalled. *Christ!* His father had been successful too and could have built Grandma Bair the big stucco house that I loved romping through on holiday visits much sooner than he had.

Sometimes Mom regretted leaving the house she'd grown up in, but Dad didn't seem to know what they'd sacrificed. In my Laramie house, I saw a classy, historic home that would give Jake some of the solidity I'd had in my childhood. Dad saw only peeled paint.

"You wouldn't recognize architectural integrity in the Taj Mahal," I said.

"Is that so?" The corners of his lips shot down into an inverted U and his brows shot up. It was his *my-aren't-we-snooty-today* look.

Then I saw, through the window behind my father, a man in a greasy parka peeing on my chain-link fence. The man was Doc, I soon learned, a local character who lived in a shack down the street and was fabled to have shrapnel lodged in his brain from Vietnam.

I DID MAKE THE HOUSE BEAUTIFUL, I thought, returning to Laramie after my three-day trip to Kansas that August. It might have taken me eight years, but I'd done it. I'd spent the first summers sanding the exterior, then slathered the clapboard in shiny ivory with coral and sagebrush trim. Jake and his friend Andrew helped me sand down the columns on the front porch, which I'd varnished at the same time I did the porch's floorboards. With the honeysuckle vine I'd planted pouring over the front fence and my xeriscaped garden of wildflowers, the house now had an open-armed, welcoming look that surpassed even my memories of the farmhouse.

I wished my father could see the house now, but he lay buried in Kansas, beneath a tombstone with a wheat stalk carved on it. Anyway, as much as I wanted to impress him, there wasn't much I could do about the neighborhood. I really hadn't chosen the best part of town. Before signing the offer, I'd consulted with a future colleague, who assured me there were no bad neighborhoods in Laramie. Little did he know. Even though Doc had since died and his shack had burned down, leaving a welcome gap on the street, Jake had witnessed many ugly things in the families of his friends here. Abuse, neglect, alcohol- and drug-addicted parents.

To compensate, I'd enrolled him in a model elementary school on campus, staffed by master teachers. He made some good friends there. The summer before they started high school, they'd formed a punk-rock band together.

When they practiced in my basement, the house shook. Some parents would have objected to the bedlam, but Jake drummed with thrilling enthusiasm. I loved how he poured himself into the music. And I looked to his friendships with professors' kids for reassurance that he was fine despite my single parenting, his missing father, and all he'd seen in our lousy neighborhood.

I dropped my bag in the entryway. He was lying on the couch watching TV. His velvet-eared, doe-eyed beagle, Regina, jumped off his chest onto the coffee table, then into my arms. I kissed the white splotch on her head, then leaned over and did the same to Jake's forehead, an inch below his self-inflicted Mohawk. "Hi, Mom," he said, as if he had no reason to feel guilty. It was only four o'clock, and he wasn't supposed to get off work until five. Jake had probably the coolest job in town for a teenager, pretending to be a gunslinger from Laramie's Old West days, and he just blew it off?

He was wearing an old tank top of mine from twenty years ago. Cracking vinyl paint on the front of it showed a surfer riding a wave. On the side of his left calf, below the brown jeans he'd cut off—with pride, it seemed, in how jagged he could make them—I noticed a self-administered tattoo of a crooked star.

"Oh Jake," I said, reaching to touch what amounted, in my maternal opinion, to a stain on his innocence.

He covered it with his palm. "You weren't supposed to see that."

"How was I going to miss it?"

He pretended to return his focus to the TV.

I flicked it off.

"Gee, Mom, don't you think I'm a little old for you to take away TV?"

"Why aren't you at work?"

"I overslept, I guess."

"You overslept. By how much?"

"I don't know. That alarm clock doesn't go off. It's happened two times now."

At times like these, I longed for a man to step in and set Jake straight. It went against all my feminist principles to want this, but I did anyway. Dad would never have put up with this kind of behavior in his sons. Not that I did. I let Jake know that he would lose his driving privileges if he skipped another day of work.

THE NEXT MORNING HE DIDN'T GET OUT of bed until after my fourth knock. Too late for the breakfast I'd cooked for him, he shoved his park-issued cowboy hat over his questionable hair and left for the tourist park.

I sat down at my computer. If that water I'd seen four days ago in the Little Beaver could talk, what would it say? Above my desk hung a Charles Russell print—a caravan of Plains Indians crossing a creek. Russell had depicted the riders in the rear as transparent and ghostlike, as if fading into history. They might have been crossing the Little Beaver, the water that had supplied them now as diminished and ghostly as they.

Farmers said they had no choice in how much water they pumped. *Use it or lose it!* my father used to say whenever I complained about how much he drew out. Kansas, like most dry western states, had a law requiring that those holding water rights take advantage of them to their fullest, or lose what they didn't use so someone else could access the water before it flowed, or seeped, into the next state. It hadn't occurred to early legislators that water could be lost through too much use. Now the law was codified by long practice and the rights holders were powerful vested interests with political clout. It would be nearly impossible to change how the Ogallala was managed. Still, I wanted to see new laws passed that aggressively protected the water.

I emptied the pencil sharpener, played with paper clips, and searched for an argument that would penetrate the armor of the most dyed-in-the-wool pragmatist.

> *My father died thinking that he and his farm neighbors were the same people they'd always been, descendants of pioneers adhering to frugal pioneer values. But since his childhood, he'd gone from horse-pulled plows to tractors that pulled forty-foot-wide chemical spray rigs. He'd gone from windmills that pumped ten gallons a minute to centrifugal pumps that could lift twelve hundred gallons in that brief amount of time. He'd gone from intense labor that broke men's and women's backs to intense pillage and poison that broke the earth's.*

Staring at me from my bulletin board was a self-portrait Jake had penciled on the back of an envelope when he was ten. It was an accurate portrayal of him then. The wide, clear forehead. His trusting gaze and crooked, close-lipped smile. No matter how much turmoil he'd put himself through lately, by resisting school, work, me, he was still fundamentally the same kid. Under his rebellion, the soul of him was trust. He and his generation deserved far better than what my father's generation had bequeathed mine.

Make that *his children* would deserve better. On the geologists' maps of the aquifer, our county, Sherman, was still mostly orange, for reductions of 15 to 30 percent. It hadn't taken me long to do the math, figuring how much water we had left on our farm if we continued pumping at current rates. About eighty-five years' worth, I estimated. I would be dead. As difficult as it was to contemplate, so would Jake. We would have "gotten ours," as my father liked to say he had.

What I'd written moments before now seemed overblown. It had the same self-righteous tone I'd taken with my father when I was younger. But after inheriting part of the land I had always accused him of abusing, I had quit my teaching job. Thanks to the Ogallala, I was now able to write full time. I had no right to point my finger anymore.

I went back and crossed out all the "he"s and put in "we"s.

I WOULD STIR-FRY SOME BROCCOLI AND MUSHROOMS with hamburger. Jake liked that. At the front gate, I looked down the street, hoping to see his beater pickup approaching. Not yet. I opened the mailbox and was surprised to find not only the usual assortment of pizza flyers and bills but also a hand-addressed white envelope.

Seeing the postmark, I smiled. So soon? Ward must have written and mailed it the day after we met. I hurried up to my bedroom, closing the door and locking it lest Jake return and interrupt me.

Black fountain-pen script flowed confidently onto fire-orange paper. *You may not have given a second thought to our chance encounter. I, on the other hand, have revisited it often.* At the bottom of the page, he'd rendered a cowboy riding a sorrel in watercolors that strayed beyond the lines. The horse was about to gallop over a prickly pear cactus, in purple bloom.

As I read, I felt as if I were the one being painted—back into vivid existence, coming alive to a type of excitement I hadn't felt in years.

Tap-eta, tap-eta, tap! Jake's customary knock, his fingernails on my door. I leaped up.

"Mom? Can I come in?"

I shoved the letter under my bed and slid the lock open as quietly as possible. His hat was tilted back as if he were a real cowboy, tired from a day riding the range. "Why are you sittin' in here with the door locked?"

Caught. Sometimes I felt like the kid. "Old habit, I guess. Your Mohawk is showing."

Jake looked at me suspiciously. "You're looking pretty punk yourself, Mom. Did you know your hair has a paper clip in it?"

3

I PULLED MY BAG ONTO THE ESCALATOR AND TRIED TO FIX THE PERFECT SMILE, NOT TOO EAGER, YET WARM, RECEPTIVE. We were supposed to meet by the fountain, but I wanted to be ready in case he was waiting where passengers first spilled into the terminal. Denver was about halfway between our homes, and I was stopping here on my way back from Omaha, where I'd presented my essay on the Ogallala at a literary conference. We would have a day and a half together, then I would fly the rest of the way home to Laramie. Not seeing him, I continued over to the "Mountain Mirage."

Clear, perpetual glacier melt, funneled down from mountain reservoirs, then forced through hidden pipes, spouted up from hundreds of holes in the marble floor. The water put oxygen into the air and soothed travel-weary nerves with the sound of itself. Elegant compared with the cow pond we met beside in August. We'd exchanged two long letters, then switched to cybercorrespondence. That's when my disciplined morning writing routine had come unraveled. Ding! Better check. It might be a word from Ward.

I allowed myself one slow scan of the crowd. Not seeing him, I began to wonder if I'd scared him off somehow. But he'd called me the night before I left for the conference and had sounded fine then. "I thought I'd better speak to you at least once before our date. Otherwise I'd get tongue-tied." It was the first time we'd talked since we met. I had been worrying about the same thing. Take that word "date." I was relieved to hear him say it out loud, as if it were the most natural thing in the world for two people entering their fifth decade to go out on one.

It's hard, I'd written, *not to anticipate the whole soaring, predictable plot based on one charmed meeting. The same way we hum a whole song after hearing a single bar. Disappointment is inevitable.*

Why had I considered it necessary to hedge my romantic bets? I wondered. I regretted having tossed that discordant thought into the mix. It had caused him to agree, and that was the last thing I wanted.

When it comes to the disappointment factor, he'd responded, *my experience has proven you right, but I'm kind of like Pea in* Lonesome Dove: *"'Though loyal and able and brave, Pea had never displayed the slightest ability to learn from his experience, though his experience was considerable. Time and again he would walk up on the wrong side of a horse that was known to kick, and then look surprised when he got kicked.'"*

For the most part, we'd stuck to safe topics. He wrote a gripping account of riding a runaway horse when he was a kid. *It's always been a mystery to me how it managed to brush me off on the only tree between the Smoky Hill River and Oklahoma. I've had plenty of near-death experiences on horses since then, but that one is still the benchmark.* We recommended books on Cheyenne Indian history to each other, and I shared drafts of my essay. He'd proven to be a perceptive critic.

I scanned the terminal again, a full 360 this time, then looked into the airiness overhead—the hollow undersurface of white peaks that were supposed to resemble mountains. No matter how distinctive the architecture, the scale of it dwarfed a person.

Waiting for him like this made me regret the one confiding e-mail I did send, telling him that because I'd grown up twenty miles out in the country, I hadn't developed many social skills. High school had consequently been rough—part of the reason, probably, that I'd gotten married so young, at eighteen. After that first divorce, I'd been shocked to discover I didn't know how to make friends. I'd since become much better at that, but as I'd written, *By myself in the house at night, with Jake gone somewhere, the lonely ache still creeps up on me sometimes, as if a door has been left open onto subzero cold.*

Waiting. What had he revealed in turn? He'd said that all of his past relationships had been good, even if none had lasted. What made them good, then? He wrote that *trying to describe my abiding interest in horses would be like boiling a religion down to a few words. And in case you were wondering, as for religion, I don't follow any standard-issue faith but firmly believe death isn't our final end.* I was glad he felt that way, I responded, although I couldn't claim as firm a belief.

Ward had been somewhat revealing when, *in the interests of honesty in advertising*, he listed his faults. He said that he procrastinated too much, and this kept him from achieving the degree of success he wanted. The admission worried me a little. He also confessed that his friends considered him *very independent. I'm not proud of that, but there it is.*

Why does he consider that a fault? I wondered. I did take pride in my independence. When I'd told him about going back to Kansas to have Jake after my second marriage ended, had I given him the mistaken impression that I was of a more dependent nature?

But courtship is a fine institution, he added. Had he been trying to warn me?

I must have written something disparaging about conservative politicians, because he also said, *I can tell from your last letter that we see things differently in some regards.* We'd since acknowledged our political differences. Could we talk these out without rancor or insults? We weren't sure, but we were already committed to trying.

Actually, we didn't really seem to care what our differences were. *It's way too soon to be thinking the way I'm thinking*, Ward wrote in his last e-mail, before he'd called. *This is INSANE. What is going to happen when we wake up?*

I guess it's this, I thought, letting out a huff of cynical despair. This is what's going to happen. I scanned the high walls for a clock. How long should I wait for him? Fifteen minutes? Thirty? Then what? See if I could catch an earlier flight back to Laramie? I was like Pea too. Always walking up on the wrong side of romance. When had it ever not kicked me flat?

Just as I spotted the clock and discovered it was ten minutes past the time we were supposed to meet, I felt a tap on my shoulder.

He stood grinning beside me, wearing a black cowboy hat. We hugged briefly. "I waited on the mezzanine," he said. "Thought I could see better from up there. Then I missed you altogether." His exotic eyes had a mischievous glint in them.

Why on the mezzanine instead of where we'd agreed? He'd wanted to play me a little, apparently, and it had worked. The minutes of anxiety he'd put me through seemed deliciously excruciating now that they were over.

AFTER DRESSING FOR DINNER IN OUR SEPARATE rooms, we met in the hotel lobby. Ward was wearing a brown suit, a pale-green shirt and a regulation brown tie with a yellow stripe. He said, "I know you probably expected something western, but what I think you want here is a date, not a cardboard cutout."

In the pasture, he had reminded me a bit of a blond John Wayne, but dressed this way, the high ovals of baldness on his forehead exposed, he reminded me more of my farmer father ready for a night at the Elks Club. Or for Easter Sunday, when he would indulge my mother by going to church. I was sure that Ward's callused hands had seldom felt the brush of a suit cuff. Like my father, he was an outdoor working man who'd endured and been shaped by weather.

Ward hadn't gotten his tan in a leisurely way, recreating. He'd gotten it the honest way, working. Each day he breathed the dust I'd breathed growing up. He felt the heat and cold I'd felt. Smelled the same smells. His eyes looked restless in the restaurant surroundings of plush carpets and rich brocades, and I knew that his vision had been honed, as mine had, on distances and pastels.

The male university professors I knew in Laramie seemed effete by comparison. For exercise, they rode bicycles and, like me, were willing to drive sixty miles to Colorado to shop at Whole Foods. Ward would probably melt like the Wicked Witch of the West if I suggested he ride a bike or visit Whole Foods. If the Parmesan and walnut-encrusted tofu I wanted him to try didn't do him in, the sun-dried tomato tapenade on a gluten-free, whole-grain wafer would. Indeed, his waistline suggested that he was still nourished on beef and potatoes.

I would have to deal with some things, I thought. I wouldn't be surprised if, among men, he told the same kinds of sexist jokes that my father had. But then again, he loved my book and the grasslands. He cared enough about the past in our mutual home to be excited when I'd suggested we go to the Denver library the next morning to look at old maps of the region. He wrote well. He stood open to me, like a door onto another self. The Kansas farm girl who, with all her worldly experience, had never quite left home.

If romance has a color, it is burgundy. I don't remember what either of us ate, but I do recall the sensuous, round-bellied goblet in my hand and the chime it made when we clinked. While we waited for the contents of our glasses to loosen our tongues, we fleshed out some details from our pasts. I knew from his letters that he had studied history in college. But now he told me how important it had been to him to pay his own way through, working for a large-animal veterinary practice. A close family friend who had graduated from high school before him had almost busted his parents' bank account going to school, then had flunked out. "I was bound and *determined* not to be like him," Ward said.

My father had paid his way through college too, I told him. "I admire people who do that."

"If I was going to flunk out," Ward explained, "I wanted to do it on my own dime. I was more interested in my job than colonial politics, but I stuck it out and made a pretty good showing." After getting a teaching degree, he'd been hired by a small Colorado high school.

He still faulted himself for lacking patience, not wanting to "hold those kids' hands."

"Why should you have?"

He reached over and squeezed *my* hand, which I'd placed strategically, on the table between us. "Thank you, darlin', but we all deserve, well, need some hand holding from time to time, especially when we're young. I just wasn't the one to do it. I've never been so unhappy in my life, before or since."

I watched the frown leave his face as he returned to the present. He confessed that when he'd told his friends how excited he was about our date, they'd advised him to put on the brakes. "They think I don't really know you, but they don't understand how many words we've written to each other. They're not like me. Most of my buddies would rather walk a mile barefoot through a sticker patch than write a letter."

After Ward quit teaching, he moved to Denver and sold real estate, but that job hadn't lasted long either. He now earned the greater share of his income selling ranching products—pipe corrals, water tanks, loading chutes, while grazing some cattle himself. "Cows and sales might make my living, but horses give me a life." He'd moved back to Kansas because his family's land would afford him the privilege of spending the rest of his life around the animals. "I never met a horse who didn't have a decent heart. Some of them have been frightened by bad treatment, but you can win back their trust."

"Unlike humans?" I asked.

"I haven't had as much luck with them," he confessed. I reminded him what he'd written—that he'd never been in a bad relationship.

"They weren't 'bad,' they just didn't work out."

"Did you leave or did they leave?" I asked.

He picked up his glass, took a sip—to buy time? "Usually I did," he said.

My smile must have flattened, as he grasped my hand harder this time. "Because, Julene, they weren't you. This is different."

We held hands all the way back to the hotel, and when the elevator came to my floor, he stepped off with me. I'd wondered if he would and wasn't sure whether I wanted him to. Nine tenths of poise is pretense, I reminded myself as we stopped at my door.

"Well," he said, holding out his arms for a goodnight hug.

He wore aftershave. No man I'd dated since leaving Kansas had worn aftershave. I took a deep whiff. "Mmm."

He accepted that invitation with a devouring kiss. Stunned, I returned it. My body was rising to him like a vine lacing itself around a post. How is this happening? I thought. He's from *there*. I'm kissing a man from *there*.

I swiped my key and held the door open for him.

"Not tonight, sweetheart. I don't want to rush this."

"Rushing's good when you're in a hurry," I said.

"Let's have breakfast at nine, then go over to the library, look at those maps."

"Are you forgetting I have a son? I don't know when I'll be able to see you next."

He grinned. "Tomorrow is also a whole new day. Let's see what it brings."

The room was freezing, and I couldn't find a thermostat. After vainly searching the closets and drawers for an extra blanket, I lay awake and alone on the giant bed, less certain than I'd been since we met.

It had happened twice now. He'd offered then withheld himself, promising to meet by the fountain and waiting instead on the mezzanine, now tantalizing me with the greatest kiss of my life, then leaving. I had feared I wouldn't want him. I now knew that I did. But how much did he want me? What had he said about courtship? It was a "fine institution." If this was a game to him, he'd won the first round.

 4

IN THE LIBRARY'S RARE-MAP ROOM, WE OPENED THE LONG, FLAT DRAWERS AND LIFTED OUT THE TREASURES ONE BY ONE. Most of the old maps showed nothing at all in our remote region—no roads or rivers or topographical marks. "I kind of like living in a part of this sad old world so empty they use it to print the legend," Ward said.

"Those are the best places," I agreed. Finally, we seemed to be getting back in sync. In the mirror that morning, after a sleepless night in my freezing room, my face had looked drawn, and my eyes had dark circles under them. I'd never done well on little or no sleep. Talking over breakfast, I'd felt like I was tiptoeing through broken glass. Each word I uttered seemed to shatter on impact with his. We hadn't connected well, but now the bad spell his refusal had cast over us seemed to be lifting. Perhaps he's just old-fashioned when it comes to sex, I thought.

"Look how big we once were," Ward said, pointing at a map of Kansas Territory. Until 1861, Kansas had reached from the Missouri River all the way to the Rockies. Our eyes were drawn to the Smoky Hill River, where Ward lived, and to the Middle and Little Beavers, whose dry beds had both wound through the countryside where I grew up. The Smoky appeared much more often on the maps because it had always had reliable water in it. In the late 1850s, when gold was discovered in Colorado, the Smoky Hill Trail had been the most direct route to Denver. It had also been the most dangerous. The Cheyenne, who camped and hunted on the plains, were understandably threatened by the incursion. They were prone to burning stage stations and torturing and killing the passengers.

Despite these dangers, instead of crossing Nebraska on the Oregon Trail, some travelers headed for the far West came through Kansas, then turned north onto the Overland Trail, which ran along the eastern face of the Rockies.

I traced my finger from Laramie south along the Overland to Denver. "Our paths join."

Ward gave me a sideways hug. Standing that close to him after a sleepless night grounded me, like leaning against a sun-warmed tree trunk. He removed his hand from my shoulder and lifted another map from the stack we'd made. Close to where we met on the Little Beaver, I spotted a north-south dotted line. "The Ladder of Rivers!" I said.

Tribe after tribe had climbed the ladder across the High Plains, going from one watering hole to the next as they hunted bison. Some had settled beside the springs long enough to grow corn and squash— all thanks to the gift of surface water. Even my modest Little Beaver had been a rung on the ladder. Along with Ward's Smoky Hill and the mightier Platte and Arkansas, it had made High Plains trade and travel possible all the way back to the Paleo-Indian Clovis culture.

"The Ladder of Rivers," Ward mused. "That phrase sounds familiar. I think I ran across it in that book I sent you about Dull Knife's escape from Oklahoma."

He was referring to the epic flight, in 1878, of the Northern Cheyenne from Oklahoma. The military had coerced them to move there, onto the Southern Cheyenne reservation. But the northerners escaped, fighting their way through Kansas and Nebraska, fending off the attacks of better-armed, more numerous cavalry. Some of the tribe had made it to their home in the Black Hills, but many had died in Nebraska, gunned down as they huddled in the freezing hills.

"It was terrible what we did to the Indians," I said.

"I know just what you mean, even if I did always root for the cowboys in the shoot 'em ups."

"I rooted for the Indians," I said.

"I never would have guessed." He softened the sarcasm with an affectionate smile.

"I want to go to all these streams," I said. "I want to find the springs where the Indians camped and the pioneers settled. I'm drawn to those places."

"I would be honored to join you in that. Dull Knife's band crossed the Smoky not far from my place. I'll take you there."

"That would be great!" I stifled a yawn.

Ward studied me for a second. "You know, I can see I've worn you out. Let's go back to the hotel and rest."

I SANK INTO THE LEATHER PASSENGER SEAT of his vintage Continental, the kind of car you'd expect to see a cigar-chewing, country real estate agent driving. Except for its color: powder blue. "My buddies rib me about it," he said, "but at least it's not pink."

At the stoplight, I closed my eyes. "Make yourself at home. Lean back," he said, pushing a button on the console to tilt the seat.

I trusted him to bear me along on this cushion, then up the elevator to his room. I would sleep, or we would make love. Both sounded equally appealing. We could linger the rest of the day. I didn't care if I missed my plane. There'd be another one in the evening. I could call my friend Diane and ask her to stay another night at my house. After Jake had skipped work when I was away in August, I'd resolved not to leave him home alone again until he'd proven he was responsible.

Behind thick curtains in his darkened room, Ward kissed me deeply and deliciously, as he had the night before. But much sooner than I expected, he began undoing my buttons. He pulled his T-shirt over his head, then guided me onto the bed and took off my jeans and underpants, tossing them aside like weeds. Quickly, he took off his own jeans and lay down beside me.

Here was the reality of him. The wiry, gray-blond chest hair, shoulders broad as a truck making his belly irrelevant. A thrilling shock, this sudden nakedness. The reality of both of us. A little embarrassed to be making love in daylight, I reached for an embrace. He rolled on top of me.

I tried to slow him down through body language—a hand on his forearm, messaging, "We have time," but he was oblivious to my signals. Even his kisses were hurried and incomplete.

How to convey the shock of this suddenness? It was like being invited to dinner and having the food thrown at me, or finding that I was the dinner and my own appetite was not even secondary but inconsequential. I hadn't experienced such selfishness in a male since I was sixteen. His hotel room might have been my first boyfriend's Chevy Impala on a gray road between square wheat fields. I might have been lying on a cold vinyl seat, trying to feel what I wanted to feel—passionate, in love—while my boyfriend had sex.

I had, in fact, been falling in love with Ward just moments before, but the feeling evaporated under this onslaught. After he rolled off me, I got up just as perfunctorily. Glimpsing confusion on his face, I feigned cheerful regret. "Got a plane to catch." My hands shook as I buttoned my blouse. "I'll go pack."

In my room, I threw all visible items into my suitcase and didn't bother to look behind the shower curtain or under the bed. I wanted to get out of the hotel before he caught up with me—if he was planning to do that, if there was any pretense of love left in him at all. If so, I thought, Let him wonder. Let him rot. I flagged a cab, paying thirty dollars for a ride to the airport that would have cost five on the bus, and went through security—again, before he could catch up with me. Beyond the checkpoint, I did feel more secure than I had before, on his terroristic side of that line. How dare he! *Bastard!* my mind shouted as I rode the train to the gate.

I sat in the empty waiting area, two hours early for my flight, sorrow welling up like slow poison. It was truth rising in me, time for a reckoning. I'd lowered myself for a man who didn't warrant a second glance, and now I would have to go through the recovery period and return to a reality that looked grim after entertaining fantasies of transformative love. With a Kansas guy, no less. Had I forgotten why I'd left, at eighteen, and again at thirty-seven? Going back would retrace every step of my evolution, erasing each gain. But this reasoning didn't prevent me from hugging myself and folding double. I sat up only as I realized that the waiting area was beginning to fill. A child sitting in the bank of molded-plastic chairs opposite me grabbed his mother's sleeve, then pointed at me as if to say, "What's wrong with that lady?"

How had Ward become so important to me so quickly? Now it was as if I'd never been disappointed before, as if he were the first cad I'd ever met. What a fool I'd been!

AT THE TINY AIRPORT IN LARAMIE, THE sky was spitting snow bullets sideways. Why today? Why couldn't the sun shine, as the state boasted it did more than three hundred days of the year? I wanted to see the luminous peaks of the Snowy Range rising above a panorama of soft-green, short-grass prairie. I needed to breathe the high valley's sunny clear air to forget Ward and all he stood for—that ancient history of mine that I'd rejected long ago. Instead, I felt his absence as bitterly as I might an extinguished fire in the dead of a winter.

On the way to the house, I spotted Jake's pickup pulling into a convenience-store gas station. I glanced at the clock. He was supposed to be in school. We'd named his beagle Regina, Latin for "queen," with good reason. She rode in the queenly way she always did, her paws on the passenger windowsill, long beagle ears framing big beagle eyes, but she fell back as the truck bounced into the lot. He'd been driving too fast. *Hell-bent on having fun*, Dad would have said. What a sudden return to reality this was, being reminded, immediately after an absence that I thought was going to change my life, where my love really lay, and what the problems of that love were.

My yard looked untended, buried in a week's worth of leaves, and the house seemed cold and dingy. A plastic cup lay on its side on the coffee table, oozing Coke glue. McDonald's wrappers littered the floor, licked clean by Regina. I leaned over the couch to open the drapes that Jake was always closing so he could watch TV in the daytime.

To my surprise, a powder-blue car was pulling up to the curb. I'd been so convinced all was over between Ward and me that I hadn't even considered the possibility he would follow me. Now I felt like a child in a movie, seeing a dead hero return to life.

I ran to the bathroom to comb my hair. Calm down, I told myself. Even if he was gallant, driving 120 miles from Denver to Laramie to make things right, he was still clueless. And how could that be? Had relations between men and women really not changed one iota in Kansas since the 1960s? Didn't the world leak in through television and films?

I opened the door. He wore a long-sleeved, blue Levi's shirt, and his belt buckle sat squarely in place again. "You left without saying good-bye."

"If Jake comes home, you'll have to sneak out. I'm not ready to introduce you."

In my bedroom, I chose the wingback chair I'd bought recently at a used furniture store, thinking of weekends when Ward would be visiting me, if things had kept going the way I thought they were then.

This put him on the corner of my bed. "I was afraid you wouldn't let me in."

I probably shouldn't have, I thought.

"What did I do wrong?" He looked sad, his lips curved down under his mustache, his eyes still sexy in their extraordinary greenness.

"You really don't know?"

"No."

That he didn't think my sexuality was as important as his didn't just infuriate me, I realized. It threatened me. It had taken years after leaving Kansas for me to develop the courage to accept that I had my own needs and to assert them. The repression was a prison I didn't want to reenter. No way was I going back to that darkness. But I also remembered how I'd felt an hour ago, getting off the plane into thin, stinging snow. I remembered Jake careening into that parking lot and worry descending over me along with the gray light. If I wanted love, and if I wanted a man's love for Jake before he was completely grown, this was my chance. But how I must look! Anguished, fragmented by tension, exhaustion, and indecision, I imagined myself as one of Picasso's cubist women, my face pasted together at sharp angles.

"I know I should apologize, but I don't know for what," Ward said.

"It's not what you did." My voice was squeaky, which I hated. I motioned for a pause, gathered myself and began again in a more even tone. "It's what you didn't do. You don't know how hard this is to say, Ward. But what about me? As soon as we started, I could see it was all going to be about you. That was like—" I closed my eyes to find the right words and blurted out what I saw—"a door slammed shut in my face." That was it exactly. The door that had stood open the night before, when I first glimpsed him in that suit, had closed in the exact moment I'd begun to walk through it.

As much as I'd tried to hold back tears, my eyes weren't cooperating. Ward leaned forward. "I know you don't want to be held, but will you please scoot a little closer?"

I wriggled my chair toward the bed but not close enough for him to touch me.

He dropped his hands onto his lap. "Okay. Jesus. I really hurt you, didn't I?"

I nodded, unable to speak.

"I'm sorry. Jesus, I'm so sorry. But I thought you wanted it to go fast."

I looked at him in disbelief.

"You know, last night, when you said it was good to rush? I thought that's what you wanted."

I felt my anger begin to fade. Could it be he'd really taken that literally? "I didn't mean wham bam. I meant why not go for it? When you're feeling passionate, why wait?"

"You see, Julene, I totally misunderstood that. Don't get me wrong. I'm not trying to sidestep this, but you could have said something. You could have slowed things down or stopped them altogether."

But I had tried! At least I thought I had, with my body language. Apparently, my signals had been too subtle for Ward. What did a man like him need? I expected nuance in lovemaking. It was supposed to be mutual, intuitive, a communion. Yet why hadn't I asserted myself more? Insisted even? Maybe *that's* what threatened me—my own failure to stand up for myself.

"Will you come here, please? Lie down with me, let me hold you?"

I looked into his contrite eyes. "I don't want any kisses."

"That's not what I want right now either."

I lay down with my back to him, but there was no way to hide the emotion coursing through me. It was pouring out of my eyes. He put his arm around me. "Will you ever run out of tears?"

"I don't know where they're coming from. I hate that I'm acting like this." Clearly, my heart believed that the lonely years were behind us, that finally we could open again, but it was too soon and too dangerous to act this way.

"Without your tears, I'd be on my way home by now. I never would have known how you felt. And this is the only place I want to be."

"Me too," I admitted, amazed at the truth of it. I thought, I am lying here with a man who isn't shaped right, for me. He doesn't think right, as far as I believe. He lives in a place I can't return to. And yet I don't want him to leave.

I sighed. "There's too much against us. We live too far apart. I'm not going to work on sex with you. And I'm not going back to Kansas. I left all that ten thousand years ago."

"This may be a corny thing to say, but I don't really think we have a choice. This is bigger than us."

"Uh-huh," I said, as if unconvinced. But what else could explain my inability to get up from the bed?

"Besides," Ward added. "My place might be different from what you think."

"I already know what your house looks like. I bet it's full of knotty pine and pictures of cowboys on horses and that you use horseshoes for coat hooks."

"Okay. I guess you do know."

"I'm a card-carrying member of the Sierra Club."

"So?"

"I have friends who are gay."

For a second, he didn't move or breathe. "Am I supposed to be shocked at that?"

We laughed together. He said, "Before you list any more of your faults, would you let me hold you for a while longer?"

"My faults?"

"Or mine. Which have you."

I rolled over and laid my head on his shoulder. "I think that door that slammed shut this morning is opening."

His chin moved up and down against my forehead. "And for once in my life, I have the sense to go through it."

"What would you have done in the past?"

"I would have run."

I nodded in self-recognition. Wasn't that what I'd spent the morning doing? At the first indication of a problem, I had turned tail. But a strange miracle had taken place on this bed. It had been like Alice's precipitous fall down the rabbit hole. On landing, we'd both found ourselves in an alternate universe, and now it was as if we'd inhaled some secondary smoke from the caterpillar's hookah. I'd lain down of one heart and now I was of another, willing to work on anything.

When Ward took my hand and led me down the stairs, it was as if every cell in my body aligned itself in his direction. It had been so long since a man had taken my hand with confidence and led me anywhere, so long since, if one had tried, I would have been willing to follow.

The sun was setting and he had five hours to drive, cows to check on and horses to feed. Jake might come home any minute. We said our good-byes on the porch, and I watched the taillights of his Continental until he turned onto the bridge that would lead him to I-80, the old Oregon Trail. He would travel east into Nebraska, then drop down the Ladder of Rivers, to his home on the Smoky.

5

ON THANKSGIVING MORNING, JAKE SLEPT AS HE ALWAYS DID ON OUR TRIPS TO KANSAS, A PILLOW WEDGED BETWEEN HIS HEAD AND THE WINDOW GLASS AND THE QUILT THAT HIS GRANDMOTHER HAD STITCHED FOR HIM WHEN HE WAS IN KINDERGARTEN WRAPPED AROUND HIM. It barely covered his upper half anymore. His dirty ball cap had fallen off, revealing his patchy Mohawk.

As I drove, I snatched glimpses of the dawn-gilded Never Summer range. The mountains had all the luster I'd wished for that grim afternoon the month before when, unloved and unsaved, I'd returned to Laramie and my imperfect life after rushing out of the Denver hotel. But Ward had followed me, then left me caressed and transformed. Ever since, I'd taken a new lover's delight in beauty. The gray-green rabbit brush against a gentle pink sky and the ponderosa pines and boulders dusted in snow made me downright nirvanic. I could hardly resist waking Jake. "Behold!" I wanted to say.

For the last several years, especially since my father died, I had dreaded holidays in Kansas. They never delivered all I wanted for Jake, all I thought he needed. But for the last two weeks, I'd been giddy about this approaching trip home because I would finally get to see Ward again. It had been difficult not to share my excitement with Jake over the past month. So far I'd told him little. He knew only that I'd met Ward when I went home alone in August and that he was coming to dinner.

Jake finally unfolded from his cocoon as we dropped into Fort Collins, the town north of Denver. "Morning, sleepyhead," I said.

"Morning." His tone was still laced with grumpiness from having to get up so early.

"Your grandfather went to ag school here when it was a little college town. Now look at it, all condos and McMansions."

"I like our house better," Jake said.

"Man, me too."

"Can I drive?"

"After Denver. Let's wait until—"

"Whatever," he said, before I could remind him of the tricky interchange coming up. He turned toward the window and a new sleeping position. He was wearing one of the white undershirts he'd stenciled with the day of the week. This one said Sunday, even though it was Thursday. It had brown stains and a tear where he'd ripped out the label. Only by pleading had I gotten him to wear plain jeans, not the pair he'd drawn psychedelic designs on and refused to let me wash.

What would Ward think? I hoped that he had enough wisdom to see past Jake's clothes. I hoped that he could read his eyes. Jake had the kindest, brownest brown eyes. He hadn't been very kind to me lately, but that was to be expected at this age, wasn't it? It comforted me that his teachers still praised his compassion, saying it was surprising in a boy.

After we'd rolled onto the plains, I dutifully exited at Deer Trail, a tiny town east of Denver. Jake took the wheel, and I tried not to seem too observant as he pulled onto the interstate.

He thought he was invincible. Closing my eyes, I imagined him standing on an on-ramp like this one, army-surplus pack on his back and his thumb out, going in search of his father. While I would do anything I could to prevent that, he didn't believe in the dangers I warned him about. And his desire for a father had been relentless ever since he was a toddler. Only when he hit his teens had the yearning become less evident, but I knew it was there. He still had a child's trusting heart, open despite the pain that had been inflicted on it.

Jake's father had sent him only a couple of letters over the years and had phoned only a few times. Then he deigned to visit him once, when Jake was twelve. He'd planned to come through Laramie anyway, with some motorcycle buddies. He was several hours late. It had pulverized my emotions to watch Jake wait for his dad's arrival. Then, when Stefan decided not to stay for the weekend as he'd promised, I'd had to watch Jake's joy turn to disappointment. Stefan was having engine trouble. Worried that he would break down, he continued on with the others.

Jake flicked on the radio and tuned it to his favorite Denver station.

"Not too loud," I said, although my newly opened heart was receptive to virtually any music. I grooved on the head-banging rhythm and raw emotion in the angry male voices. Their vocal cords might have been ground glass. Let it out, I thought. Feel it.

When the low-wattage station faded, it was my turn to choose. We sang along with "Eleanor Rigby," Jake's voice hitting the high note in *"where do they all come from?"* with ease. I missed the note every time, but neither of us cared. We were getting into the holiday breakaway spirit, thank providence. We could count on a car trip as recess from the mother-son wars.

Halfway between Denver and the Kansas border, I could still see the snowy cap of Pike's Peak hovering ghostlike in my side mirror. Otherwise, nothing but smooth grasslands defined the circular horizon. The land lifted and fell gently, meandering along dry streambeds. Two pearlescent cloud wings stretched toward us from our destination, where morning rimmed the earth in turquoise. The dry air evaporated haze, giving the sky its clarity and inspiring a feeling in the chest that the early Plains explorer Richard I. Dodge described best: *the magnificence of being.*

"I love this point in the trip," I said.

"I know," Jake said. "You always tell me that."

All flesh is grass, it said somewhere in the Bible. Grass makes flesh, and a century and a half ago we would have seen herds of antelope wheeling over the land like flocks of birds, as we often saw them do in Wyoming, veering suddenly to pour down a valley or around a long, low hill. But the only grass-turned-flesh we'd seen that day had been cattle.

And as we approached the Kansas border, all I could tune in on the radio was a moralizing talk-show hostess. "What did you think would happen when you married an alcoholic? Alcoholism is a disease, Emily, a disease. Do you remember your vows? In sickness and in—." I cut her power off midsentence.

"Amen," Jake said. Noise from the Subaru's leaking windows filled the silence.

The land was flatter now, and the grass had vanished. The earth had been human stitched into a patchwork of monotones—squares and circles of bare dirt, corn stubble, and winter wheat. Many of the fields had irrigation sprinklers. Some of the sprinklers were running, unusual this late in the year. The High Plains were in the midst of a drought, but having the Ogallala Aquifer to tap into was like having a goose that laid golden eggs. Except, of course, we were doing what people always did, killing the goose.

Ward was a rancher, not a farmer. An important distinction. Much of his land would be in grass. In a letter, he'd described his place *as honestly as I know how*, saying it looked, at first glance, *like any damned ol' farm.*

Why our ancestors thought it necessary to plow up most of the prairie, I'll never understand. I'm just thankful that I do own some grass. You can still ride a horse here and imagine it the way it used to be and was meant to be. I can't wait to show it to you, Julene. That longed-for moment was upon us. I would see his place the next day. Finally. His hand would envelope mine again.

"So are you going to marry this guy?" Jake asked.

Had he been silent all this time because he was mulling over the radio diatribe? Had he connected that poor Emily's husband to his dad, whose drinking had led to our divorce, then to "this guy," who, as far as he knew, could be a drinker too? "Gee, Jake," I said, "we're nowhere near that point. For now, I just hope you'll like him."

"You think I will?"

I paused. "I want you to, but I can't promise."

He greeted this with no words, only silence that I could read too well. I reached across and squeezed his shoulder. "You're the best thing that ever happened to me, sweetie."

"Thanks, Mom. I know. I don't have to like him. I just want you to be happy." He blessed me with a smile.

SHORTLY AFTER CROSSING THE KANSAS BORDER, WE exited the interstate. With a population of five thousand, Goodland was the largest town since Denver. We shot past the new Walmart Supercenter, which had put all three grocery stores and half the other stores on Main Street out of business.

After the Farmer's Co-op, where my dad used to fuel his pickup before heading out to the farm, we zoomed over the railroad tracks past peeling white grain elevators, then threaded the grid of square corners and straight streets. Paint had weathered off the older clapboard houses. Many had for-sale signs in their front yards.

The town was as predictable as tic-tac-toe. On the west side came Sherman Street, then Custer. Naturally, I thought. Two generals in the war against the Plains Indians. The settlers had named the county after Sherman too. I'd never made the connection as a child, but this seemed entirely appropriate to me now. The army's chief commander had taken the flat, arable land from the Cheyenne and delivered it to us on a silver platter.

We rumbled down brick-paved Main Street. When I was Jake's age, Goodland had been a bustling town. Back then mannequins with aquiline features and long, expressive hands posed in the many clothing-store windows. The only downtown store that sold clothes now was a Penney's. I pointed to the fried-chicken take-out place. "You won't believe this, Jake, but when that building was a shoe store, they had an X-ray machine you could stand on and look at the bones in your feet. I must have done it a hundred times."

"No kidding? It's amazing you didn't get toe cancer or something."

"We used to eat there," I said, pointing to the once elegant, now seedy, Waters Hotel. We would go on the rare Sundays Dad had joined the rest of us for church. I remembered linen tablecloths, heavy silverware, and other diners stopping by to tease my father. *Did she have to bribe you with dinner to get you off the farm, Harold?*

"If I could eat like this every Sunday, I'd become a holy roller."

The store where we'd bought our first TV, when I was six, had been taken over by a Mexican vendor of candies and other *"cosas de México."* Mexicans had come with irrigation, to hoe weeds from between row crops. They'd stayed and prospered, in relative terms.

The previous summer, when I'd dared mention my concerns for the Ogallala to one of our old farm neighbors, he'd warned that I shouldn't knock irrigation. It had been "good for Goodland."

I'd nodded politely. I didn't want to alienate this old family friend, who took time out of his busy schedule, running a large farm, to pay regular visits to my mother.

"If they'd put through that zero depletion," he said, "you could shoot a bullet down Main Street and not hit anyone." Zero depletion had been a water-control policy proposed in the early nineties that would have reduced the amount farmers could pump until the withdrawal rate reached a sustainable level, meaning no more would be taken out of the aquifer than rain and snowmelt returned to it each year. The plan hadn't gone over well among irrigators, but having completed our tour of Main Street, I could see that a bullet's hiting anyone was less likely than ever before.

Goodland was dying despite irrigation, and to some extent, because of it. As irrigators drained the aquifer, irrigation drained the countryside of farmers. In order to pay for sprinkler systems—and compete in the depressed grain markets caused by overproduction, due partly to irrigation—they had to "get big or get out," as Ezra Taft Benson, President Eisenhower's secretary of agriculture, had famously advised farmers to do. My aunts and uncles who'd sold their land and left in my early teens were among the many lacking the will or the means to get big. So they got out. The stores had gone the way of the farmers.

I glanced at the clock. Eleven a.m. We were close. A few more blocks to the house, then one hour before Ward was due to arrive. My heart swelled with my unbelievable good fortune. Who would have thought I could love a rural Kansan?

As usual, Jake failed to slow down for the dips that served as the newer east side's drainage system. We almost bottomed out on one of them, and the tires squealed as he rounded the turn at the First Christian Church, with its swooping roof. Our journey ended as it always did, at Mom's house. "Where's that smoke coming from?" I asked. I opened my door, peered under the car. "Oh my God! The tires are on fire." My brother Bruce had arrived before us, I saw. His "road hog," as he called his twenty-year-old Pontiac, was parked at the curb.

"I was going the speed limit," protested my son.

6

JAKE CARRIED ALL OUR BAGS IN AT ONCE AND DROPPED THEM IN THE ENTRYWAY. We exchanged whispery hugs with my mother and heartier ones with my more substantial, unreserved sister-in-law, Kris, and niece, Abby.

Bruce was sitting on the couch, his twelve-string guitar leaning beside him. "Hi, Uncle Bruce," Jake said.

"Hello." He wore his usual scruffy attire. Loose-fitting jeans, old work shoes. The laces didn't match. What was left of his hair hung below his collar, and he still had his hippie beard, although he kept it trimmed better than he used to.

"Is that a new guitar?" Jake asked.

"No, just the same ol' noisemaker," Bruce said, holding it out for Jake, who took it and started strumming the few chords he knew.

"Show Bruce that song you wrote," I said to Jake.

"Oh," Bruce groaned. "Sure, show me what you've got."

I kicked myself for submitting Jake to his uncle's seeming disdain. He put the guitar down. "Nah. Maybe later. Where's Josh?"

Josh was Bruce's twenty-two-year-old son. He was at the motel, Bruce said, with his girlfriend and their toddler daughter, who loved the motel pool. "Don't worry. They'll get here in time for gobbler."

Kris and Mom had returned to the kitchen, which seemed like a safer place. I stood in the doorway for a moment and watched Kris convey herself between the counters with her customary flat footfall, serious intention, and efficiency. Mom was mincing broccoli with a food processor. She wore one of the outfits she'd sewn in the sixties. Bright-orange polyester pants with a vest in the same color over a flowery pink, voluminously sleeved blouse. All of her old clothes still fit her. On my parents' fiftieth wedding anniversary, I'd persuaded her to put on the tiny lavender party dress she'd gotten married in. To save money, they'd eloped. It had been the final year of the Dust Bowl, or the Dirty Thirties. They were poor then. *We got ours by going without!* Dad.

Now, more than sixty years later, Mom still looked great. Her hair wasn't really gray, but silvery blond, the same color mine had begun to turn in my late thirties. It was from her that I'd gotten my Scandinavian features. We had high cheekbones, fine noses. But her skin still shone like porcelain, while mine had begun to show sun damage.

Her needlepoint pictures competed for wall space everywhere in the house. Here, above the picture rail, she'd hung the cute ones. Snoopy slept on his doghouse roof, big-eyed cows munched flowers, kittens played with balls of yarn. "Shall we set the table, Mom?"

"Oh sure, I guess it's time."

I rescued Jake and took him with me into the dining room. First we pulled the gold tablecloth from the blond, built-in hutch, then we draped it, making sure the edges were even. This was our job. We'd done it dozens of times before. Getting out the good china plates with the autumn leaf pattern, we did the tally—Bruce and Kris; my niece, Abby; nephew, Josh; and his little family. Mom, Jake, me. There would be nine of us.

No plate for Dad. I looked over at his college graduation picture on the buffet. His dark eyes, under heavy brows and set in a young, smooth face, stared fixedly into a future now spent. "Just look at that handsome rascal," my mother liked to say, as she gazed at the picture. "Is there any wonder why I married him?"

But without the cap and tassel, Dad wouldn't have looked so rakish, even back then. Mat burns he'd suffered in a high school wrestling match had caused the hair on top of his head to fall out, and it never grew back. We'd razzed him about his baldness. He always played along. Like the gold teeth that accented his smile, a vein of humor glinted in him despite his serious approach to work and what one of my aunts called his hard-assed opinions.

He could not abide what he considered sloth in others. I remembered him pacing the sidewalk outside our farmhouse when my brothers and the hired men tarried over dinner, the noon meal. With his thudding gait and hulking shoulders, his bulb-toed work boots, and the crooked brimmed work hat he jammed low over his ears, he was a caricature of frustrated ambition. "Go in there and tell them to get their lazy butts in gear," he would command me. In I would go, repeating his orders, eliciting laughter and a shuffle of boots and chairs. Empowered by my father, I'd felt like a toy poodle herding bulls.

No plate for my brother Clark either. If he'd lived, would we be setting a place for Noelle, the woman who drove to meet him after his 1988 bicycle trip down the California coast? When he didn't show up, she made the calls to all the local hospitals, then performed the dreaded task, identifying his body in the morgue.

Clark, the eldest. He had been my protector when we were kids. According to family legend, he had even saved me from getting killed when we were traveling in Arizona and I'd toddled onto the highway in front of an oncoming truck. Then all those years later he slipped on a gravel shoulder and was himself hit, by a lumber truck. In the stoic way of farm families, we had absorbed the shock of his death into our interiors and moved on. But the loss was an untended wound.

Jake opened the velvet-lined, wooden box of silver. Watching him work his way around the table, I recalled the Thanksgiving when Clark had apologized to me for not helping in the kitchen. "I want to," he said, "but if I did, Dad would think I was a homo." Screw that! had been my attitude. Ever since Jake was little, I had made it a point to insist on his helping with every meal at Grandma's house.

"Don't be late." I heard Kris command. She was speaking to Josh on the kitchen phone. "Julie's new boyfriend's coming to dinner."

Jake looked at me and pressed his lips together in a flat smile.

Clark and Noelle hadn't married, although Noelle told us that they'd been on a marriage track. "Wouldn't that have been wonderful?" Mom had said many times. Was my family feeling hopeful on my behalf now? Did they envision Jake and me made more complete by the balance Ward would bring to our lives? A fork on the left to accompany our knife and spoon on the right? I envisioned that myself, but at no time more than now, here.

WE SAT IN THE LIVING ROOM, WAITING for the oven timer to go off. Here Mom hung her more serious needlepoint efforts. A replica of John Millet's *The Gleaners*, in which peasant women collected stalks of wheat left behind by a rich farmer's harvest wagons. A large-antlered bull elk. And a romantic rendering of our old farmhouse, the one her father had built and that we'd both grown up in. "If I'd known they would burn it down, I never would have left it," she often said.

I hoped the conversation wouldn't stray into politics while Ward was here. I'd tried to warn him that he'd be entering a den of liberals. He'd said not to worry, it wouldn't be his first rodeo. But I didn't think we were ready for any rodeos yet.

Secretly I believed I could sway Ward over to our side. After all, I'd openly stated my views in my book, and he'd been a fan of that before we met. He didn't seem to see the contradictions in himself that I did. A poetic soul, I reasoned, trapped in a prosaic, repressive region.

I didn't need my atypical family exacerbating our differences. Maybe I could defuse the bomb before Ward arrived. Bracing myself, I asked, "So what do you think of our man in the White House now, Bruce?"

He stopped strumming. "Oh," he groaned in his usual fashion. He went back to practicing a short riff. I waited. He'd spent most of his adult life as a newspaper reporter. His cynicism suited the profession, but not the small-town papers he'd worked for. "I went to a city council meeting and wrote what I heard," he'd said when I asked him what had caused his last dismissal. Now he managed the farm Dad had left us. He could do that even though he lived more than a hundred miles east of Goodland because the excellent farming couple Dad had hired years before his death still did all the real work.

Finally, he put his guitar down and sighed. One side of his mouth lifted wryly, revealing a crooked canine. "I can't say what I think about our president. I could get arrested."

I said, "It might get better. We might win next year in the midterms."

"I'm not kidding!" Bruce yelled. "I could!"

"That, that . . . ," Mom said. She paused to search for sufficiently disparaging words. "Idiot! He calls himself a Christian. I can't even stand to look at him."

Mom and Dad had voted for Eisenhower and Nixon. They'd disliked Kennedy, whom Dad scorned as a "choirboy" Catholic, and were charmed by Reagan. "Such a likable fella," Dad used to say. But being religious, Mom admired Jimmy Carter, and during George Bush Sr.'s tenure she started saying, "That stinking Rush Limbaugh is driving me over to the Democrats. I'm sick of his stupid bullshit." She caused consternation in many who didn't expect such a nice-looking grandma to cuss.

Abby laughed. "You had to ask." She leaned down to pick up a section of newspaper.

Jake said, "Can I see your tattoo, Ab?"

She turned in her chair and lifted her short black hair with the raspberry-red stripe in it. Last year her hair had been auburn and long. On the back of her neck, hieroglyphs encircled a sun emblem. Jake touched it. "Is it new?"

"Oh no. I've been hiding it for something like ten years." She was twenty-six, well into official adulthood and ready to take on the world.

Mom and Kris shook their heads at each other in maternal defeat.

The cuckoo clock clicked to twelve, but the little bird didn't pop out. That mechanism hadn't worked in fifteen years. Clark had sent my mother the clock when he lived in Germany, where he taught chemistry to U.S. Army kids for a while. So it still hung on the wall, the shuttered cuckoo reminding us of the absence we seldom spoke about.

"Ward should be here any minute," I said.

"Where's he from?" Kris asked.

"Plum Springs."

"My aunt Julie is dating a man from Plum Springs?" Abby said, incredulous.

They hadn't been gossiping about us at all, I was disappointed to realize. No one even knew that Ward was local. But it flattered me that Abby had me pegged as cosmopolitan and beyond any such backsliding. "From near there," I said.

"So how'd you meet him?" Abby asked.

"In a cow pasture along the Little Beaver. I was looking for springs."

"Why?" Bruce asked. He seemed genuinely, if guardedly, curious.

I spit it out without hedging. "I thought it was high time I educated myself about what we're doing to the Ogallala Aquifer."

Bruce's eyes gleamed with orneriness that hadn't abated since he was twelve, when I'd followed him around the farmstead as he ignited stink bombs he'd made from powdered sulfur. "What are we doing to the Ogallala?" he asked with a hint of the same mimicking tone he'd gored me with then.

"Bleeding it dry."

"Oh that." He wasn't surprised at my zealotry. I'd always been the family idealist, and I'd been complaining about wasteful irrigation practices for years.

"I've got a gripe about the way people use water," Mom began.

Bruce beamed at me conspiratorially, as if to say, "Here she goes."

"I just hate the way my neighbors let it run down the street!" she exclaimed. "They water their lawns all day and let it run and run. My parents taught me that water is precious. We had a tin cup hanging on the windmill and if we filled it up, we had to drink it all!"

"That lawn water's nothin' compared with what we waste on the farm, Mom," I said.

"You saved water because you didn't have an electric pump on the windmill," said Bruce, who had a penchant for cutting through other people's delusions. "You had to conserve it because the wind didn't always blow." Then to me, "Better be careful. If you singlehandedly put an end to irrigation, you'll cut your own income by two thirds. Not to mention mine. Don't touch mine."

"Don't worry," I said. "No one's going to listen to me."

The doorbell chimed. "There he is!" Abby said.

Jake smiled reassuringly at me as Abby leaned sideways in her chair to look into the entryway. Through the three offset panes of the front door, my niece's first glimpse of "Julie's new boyfriend" was half of his mustached face, a full square of his red-and-white pinstriped shirt, his blue-jeaned hip, and half of the calf roper who cinched his middle.

I stepped outside and pulled him away from the door. He placed his hands on my waist. I laid mine on his arms and he looked into me out of his sea-green eyes. I was centered again, at home in a way that home hadn't made me feel in years. I was a wheel in a groove, a bird in its nest, a woman with the kind of lover she hadn't known enough to wait for.

7

INTRODUCED **WARD** TO **JAKE** FIRST. Jake rose, and Ward strode across the room to shake his hand, man to man. When Josh finally arrived and dinner was served, Ward actually held a chair out for me before sitting down himself. No man had ever done that in this house. Jake sat on one side of me, Ward on the other. Abby grabbed the chair at the head of the table opposite Mom, which Bruce made a point to avoid. He wasn't into traditional symbolism.

Ward had gotten a haircut recently. I longed to stroke the shiny V in the blond bristles on the back of his head. His hat had left a ridge in his hair. I couldn't imagine my father in a cowboy hat. He would have looked foolish. And Ward would have looked comical and out of character in the derby Dad had worn when dressing up. Yet both men had the anchoring presence of their largeness. It was as if the house had been a listing boat, and Ward's stepping on deck had set it to rights.

Was he shocked at our incivility? We didn't say a prayer, just started handing the platters around. If Mom had called the shots when we were growing up, she would have set a different, more reverent tone in her household. Dad hadn't gone in for all that "holy, holy, holy." Yet he'd had more social grace than all of us put together. "Grace" was not a word that leaped to mind for a man of such blunt and coarse opinions. He did, in fact, worry that Clark was gay. He did call undermotivated hired men lazy so and so's. But if he were still with us, we wouldn't have been handing platters around the table in silence. He would have sparked a conversation with a tidbit of gossip or an odd fact he'd read in *National Geographic*. He would have plied us with questions about our lives, asking Jake how school was treating him and offering sage advice it pleased me to hear. *Don't let those grades start slippin'. Pretty soon they'll be down so far you'll need a bucket and a rope to get them back up.*

"Now Jasmin," Ward said, "did you grow these pickles yourself?"

Mom perked up at this attention from the new man at her table. "Oh no, I didn't. But I used to grow all my pickles. Even after we moved to town. You should have seen that downstairs closet in the furnace room. It used to be plumb full of vegetables I'd canned."

"I miss that food, don't you?" Ward said.

"I saw some pretty good clouds down your way last week," Bruce said, before she could answer. "You guys squeeze any moisture out of them?"

"Not a drop," Ward said.

Bruce sighed. "Dry sponges. Oh well. Who needs rain when we've got the government?" He explained that the drought-relief package Congress had passed coincided with his taking out government crop insurance. "Like doubling down in blackjack," he said. Gleefully he threw up his hands. "And winning!" He revealed both crooked canines this time. "That never worked for me in Vegas, but in Washington, the odds are stacked our way."

A landslide of cash had poured in, so much, he explained to Ward, that he was planning to buy a new tractor before year end, to reap the investment tax credit. "The government gives it to us. We give it back. They give it to us."

"That's the merry-go-round all right," Ward said.

"I had a dream about your father," Mom said. "He told me we didn't need that new tractor." She'd described the dream to me before. She'd been sitting in the tub, naked, I assume. Was there any other way to sit in a tub full of water? He'd been washing her back. That this must have been a common ritual between them amazed me. Growing up, I rarely saw my parents display affection. There were no spoken endearments, no touches other than her patting his bald head on occasion or him slapping her bottom as she washed the dishes. "Oh Harold!" I could still hear her grumble, as if truly angry.

Discovering that my parents had been that intimate in their private lives touched me. But it couldn't have been easy for my father to make such a vivid appearance in Mom's dreams, especially for a man who hadn't believed in an afterlife. He must have felt a mighty need to convey his advice. I was accustomed to thinking my father correct in all things farm related. Was Bruce frittering away Dad's money on fancy equipment we didn't need? Were we destined for financial ruin? It really did scare me.

Bruce ignored Mom and her oft-repeated dream. Ward's starched shirt and dark-blue jeans were a dead giveaway. My brother knew he had a Republican sitting between the sights of his piercing brown eyes, and he'd clearly been waiting to move in for the kill. "I've got an idea. The government can get out of the lives of everyone who voted for Newt Gingrich and his buds in Congress. The rest of us'll take our Farm Program checks."

"Okay, Bruce," Ward said. "Let me know if you can spare a couple bucks."

Bruce leaned back in his chair and broke into appreciative laughter. "Score!" he shouted. He was nothing if not fair minded. A wave of relief passed around the table.

"Well I just don't know about that Bush," Mom began.

Time to change the subject. "Did you have fun swimming, Jess?" I asked my grand-niece. She nodded and paddled her arms over her head.

"WHAT CAN I DO TO HELP, LADIES?" Ward asked after dinner.

"Oh nothing," Mom said. She suggested he go down to the basement and watch the game with Bruce and the kids.

He took the dishes she was stacking out of her hands. "No, you go sit."

"Well okay, if you insist," she said brightly.

How about that. A new paradigm in the Bair household. I tried to imagine Dad questioning Ward's manhood. He was too rugged and confident. It would just never happen.

Once finished cleaning up, we left the dishwasher churning and descended the stairs. "You might want to shade your eyes," I said.

"Well isn't this something? It's a whole other world down here." Ward courteously refrained from commenting on the bold-print, chartreuse indoor-outdoor carpet laid when the house was new. Mom had completed the decor with green-and-gold striped wallpaper. The green stripes were flocked.

Bruce was propped in one lounger, Abby in the other. Jake and Josh sat in the chairs closer to the TV, Jake trying to be interested in football. Bruce picked up the remote and turned the volume down. "Get up, Abby," he commanded.

"Now, don't bother," Ward said. "I'll just—"

"Oh it's all right," Bruce said.

I sat down on the end of the couch nearest Ward. "I always thought this had to be the ugliest couch in the world. Dad called it shitmuckle brown."

"He called every shade of brown shitmuckle," drolled Abby.

Jake laughed and examined the matching chair he sat in. "Didn't Grandma and Grandpa get these like forty years ago, when you lived on the farm?"

"Those sonsabitches'll never wear out," Bruce said. "You kids can save some of Harold's money by marking our graves with them instead of headstones."

"If we don't lose it all before then," I said.

"We're doing fine," Bruce said. "The new ground averaged better than anything." He was referring to the wheat yield on some land for which he'd traded our father's largest pasture. The pasture had been rough prairie, sliced in two by a dry creek like the one in our childhood canyon pasture, while the new ground had been ideal for wheat. *Flat as the day is long*, Dad used to say about such land. "That's a half section of new wheat we've got coming into the coffers," Bruce added. "Twelve thousand bushels in a good year."

I was accustomed to bluffing my way through conversations with Bruce, pretending not to need his approval, but now his dark eyes brimmed with pent-up unsaid things. Was it possible he doubted himself? Did he need my approval too? Is that what he was signaling? I said, "It was a good decision, Bruce. I know that."

Here was the machine that was our family working in its best, limping fashion. "What choice did I have?" Bruce said. "We don't run livestock anymore. I could have kept it just so that cowboy bastard we were renting to could play out the romance of the dying breed, or I could make us some real money."

I glanced at my cowboy boyfriend, who smiled lopsidedly at me and shook his head slightly, as if to say, "Don't worry. Water off a duck's back."

"You sold the pasture that had the cement stock tank in it?" Abby broke in.

"Yes," Bruce said.

"God, Aunt Julie," Abby said. "Remember the time you took us swimming in that stock tank and I couldn't get out? You almost killed me!"

I'd returned and was living on Dad's farm then. Jake was a baby. "You just thought you couldn't get out," I said. "You were thirteen and going through a phase of girlish weakness. I had to get back in and push up on your bottom."

My father had inherited that pasture and some of the land around it from his father. When the grass got too short in the canyon pasture on the Carlson farm, he would drive his sheep ten miles across the county to his own place, where he, Mom, and my brothers had lived before I was born. I would ride on the bench seat of his pickup as we bounced across neighbors' fields, cutting and mending barbed-wire fences as we went, honking the horn and thumping the outside of our doors until we finally herded the sheep into the other barnyard, then out into that pasture.

Jake's memories of the pasture were probably not as pleasant. When he was six and we'd come home for a visit, Dad invited us to ride with him to survey his heifers. Rex, our dog at the time, jumped out of the pickup bed and began chasing them. This was a high-stakes catastrophe. In ten minutes, he could run a week's worth of weight gain off the heifers. Dad barreled over the hills, threatening to run Rex over. "Don't kill my dog!" Jake wailed.

"Drive away! Fast!" I shouted. Rex, fearing abandonment, ran after us. We rode in silence back to the farmstead, my heart rate returning to normal only as Dad's anger subsided. It wouldn't have been the first time he'd killed a family dog. He treated his sheepdogs like kings, but didn't suffer chicken eaters or cow chasers. In this way and a thousand others, my brothers and I had learned from him our society's values, rooted in production and finance.

Killing the dog to protect our financial interests. It was the same value system that Bruce had exercised selling the pasture. We both had romantic ties to that grass. It was one of the last places in our corner of the county where you could still imagine what the original Kansas had been like. But he was trying to fill the shoes of a father whose only focus had been the bottom line.

Hang on to your land! Dad had always commanded us. If we didn't, he warned that we would die broke, just as he predicted our aunts and uncles who'd sold out would do. He'd been right. Many of them had. But in trading for the wheat ground, Bruce had not only improved our financial security, he'd also demonstrated that we were still in the game. He hadn't let Harold down, as just about everyone had expected him to do.

Bruce retrained his gaze on Ward, who hadn't folded the recliner back, but looked comfortable, resting one polished boot on his knee. "You're a grass man, I suppose?"

"I have some cattle and I breed horses," Ward said. "Grass doesn't make you money the way farmland does though."

"Right," Bruce said. "I hated to sell the pasture, but renting it out was one helluva drag." He explained that the cowboy renter neglected the fence and his cows were always getting out. The neighbors would call Bruce, complaining, so he insisted that the renter put in all new posts and wire. Then the Errington "girls," as Dad, and now Bruce, called them, put that section of good wheat ground up for sale. Dad had lusted after that land his whole life. Bruce couldn't resist. He worked out a like-kind exchange, trading the pasture for the farmland and avoiding capital gains taxes in the process.

"It made our renter pretty mad," he said. "The bank trust department that handles Dad's estate didn't like it either. You know, people in this country form alliances. There're the insiders and the outsiders, the ones who drink together out at the country club and cook up land schemes and get rich off each other, and the ones like us who've always gone along by ourselves, making money the dumb way."

"Insiders. Outsiders. That'd be how a lot of folks see it," Ward said. He didn't point out that he sold horse tack and water troughs to real estate agents and bankers. He played golf and roped calves with them too, but had somehow failed to get rich.

"To tell you the truth, I'm not sure what the future holds for the Bair Farm," Bruce said.

I caught my breath. Our forbidden topic was being broached. Just look at us, I thought. To Ward, we must have seemed less like a farm family than any he'd ever known. With the exception of Mom, asleep upstairs under the quilt she'd made from gaudy polyester squares, not one of us had a Norman Rockwell glow. We didn't speak the vernacular. The older among us voted for liberal presidents. The younger dyed their hair funny colors and cut it into weird shapes and got tattoos. But our patriarch's blood ran thick in our veins. He'd implanted his values in my brothers and me by the time we were three, the most important one being that first commandment, *Hang on to your land!*

Whether we kids would find the wherewithal to obey it had hung in the air our whole lives. Even Harold's grandkids had drunk the commandment with their baby milk. Of the three, only Jake showed overt interest in our conversation. He leaned toward us with his arms planted on his knees, making himself available should there be an opening for him. But I knew that Abby and Josh were listening too. It didn't matter that the Raiders had just scored a touchdown on TV. Every one of Bruce's and my words, when we talked about the farm's future, lofted through the air into the ears of surefire receivers.

"We'd have to be fools and ingrates to complain," Bruce went on, "but I spent too many years being Dad's tractor dog. I told him a long time ago, I really don't want to farm. Neither does Julie." He looked at me. "I don't think."

I shook my head reluctantly.

"Hell," Bruce continued, "neither of us can farm it. All I can do is watch the grain markets on my computer screen and call our guy on the farm once in a while. He lets me think I'm the boss. I don't have the stamina for farm work. Too old. Arthritis. I can put myself out of commission for a week throwing a Frisbee for my dog. And Julie doesn't know enough." He looked at me. "No offense."

His smirk irritated me. "I do know a little," I said. During those years I'd spent on the farm when Jake was a baby, then a toddler, Dad had taught me all he could. He'd even entertained the idea of me as his successor.

Bruce flung his arm in Jake's and Josh's direction. "Our boys weren't raised to farm." Jake glowered at this, making eye contact with me. If you were among my father's descendants, you soaked up his conceit, that farming was the only valid work in the world. It didn't matter that Jake had never driven a tractor, or that he made fun of Garth Brooks, or that he played drums in a punk-rock band that went by an absurd moniker—the Kilted Monarchs. None of that immunized him any more than the Beatles and Bob Dylan had spared Bruce and me.

Thinking this, I realized that my nephew, Josh, looked like John Lennon. Dark eyes behind wire rims, the long Grecian nose, the tender, intelligent mien. Except that now his lips had pressed together with a bitterness I'd never seen in him before.

Abby sat frozen too. Had she noticed that her father had made no mention of her?

Bruce seemed unaware of Jake's reaction or of Abby's and Josh's studied nonreactions. "Ron, the guy who lives there and does the real work, isn't getting any younger," he went on.

"What will we do if he gets sick?" I added.

"If he gets sicker," Bruce said. "He has emphysema."

"Farm dust, or cigarettes?" Ward asked.

"Both. Julie's right. It would be a catastrophe if he had to go to the hospital in the summer, when irrigation's in full swing. I don't know how fast we could find a renter."

"Even if you did, there'd be no tellin' how it would work out," Ward said. "You don't know the proof of that pudding until it's congealed and all you've got is lumps."

"It's an age-old question," Bruce said. "What to do with the farm." He allowed a dramatic pause. "Do you want to manage a thirty-five-hundred-acre dryland wheat and irrigated farm?" He was being facetious, but also a tad bit serious, honoring Ward and messaging approval to me. Did he think I'd finally made a sane choice in a man?

"I'm afraid I've never been much of a manager, Bruce," Ward said.

As Harold's daughter, it baffled me how a man could say such a thing about himself. Was it just his humility talking? My brother only nodded. Subject closed, for now.

8

CAN IT, SPIDER!" Ward shouted out his open window. The dog was growling just as he had in the summer, when he first laid eyes on me. I stepped around the back of Ward's pickup. We'd met at a country intersection. He said he wanted to show me something before he took me to his house, our planned post-Thanksgiving rendezvous.

"Pardon my idiot friend," Ward said as I got in, "He's on a mission to fend off any woman who tries to come near me."

"Poor dog. Must have his hands full." It was drizzling lightly, and I'd gotten a little damp. Not all bad, I mused. Although I hoped the drought was ending, my focus right now was on my appearance. Every plainswoman knew she looked better when the normally dry air had moisture in it. My hair would pouf up and have more body. My wrinkles would soften. I was three years older than Ward. All of his past girl-friends had been younger than him. This troubled me even more than knowing he might be an irremediable bachelor. He'd come close to marrying once, in his early twenties, he'd told me, but had bolted shortly after his town's newspaper, the *Handshake*, ran the announcement of his and the local girl's engagement.

We rode together in his pickup, which doubled as his office, apparently. Receipts stuck out from beneath both visors. *American Quarter Horse Journals* littered the floor behind the seats. He turned onto a narrow trail between fields of wheat stubble left from the previous harvest.

Suddenly the land dropped away and we were bouncing down a road carved into a bluff. Before us yawned the Smoky Valley, the river concealed by cottonwood trees, their branches bare. I rolled my window down and Ward followed suit. He threw his head back, swilling the air into his lungs. "Wet grass on a fall morning," he said. "I haven't smelled that in *so* long."

Me neither. The smell was intoxicating, restorative, and pungent due to the willows that hugged the gullies leading to the river. They were leafless like the trees, but their burgundy branches, streaked in orange, flamed against the yellow prairie. The grass was tall for our part of Kansas, calf high on the hills and deeper along the edges of the trees and willows. In one place far up the valley, where the sun smiled through the clouds, the grass smiled back. The innocent color of a toddler's blond hair, it literally glowed.

I have remembered that moment ever since as the beginning of my love affair with Ward's Smoky Valley ranch. Visiting his pastures reassured me the way visiting my mother did. She was old. She couldn't do all the things she used to do, but she was at least still with us, very much alive. Knowing this was a creature comfort. The same was true of that valley swath of intact prairie. Its beauty and smells gave me respite from the loss I felt on the tablelands where I'd grown up.

I envied Ward for being able to ride in these pastures as a kid. His family had lived in town, but he'd come here to play with his cousins for as long as he could remember. When his uncle died, his aunt, wanting to move to Arizona for the warm winters and to be near her kids, had put the land up for sale. "I couldn't stand seeing the place leave the family," he said. He'd bought the headquarters and valley pastures.

There was farmland too, but his aunt had hung on to it and rented it out to a neighbor.

He had taken me there to see his mares. About twelve of them came trotting out of the nearest copse when he banged a bucket and called, "C'meat!" It took me a while to realize he was saying "Come eat." He moved casually among the herd, pouring grain in piles as the mares jockeyed for position. "Take it easy, sisters," he said. "Whoa, Alice."

I breathed deeply, relishing the fragrance of wet horses, willow, and grass all mixed together. *"'Las yeguas jóvenes, las yeguas salvajes y ardientes,'"* I said. Cormac McCarthy's hero had whispered the erotic phrase into the cocked ear of a high-strung, pure-blooded stallion he'd ridden to a lather.

"And that means?" Ward asked as he emptied the bucket into a final pile.

"The young mares, the wild and ardent mares," I purred.

"Gr-r-r-r," Ward said, grabbing me around the waist and jamming me against his hip as we walked. Oh, the deliciousness of desire. It had been too long since I'd wanted anyone like this. He led me to stand before what seemed to be the lead mare, a bay. I noted her wide belly. "She's pregnant?"

"All of them took this year. A record." We stepped back as the mare squealed and nipped at the roan beside her. Ward said, "If this one didn't have the best blood in the herd, I'd sell her in a whinny. She's got the temperament of a rattlesnake."

An apt description, I thought. With her ears laid back on her long neck, her nostrils flared, and her teeth bared, she had looked like a snake.

"The bitchiest mares make the best mothers though. They really defend their babies. Now watch out, stand back so you don't get kicked." Bitchier, that's what I need to be, I thought. I needed to boss Jake more and keep those invaders—drugs, alcohol, bad influences—at bay. Of course he already thought I was the parent from hell, insisting on obsolete concepts like homework and curfews. But where were the horse dads? How come we human animals supposedly needed two parents, while others got by with one?

"Some breeders don't pay much attention to the dam," Ward said, "but I think the mother is actually more important."

"Huh," I said noncommittally. "Why's that?" Had he read my mind? Was he making a bow toward Jake's fatherlessness?

"She's half the bloodline, and she also establishes her offspring's position in the herd. You want to buy a lead horse, not a follower. They're more competitive, if you're into roping or barrels, anything like that. And they're more confident too. Less likely to get scared or blow up in the middle of whatever work you're trying to do."

"So this one's Alice?"

"They're all Alice. That's just what I call 'em. They have their own names too. Here," he said, leading me to the end of the line. "I want you to meet Virginia."

"Virginia must be low gal on the totem pole. She got the last pile of grain."

"They lose rank as they age. It's just nature's way."

I'd never seen a horse quite like her—smoky gray with a black stripe down her withers and black bars on her front legs. "She's a grullo," Ward said. "The horse folks along the Front Range will trade their jodhpurs for this color, but I could never bring myself to sell her." He reached down with a leather-gloved hand and scratched the mare's ears. "Virginia's my oldest girl. She's thrown ten foals and still goin' strong. Easy labor. No misses."

I felt his eyes move on to me. "You know, Julene, it's always made me uncomfortable when a woman wanted to visit me here. But you're different. I couldn't wait to show you everything. I want you to know everything about me."

"Really? Everything?" I teased. Was he trying to flatter me? Why would he not want his prior girlfriends to come here? Wouldn't he want to impress them? It was all pure sex appeal. Horses and hats.

Ward whistled one short note through his teeth. In response, Spider leaped off the bed of the pickup and bounded ahead of us as we threaded our way into the woods along a trail the horses had made. The drizzle was getting heavier, droplets falling from the brim of Ward's hat and darkening the back of his canvas jacket in a V. I wore my impervious Gortex parka and waterproof hiking boots self-consciously. I knew the local opinion of people who bought special equipment for hiking. Western Kansans didn't hike. They walked, but only when they couldn't take their pickups.

We stepped through downed limbs, tall yellow grass, and wet drifts of fluff the cottonwoods had shed. A forest was a veritable paradise on the plains, where a single tree was a rarity. As always, there was water to thank, and soon we came to a wide, sandy riverbed, sparsely strewn in yellow leaves. A shallow, narrow stream twined down the middle of the bed. It was hard to believe that the Smoky was once plentiful enough to water thousands of Cheyenne, not to mention the horses they kept in numbers many times their own and the buffalo that had sustained them.

"We used to have family picnics here," Ward said. A frayed, rain-blackened rope hung from one of the trees. He pulled it to the edge of a broken-down homemade picnic table. "Us kids would take turns. 'Tarza-a-a-n!'"

Even though sand had long since filled the swimming hole, I could imagine the scene. Ward's family might have included fewer farmers than mine did. Most of the men were probably ranchers, like my grandmother Bair's brothers. From the Colorado side of the border, they wore cowboy hats and narrow trousers with triangles embroidered on the pocket corners. But I was sure that the women had all dressed like my mother and aunts used to do, in Betty Crocker housedresses they'd sewn themselves. They would have covered the old table in the food that had delighted me in childhood—fried chicken, potatoes that were first boiled then fried in butter, pies made from bright-red sour cherries picked from the tree that grew in every farmyard. The wind would have made that enchanting running-water sound through the leaves of the cottonwoods, just as it had done at Smoky Gardens, the county park some forty miles west of here on this river, where my family had gone for picnics. Those giant old trees rendered an August afternoon pleasant rather than unbearable. They didn't stop the flies from biting, though. The men ignored the flies, but the women, who had softer, more exposed skin, shooed them until they couldn't stand it any longer and began packing up.

No coals remained in the fire pit now, no bottles or cans to show it had been used in the recent past. Just coarse, grayish-pink sand. The drizzle intensified the color. As a child, I'd loved seeing the sand in the Little Beaver redden after a rain.

I walked to the center of the bed and took my knit glove off to test the rivulet that ran there. The water was as cold, on that late-November day, as the glaciers whose melt had first suffused the Ogallala formation.

By now, I'd winnowed the decipherable from the incomprehensible in several geology texts and had a basic grasp of how the formation had been created five million years ago by rivers flowing out of the Rockies. The rivers braided, unbraided, and rebraided themselves, depositing the eroding mountains over the terrain to their east. Glacier melt and rain filled the spaces between the eroded materials with water. Our "cussed wind," as Mom called it, had then deposited a couple of hundred feet of our highly prized, fertile loess over the top. Together, those rivers and the wind had made the High Plains.

In the late 1800s, the geologist who discovered the Ogallala deposits exposed in cliffs cut by the South Platte River in Nebraska had named them after a nearby town. Ogallala, the town, had gotten its name from the Oglala Sioux, who favored that region along the Platte. I'd seen "Oglala" variously translated as "spread throughout," "to scatter one's own," and "she poured out her own." All appropriate, as the aquifer was spread throughout the High Plains and scattered or poured out her own to all who lived there.

I lifted the water in my cupped palms. It was wonderfully clear. Without pumps or wells, the natives and early pioneers could only live near springs like the one where Ward and I had met, or along spring-fed streams such as the Smoky. But we were no less dependent on the Ogallala than those earlier people had been, and not just for irrigation.

Life needs water. The only water we had came from the aquifer. If we were mindful of this, we would call ourselves the Ogallala People, not after the tribe that lost its home to our invasion but in recognition of our life source. The name would cascade as water does, down stairs of years—the tribe, the town, the aquifer—onto us.

"The Cheyenne called this Bunch of Trees River," I said, standing up.

Ward looked around at the grove. "Makes sense. Did you learn that in your Dog Soldier book?"

I nodded. A couple of months ago I'd been excited when I read that the famous Cheyenne warrior society's favorite campground had been on the Smoky, only about thirty miles south of Goodland, on what was now the Colorado-Kansas border. The divide where I grew up, the sweeping prairies between the Smoky and the Republican rivers, had been their prime hunting grounds. My grandparents' deeds gave them ownership of land taken ninety years before my birth by soldiers led by the likes of General Custer, Buffalo Bill, Kit Carson, and Wild Bill Hickok.

"Was this where Dull Knife came through?" I asked.

"No, they think it was west of here. I'll take you there sometime, but this afternoon I have other plans for us."

Mmm. Other plans.

WARD'S PLACE—A NARROW, TWO-STORY HOUSE WITH A garage tacked on to it and a bunch of outbuildings beside a wooden windmill—looked like a ranch to me, not *a damned ol' farm*, as he'd lamented in his letter. The place had an old-timey feel and, positioned on a bluff overlooking the Smoky, was far more romantic than a farm. To see the valley, we had to walk behind the house, which his uncle had built facing the road instead of the river, and through a maze of weathered wood corrals, where several horses searched the ground for strands of the morning's hay. From the edge of the bluff, we looked out on the mile-wide bottomland.

It was the kind of low-key vista that could thrill only a native Kansan whose eye had not been jaded by mountains or the sensational. "Thrill" is probably the wrong word. "Satisfy" might be better, or "fulfill." Not even in my childhood had I seen so much uninterrupted prairie. This is what the Indians saw, I thought. There were no buffalo, of course. All of those had been wiped out by hide hunters—with the encouragement of the generals overseeing the Indian wars, who knew full well that the natives couldn't survive long without their food supply. "You kill the buffalo, you kill the Indian's commissary," General Philip Sheridan had cynically recommended. But the grass was the same grass that had supported the immense herds, and the trees and yucca were the same trees and yucca.

Where the cedar shelterbelt didn't break our view, the aspect in the other directions alternated between square expanses of young, green winter wheat and lusterless stubble on the fallow ground, interrupted by remnants of frost-cured buffalo grass along the serpentine gullies. Even if surrounded by farmland on three sides, the place had a "poky" feel to it. That word, one of Ward's favorites, described a certain lazy, western quiet that emanated from where cowboys lived. Here the pokiness was evident in the iron dinner bell beside the door, the solid round corral made of cottonwood limbs, the cattle-loading shoot, the brand some welder had worked into the filigree above the front gate, and the hitching post beside the garage, which Ward had converted into a tack room. I especially liked the quiet. The concepts of peace and quiet go together for good reason. I breathed the quiet in, letting the peace run through my veins.

All of the outbuildings were white stucco with green trim like the house. I appreciated the congruity. The place was a home, not a grain factory like our present-day farm. I was never able to explain to my father the ineffable qualities of old farmsteads that hadn't been demeaned by corrugated-tin sheds. "Farmerized," Ward called it.

I saw that the branches of nearby trees had scraped shingles from the house's roof. The rain gutter was beginning to come off. The green trim was peeling. He was a bachelor, I reminded myself. What had I expected?

Reading my expression, Ward said, "I've got a list. The house has never been very near the top."

He followed me as I took in the downstairs, recently cleaned. "It's nice," I said, half lying. Both the dining room and living room walls were hung, as I'd predicted, with reproductions of famous western paintings. I did like the yellow Formica-and-chrome table and chairs in the kitchen, but the olive-green linoleum and walnut-stained cabinets with the copper handles gave me the creeps.

I began mentally remodeling, tearing up the turquoise carpet in the living room, sanding and varnishing the wood floor that was probably suffocating beneath it, widening the front entrance that Ward said he never used.

"And now for my lair," Ward said. After a steep climb up a narrow stairwell, we stepped into an L-shaped sitting room that held a big recliner, a rolltop desk, and a large TV—I'd feared that his TV would be large. Coved ceilings and the overstuffed chair gave the room a cozy, nestlike feeling. The walls were real knotty pine, unlike the paneling I'd talked my parents into for my room in the Goodland house. Shelves lined one wall. The Hardy Boys, Sherlock Holmes, every book in Walter Farley's Black Stallion series. Things Ward must have read in childhood.

There were several adult books too. All of Hemingway, it looked like, most of F. Scott Fitzgerald. Nothing by Faulkner, a serious oversight for someone of the masculine-classics bent. Dickens. Some Michener. A few recent bestsellers. *Angela's Ashes. Cold Mountain. Men Are from Mars, Women Are from Venus.* What conflict had led a former girlfriend to suggest that one?

Women authors were poorly represented except for a complete set of Ayn Rand. Oh boy. Social Darwinism. Capitalism as the natural winnowing by which superior men triumphed over their inferiors. Rand's high-spirited Dominique Francon finding her alpha male in

Howard Roark. I looked down the hall. At the far end, a door stood open—his bedroom, I assumed. The edge of a green porcelain sink gleamed inside the nearer doorway. When my parents had remodeled the farmhouse, they installed green bathroom fixtures. Suddenly, it all seemed too shabbily intimate.

Like anyone who'd had a happy childhood, I was a little nostalgic, but a sense of desolation overcame me when I considered what it would be like to live in the same county where I'd grown up, in a house that my uncle had built. How could Ward stand it? What was I doing here? Why would I want to reenter my dead past?

"Brr," I said.

"Cold?"

"Just a little." My clothes were damp from the drizzle.

"We'll have to take care of that." Ward must have seen my eyes stray to the shelf. "I know I'm out of date."

"I went through an Ayn Rand phase," I said.

"I got excited about her in college, but I'm still an eager learner." He pulled me to him. "It's just I haven't had a teacher." He said this into the hair over my ear, turning my spine into an electrified rope.

There was more to a man than the books on his shelf. Besides, Ward didn't buy many books. He'd told me he read mainly out of his little town's library. That's where he'd run across my book. Unfairly, I'd led him to apologize. I backed out of the hug. "I'm such a snob, and you're so open-minded."

"Oh yeah. That'd be me all right." He walked down the hall, stopped beside the bedroom door, and turned to wait for me. He wasn't smiling.

My tongue thickened, and I could feel my heart beating as I brushed past him into the room. The oak-slatted headboard, chest of drawers, and dresser were so dark from age that I first thought they'd been stained black. The dresser had an oval mirror like the ones in old Westerns. Navy-blue curtains framed the room's one skinny window. The venetian blinds were turned open, permanently, I suspected, because what did it matter? The closest neighbors lived more than a mile away. Through the dirty glass, I could see the valley.

Say things worked out between us and I moved here. First, I would remove the blinds. Wash the window. How impressed Ward would be to see me on an extension ladder outside his house. Perhaps someday we'd enlarge the window opening and hang French doors onto a little balcony. . . .

He was standing beside me. "Julene, *Julene*," he said, pulling me close and searching for a scent on my neck. Perfume wasn't my thing, so to distract him, I turned my face up for a kiss. He gave me one, deep and all consuming, but when my body began to conform to his, the way water does to rock, he put his hand on my shoulder and turned me toward the mirror. "Later, sweetheart. I want to spend the night making up for last time. Look at how beautiful you are."

Now that I understood his game, I didn't mind being redirected. I would anticipate and savor him all the more. The mirror, hazy with its own age, blurred and flattered us. "We look good together," I said. In the low light, our hair was exactly the same color, blond without a hint of silver.

"Now here's my plan."

Following Ward's instructions, I went into the bathroom, started the water in the green tub, peeled off my damp clothes and put them outside the door. How good the hot water felt! I hadn't realized how chilled I was, but he obviously had. While I languished in the bath, letting the warmth seep into my bones, he put my clothes in the dryer, then deposited them outside the door.

"Better?" he said when I came downstairs.

"Much. Thank you." In warm, dry jeans and my soft velour sweater, I felt nothing less than well loved.

"Okay then. Let's see some sights."

9

PLUM SPRINGS TURNED OUT TO BE AN IDYLLIC PRAIRIE TOWN WITH A MUCH-MALIGNED AMENITY. A hill. Ward said that the locals complained because they had to walk up it every so often—when they were children and climbed it on their way to school or, later, when their pickups broke down. I loved the place for that hill, and for the view from it of untrammeled, rugged prairie.

He pointed out his parents' white frame house on the end of Main, where the street began to curve down into the Smoky Valley. We'd been invited to a dinner of Thanksgiving leftovers, but Ward had told his mom he wanted me all to himself today. "I promised we'd come tomorrow, though. Everyone's eager to meet you."

We ate our "dinner," which was lunch in Kansas, at a little drive-in restaurant. The only choice was between a hamburger or a "fishwich." The fish, I knew, would be a square-shaped, deep-fried, codlike substance. I chose the hamburger and made the mistake of ordering it with mayonnaise. The bun was so soaked with Miracle Whip that it fell apart. I hate Miracle Whip. I wiped my lips with my napkin and resorted to eating the burger with my fork. Ward watched me, apparently amused.

"What a slob I am, huh?" I couldn't say what I thought about the meal without offending him, and I was determined not to make the same mistake I had earlier, passing judgment on his books. Did he know how good he looked? He had changed out of his own rain-dampened clothes and now had on a button-up Pendleton shirt. The yellow plaid complemented his hair and mustache, and the chocolate-brown neckerchief he'd put on lent his black cowboy hat all the more dash. He wore cowboy clothes with flair, but I'd been happy when he told me that he considered snap-up shirts ridiculous. He wasn't into country music either. Like me, he preferred the soulful, minor-key songs of Joni Mitchell and Leonard Cohen.

After lunch, we drove north, across the interstate that I'd traveled in the morning, onto a narrow highway, then onto gravel. We took more turns than I would ever be able to retrace on my own, finally stopping beside an unmarked bridge. This creek was the Sappa, Ward informed me, the site of the Cheyenne Hole Massacre, which some people called the last battle of the Red River War.

"Want to take a look?" It was still misting outside and cold. He wore suede work gloves, and through them his grasp was the large-handed, firm one I'd yearned to feel again. It was a manly grasp, full of his own ego and volition, his own ideas of what we would do next.

We climbed a steep, yucca-strewn slope. Deep in the ravine, obscured by tree limbs, glimmered a circle of dark water, as placid and inscrutable as the eye of a horse. Here again the Ogallala was making one of her magical, life-giving appearances, this time in a death-dealing place.

"The soldiers rode in through there," Ward said, pointing to a gully that dissected the hill opposite us. His eyes grew distant as he considered the ravine again. "Anyone camping down there would have been a sitting duck."

I'd read about the Cheyenne Hole Massacre in a book Ward had sent me. The Indians had lost the Red River War, which they referred to as the War to Save the Buffalo. It had been fought south of the Oklahoma-Kansas border, and those Indians who'd camped here had been Southern Cheyenne refugees attempting to reach the Black Hills, where some bands of Northern Cheyenne still lived freely. As one historian put it, they had felt secure here, because this was the land their clans had hunted before being exiled to Oklahoma. They were the people, in other words, who had hunted the pasture hills where I grew up.

The book had included a list of the dead. They had names like Little Bull, Dirty Water, and White Bear. They had consciously taken their identity from the land, as I had done unconsciously in my childhood, from the very texture of the sand in the Little Beaver and from our craggy little canyon.

As the book was fresher in my memory than in Ward's, I told him a few of the details that I recalled. The ambush had taken place in April, when the creek was near flood stage. The soldiers' horses struggled in the crossing, alerting the Cheyenne. Half of the band climbed out of the ravine and escaped. The half that didn't were likely women encumbered by small children and the men who stayed behind to defend them. The lieutenant who led the charge claimed that nineteen warriors were killed and eight "squaws" and children. Cheyenne accounts claimed the reverse—twenty women and children and just seven braves. Of the lieutenant's forty-four men, two lost their lives.

Ward said, "You can't imagine how exciting this is to me, Julene. To be standing here. Talking like this." Yes I could. Learning the history, we were filling in the blanks in ourselves. This had been a major event in a place where we'd grown up thinking that nothing significant had ever happened. Yet no one seemed interested in memorializing it. I'd seen no historical marker, not even the creek's name posted on the bridge. A kid living on a nearby farm would have been as ignorant of the Indian past as I'd been.

My only awareness of Indians had come when my brothers or I found an arrowhead or when my father told his fantastical bedtime stories about a deep, mysterious hole in our canyon pasture. We couldn't see it by day, but Dad said it opened at night. *These ol' redskins live down there, and when the moon is full, they come out to hunt.*

Today it intrigued me that my father had placed his Indians underground, as in the deep recesses of the mind. Where else could they have gone? They'd been thoroughly vanquished on the land they'd lost to us. When I'd read about manifest destiny in high school and my history teacher made it clear, with her patriotic ramblings, that she still bought into the dated concept, I had no classmates whose resentful dark eyes in dark faces might have caused me to question her. As the North Dakota author Clay Jenkinson pointed out, you could sense *a compelling edginess* in Nebraska and the Dakotas, where there were large reservations. Not in Kansas, though. *A plains state without Indians is a dull blade*, he wrote.

Yet the Indians hadn't been vanquished from my father's psyche or from mine. Looking down into the silent accusing eye of Sappa Creek, I felt a little more centered in fact and less in the void of denial. By the simple act of beginning to learn the history, I was making slight amends. Not to the Indians—that would have been impossible—but to the violated principles of truth in my own heart.

Ward said, "Some of the history buffs I talk to think that when Dull Knife's Northern Cheyenne came through this area three years later and killed all those settlers, it was revenge for what happened here. Others think it was just savagery. They say that even if the braves had known about Cheyenne Hole, they wouldn't have cared about it. The Northern and Southern Cheyenne were two separate tribes."

"That's such bullshit," I said. The braves had killed forty settlers. But they hadn't raided anywhere else in their six-hundred-mile flight from the southern reservation. The attacks had most likely been waged here because the Cheyenne had in fact always viewed themselves as one tribe. They'd been split, north from south, only when the migration of whites began along the Platte River, on the Oregon Trail.

"Then the many paid for it," I added. One hundred fifty of the Cheyenne who'd fled with Dull Knife were apprehended and imprisoned at Fort Robinson, in Nebraska. They refused to return to Oklahoma, so the commander ordered that they be deprived of heat, food, and water. They had no choice but to break out, and when they did, soldiers shot more than half of them, whether guilty or not of raiding, whether male or female, whether adult or child.

Ward bent down to examine something on the ground. I said, "I'd like to think that we'd be a little more discerning today, as to which people we punish for which crimes, but just look at how we responded to the World Trade Center attack." Ward didn't say anything. "I mean, some people can't distinguish one Arab from another. Like our president, Ward. I know he's your guy, but if he gets his way, pretty soon we'll be fighting wars all over the Middle East."

Ward stood and dropped a triangular stone into my hand.

"Wow," I said, although I couldn't see any sign that it had been chipped into that shape.

"He's gonna go after any nation that harbors terrorists," Ward said, squeezing my hand closed over the rock and bending down to look for others. "What do you think we should do?" he asked over his shoulder. "Get together with Bin Laden and have a big powwow, talk it through?"

It was all I could do not to throw his stupid rock at his butt. "You really don't get it do you?"

He stood up. His mustache poked out over the upper corner of his wry smile. "It's a dangerous world, Julene. We need to go after 'em wherever they're hiding."

"Don't you see, Ward? A lot of innocent people will die. How is that different from what happened here?"

He put both hands on my shoulders and looked into my eyes. "I hope that doesn't happen, but there's one thing I do know."

"What's that?" I asked, prepared for him to say he couldn't go on seeing such a lily-livered liberal.

He winked at me. "I wouldn't be worth your trouble if I didn't have any reactionary opinions for you to correct."

His ability to defuse a conflict would come in handy over the years—if there were to be years. "I guess I don't have to convert you this afternoon, huh?"

"No, I guarantee you'll have plenty of time for that."

The drizzle had stopped, and puffs of gray cloud were lifting to reveal a clear strip of cellophane blue on the horizon. "Let's look up there," I said. Skirting sharp yucca spires, I climbed a wet cow trail up the hill. It was dotted in cedar trees. I'd read somewhere that these were isolated survivors from the last glacial period, when the world had been much colder. With Ward behind me, I pretended to search for arrowheads. What I really wanted was to cool off. Go lighter next time, I thought. He'd nailed it. It would take a while to loosen the hold his "reactionary" friends had on him. I poked along what looked like a promising embankment.

When I turned around, I caught Ward looking me up and down. Those eyes. They were lit up like green fire and contained a coyote's wily lust. Had our disagreement aroused him? It couldn't have been the shape of my behind that had done it. My voluminous raincoat made thoughts of it purely imaginary.

By the time we got back to the ranch, arms of mauve stretched across either side of the sun, small and white in the west. The cellophane blue that had begun to show as we left Cheyenne Hole was an amphitheater now for the appearance of the brighter, bigger moon.

Ward cut the twine on two bales of hay and I went down the line with him, tossing the square flakes and being introduced to the geldings. "This is Sam, a yearling and a half. He'll make someone a good roping horse." Next in line was a blue roan. "Thankless, I call him. He'll be on the truck next spring."

"The truck?"

"To the sale barn. Terrible disposition. You can't trust him not to bite or kick you if you turn your back on him. Of course in the sales book, I put their registered names." These would no doubt include references to the famous stud in their bloodlines. Ward favored the descendants of Doc Bar.

Over a supper of rotisserie chicken we'd picked up, I learned that he ate off Styrofoam plates with plastic cutlery so he wouldn't have to wash dishes. To avoid emptying the trash often, he kept a full-sized garbage can in his kitchen and lined it with a heavy-duty plastic bag. When I asked how he disposed of the bag, he said he burned everything in his own trash pit. I envisioned fumes from curdling plastic and Styrofoam widening the hole in the ozone layer.

"You use sunscreen?" I asked.

"Never have."

"You might want to start."

"Don't have to. I wear a hat. Don't take my clothes off except at night."

I glanced meaningfully at the dark window, then looked right into the green fire.

"C'mere," he said.

We dropped our shirts in the kitchen, my bra on the stairs, our boots in the den, and peeled off our jeans in the bedroom. When he didn't make a move to turn on a dim light of some kind, I was afraid this was going to be another, wham-bam "get this over with cause it's only for me and women aren't really interested in sex" encounter.

"Uh, do you have a candle?"

He found one, no problem, but didn't have a match in the house. He had to go down to the cold basement in his boxers and light the wick in the furnace pilot, then carefully nurture the flame all the way back up to me.

"Much better," I said. "Now let's take this slow, like you promised, Coyote."

10

ON THE SECOND STORY OF WARD'S HOUSE, IN THAT HIGH ATTIC ROOM, HE HAD THIS BIG OVERSTUFFED CHAIR THAT WE WOULD SIT IN TOGETHER ON THE NIGHTS OF MY VISITS. Upholstered in nubby fabric the pale-green color of Russian olive leaves, the chair reminded me of a couch and chair we had in my childhood, before Mom bought that awful shitmuckle-brown set that had refused to wear out.

I would squeeze in beside him, facing the back of the chair. On those nights, Ward talked freely about himself. He told me about the many men he felt beholden to. Not just his father and uncles but also neighbor men who'd taken time to instruct a young boy because they "cared about something other than their own skin." They believed in "a right way and a wrong way" and demonstrated it by their actions more than their words. Most of what they demonstrated had been about horses.

"I don't claim to be that good a trainer, but I aspire to be," he said. He'd been to clinics with masters and knew that to get a horse to do what you wanted, you had to align your will with the animal's will, unifying the two spirits. "You can't force a horse. You can't subdue it. Oh well, you can, but you'll only get what you deserve. You have to put yourself on the horse's wavelength."

Of all the western art Ward had collected, the brass base on the lamp beside that chair was the only horse in the house without a man astride it or being tossed from its back or squatting near its feet at a campfire. "Horses," he explained, "were intended to be ridden." His tastes in art reflected the arcane code of the cowboy, which had to be obscure in order to winnow the real ones from the pretenders. That was okay. It meant he belonged to a semi-intact culture and I couldn't deny that this was part of his appeal. Because that culture was based in the same land I came from, I had never shared so much basic understanding with a lover, so much place sense.

Overlaid on those fundamentals were, I had to admit, some silly customs and strictures about how to dress and what to think. These put me in mind of my cowboy students in Laramie who had worn their stiff denim jeans, long-sleeved shirts, and felt hats into the classroom even during summer sessions. They looked trussed up, in uniform. Their code was a shield. Trying to get them to accept a new idea or read an unconventional text had been like trying to toss a nickel into one of those glass dishes that rested atop big stuffed teddy bears at carnivals. The ideas just bounced out of them. Those poor kids were growing up in a world that took advantage of their western identity, linking it to a particular set of political ideas.

I didn't remember much partisan division in Kansas when I was growing up. People here had been more mainstream then. A strong current of practical common sense and reasonableness had run through both Ward's and my childhoods. We recognized it in each other. That's what made our political disagreements minor distractions, at least at first. Unlike most of those kids in my classroom, Ward's eyes lit up at new ideas. He wanted to travel more. He wanted to learn. He entertained just enough cracks in the code to be open to me.

Maybe this was because he'd gone to college, then spent those years in Denver.

"My wild oats years," Ward called them. "I skied, wheeled and dealed real estate, chased women, ran with the high rollers. Quite the desperado, you would have thought had you known me then."

I don't know when this particular conversation took place. They all bleed together in the eternal present of iconic memory. That chair, the dim light cast by the horse lamp. He usually wore a black sweatshirt and pants. I wore green silk pajamas that I bought to look sexy in, for him. "We were all full of it then," I said. "So you had a good time?"

"Oh I was flying. But you know, you talk about being lonely? I think I was, but I didn't know it. I haven't been lonely once since I came home."

"How is that? When Jake was a baby, and I lived back here, I hardly had any friends at all. That was one reason I left again."

"You can have a thousand so-called friends and still be lonely," Ward said. "I could go all year here and not see a soul, and be happier than I was in Denver." But he didn't have to go a day without seeing a friend if he didn't want to. "They might all be codgers and misfits," he said, "but we do have fun together." Most of his friendships centered on horse sales, roping, and poker, he explained, then suggested that my reading, writing, and wilderness passions had not been as widely shared.

Gradually it dawned on me that I was dating a favorite son. Whenever I visited Plum Springs with Ward, I felt as if I'd stumbled into Brigadoon, that hyperfriendly Scottish utopia made famous in a 1950s musical that, it turned out, both of our high schools had staged when we were students. Ward had not only been a budding actor then but also a good singer, and had starred in his school's production, while I hadn't even dared to try out. Men backslapped him when we went to gas stations or restaurants, and on one visit to town near Christmas, he ran into at least five ex-girlfriends, home for the holidays.

"It was only three or four," he insisted.

His last girlfriend had been a Baptist. She took him to church, which he didn't mind. "It made her happy, and I don't pretend to have the answers in that department." But then one day he woke up and knew he couldn't make her happy and make himself happy too. When he told her this, he said she turned white as a sheet and didn't say a word. This haunted him.

It troubled me too. "I never want to be in her shoes," I said.

"You don't have to worry. You won't be."

"Why not?" I wanted to know.

"She wasn't you, Julene."

I took him at face value on this because of how he enthused about me. "You don't know how much I love being with someone like you," he would say. "We can talk about everything and anything, not just about what's for dinner."

I suggested that maybe his being a man in such a male-dominated place allowed him to realize his potential without having to leave, but that's not how he saw it. "I haven't reached my potential, not nearly. Coming back was the only way I could do what I love. I know there's a bigger world out there. I'm not tied to here."

No falser words were ever spoken, I suspected. "But that's what intrigues me about you," I said. "You stayed."

"And that's what intrigues me about you. You didn't."

He came from a functional family in which everyone hugged and expressed affection openly. His two brothers, who were both married, made a point of charming me. "Why'd you ever consent to go out with this cuss? We can't shut him up about you. It's *Ju*-lene this, *Ju*-lene that." While I wouldn't have traded my iconoclastic brother's sideways love for the forthright affection between Ward and his sibs, it was nice being warmly received. One of his sisters-in-law dashed out and bought me a present when she heard I would be visiting during the Christmas holiday, a large candle that we always lit when we were making love.

I shared in his fondness for his father, a balding man who looked like so many old farmers, still strong in the shoulders, barrel-chested, his face pocked by the removal of cancerous sores. He reminded me in some ways of my own father, although Ward's dad was a humbler and less accomplished man. There were apparently advantages to this.

"He didn't work me the way your dad did your brothers. Oh, he had me on plenty of tractors, but I wasn't his tractor dog like Bruce says he was. It would be a week here, a week there, not all summer. He gave me plenty of time off to have fun."

His mother looked at me hopefully, as if I might be the one to finally capture and domesticate her eldest son. She was the fawning type, obviously in thrall of all her sons, but I sensed tension between Ward and her. He said she'd guilt tripped him and his brothers when they were growing up by complaining that she had to quit her job for the county's biggest grain merchant in order to raise them.

How dare she! I thought. Who needed a bustling office, an appreciative boss, and the world's important business to be proficient in when you could work alone at home for no pay? "Try to imagine it the other way around," I said. "A father having to give up his career to raise kids. But it doesn't work that way, does it? Or it didn't then. Dads made the money, while moms were supposed to stay at home and be happy about it."

"No matter how it worked, or should have worked, I couldn't do anything about it," Ward said.

There was clearly more hurt here than I had originally thought. "Other than take the blame?" I asked.

His lips set together so tightly that they disappeared below his mustache. He shrugged.

Sometimes the onus of motherhood terrified me. How much had I traumatized my son? "I was luckier than your mom," I said. "I had no choice but to work. So I never had to feel deprived in that way. When I was teaching and Jake would get sick and I had to stay home to take care of him, I was actually grateful." I told Ward about the chronic earaches Jake used to get. "We'd sit together for hours, like you and I do here, except it was a rocking chair. 'The rack,' I called it."

"Sounds like torture," Ward said. He gave me a warm, approving grin.

I flashed on an image of Jake as a four-year-old in his blue jammies with the feet in them. He would lie across my lap with his long legs twisted around the chair's wooden arm, and his chin would be stained with the red antibiotic syrup I'd given him. My back would strain as I held him up so the other chair arm wouldn't press into him.

"But when he finally went to sleep," I said to Ward, "his relief was my relief." I paused for a moment. "It works the other way around too, though. His pain is my pain."

"I can understand that," Ward said. "But not his failures. Those should be his alone. Don't take those on yourself."

"A parent has no choice," I said, "especially when a kid doesn't seem to care that much himself." How could that be? I wanted to know. Jake had never been a striver when it came to school or learning. The only diagnosis any of his therapists had come up with had been ADD, the blanket explanation for every childhood motivational or behavioral problem, it seemed. I'd refused to drug Jake into submission, and now that I'd caught him smoking pot more than once, it didn't seem the time to give him speed.

Ward said, "Kids need consistency. You've got to lay down the law and make it firm."

"That's easy for someone who has no kids to say," I shot back. "Believe me, I've done everything I can to be 'consistent and lay down the law.'"

"Do you think I'm judging you, Julene? Because I'm not. I know you're a great parent. I could tell that the first time I met Jake. He's a sweet kid."

"Judging." It was that word that got to me. I forced a smile, then dropped my head to hide what was happening to my face.

Ward changed the subject. "You've never said much about Jake's dad, or how you met him."

"Marrying Jake's dad was the stupidest decision I ever made, but I was riding high before that, living alone in this remote cabin in the middle of the Mojave Desert. I feel kind of like we're in the desert now." It was true. Cozy in the quiet house, with the brass horse lamp turned low and knowing that the corrals outside were full of real horses, reminded me of my Mojave rock house at night, where my two horses had grazed right outside my front door. "I always closed the curtains at night. But if I hadn't, no one was going to look in. That house was surrounded by more than a million acres of wilderness."

Ward shook his head at the wonder of it.

"I hated giving up the desert when I was pregnant with Jake and had to come back here. It was humiliating. It was mortifying, in fact, but good for me in the long run. I don't think I would know half as much about who I am if I hadn't been forced to return. I wouldn't write the things I write or care about the things I care about." I looked at the clock. It was getting late. I'd been waiting to tell Ward all of this, but starting this late, I wouldn't be able to do the story justice.

Ward patted his thigh. "C'mere."

I muttered something unspellable, a cross between a moan and a sigh.

"What?" he said.

I smiled slightly, shook my head.

He laughed. "Wha-at?"

"I love it when you say, 'C'mere,'" I confessed, climbing astraddle.

He lifted almost imperceptibly, from the hips.

A shiver ran through me and I fell on his chest. "God! What you do to me."

"Oh darlin'."

WARD'S BED WAS DIFFERENT FROM HIS CHAIR. He insisted that I think of it as our bed, not his. The same with my bed in Laramie. It was ours. Our beds felt almost sacred to him, he said, although he realized that "you have to be careful mixing religious language with sex. Tends to put a damper on things."

Our Kansas bed was the same one his aunt and uncle had slept in, part of the suite of dark furniture that caused me to imagine we were on the set of an old Western movie. Even though I'd succeeded in slowing him down, the love we made was bumbling at first. I hoped that his aunt and uncle had done better. But it took me years to become uninhibited enough to talk about sex, and—call it my prejudice—I didn't think those conversations took place often in Kansas.

"I need to tell you something about me," I murmured.

"I had a feeling we were going to have this talk."

"So you probably know what I'm going to say?"

"I think so." Ward gave me a reassuring kiss on the forehead. "But tell me anyway. You can tell me anything."

I guided his hand to the spot.

"What do you want me to do?"

Ward's other lovers all had hair triggers, he guessed. "Lucky them," I quipped. I had little doubt they'd been faking, as I had done when I was younger.

Ward reassured me that he loved me all the more because I was special in this, as in every other way. On hearing the word "special," I literally bit my tongue. I held it between my teeth until the urge to spill anger all over him subsided. But once I'd coached him, he was so responsive to my needs that the umbrage I took at that word faded, then disappeared.

In our beds, images were born in both our minds that sustained us during our long separations. One foggy March morning he awoke from a dream in which I hovered over him, wearing only the red satin jacket I'd worn when we went dancing together on New Year's Eve in Laramie.

He told me that he spent the remainder of the day in a state of grace. As he mended barbed wire in one of his far-flung pastures, the vision reappeared, warming him even as the cold mist thickened to rain and wet his clothes through to his skin. We were able to see each other only about once every month, and he had been feeling down about the seeming impossibility of our ever being together permanently. The dream buoyed him up.

I loved the stillness of his room at night, the stars out his window. His metabolism was slower than mine, calmer. When I lay on his shoulder, that calm emanated from him and into me. It brought to mind the cottonwood tree beside the spring where we'd met. He seemed as solid as that tree.

And when I pulled out of his yard, beginning the three-hundred-mile drive back to Laramie, he would stand as still as that tree, watching me go. Standing there all woebegone in his thick Carhartt jacket, he reminded me of my father in his wool-lined denim jacket, although my father never would have found himself alone at age fifty, unless Mom had died. Even then, I couldn't imagine Dad looking romantically forlorn. He was not a romantic man. The two men were very different. Yet they were formed by the same soil.

II

A BODY IN A PLACE

Emancipation from the bondage of the soil
is no freedom for the tree.

— RABINDRANATH TAGORE, "FIREFLIES"

1

CALIFORNIA, 1976. The Sierra Nevada Mountains. I am twenty-six, and my boyfriend is leading the way up a trail into the Desolation Wilderness. On my back is the olive-green pack he helped me pick out at the REI store in Berkeley. It contains my share of everything we will need over the next two days and nights—the sleeping bag and pad he also helped me choose, the set of tin dinnerware his ex-wife used when they camped together, two boxes of macaroni and cheese, one can of tuna and one of condensed milk, a round of smoked Gouda, six bagels, fuel for the stove, matches, my Swiss army knife, a comb, lip moisturizer, and a smattering of clothes. Somehow these few items add up to a shoulder-straining, back-breaking weight that I bear resentfully and in shock.

Although I moved to San Francisco in 1968 at the age of eighteen, and San Francisco is a city of many hills, I've only recently begun getting used to walking up them. On our weekends together my boyfriend and I often trundle up and down between his Telegraph Hill apartment and the North Beach coffeehouses, restaurants, and jazz clubs. But this isn't a hill. It's a mountain. Other than the windmills on our farm when I was a kid, it's the steepest thing I've climbed in my entire life. It doesn't help that my boyfriend carries a larger pack and strides ahead of me—up and over rocks and tree roots, across streams, always up, up, and up—faster than I can manage and as if it costs him no effort at all. I stare maliciously into the back of his head and his narrow shoulders, which he holds in his usual thrown-back straight manner despite the weight they carry. I wish I could focus hatred like a magnifying glass focuses the sun, causing a fire to light in his curly brown hair.

During all these city years, I have been an astronaut floating in space, the lifeline of my identity always securely fastened to Kansas, the mother ship. But I don't realize that yet. Nor do I have any way of knowing that I will eventually remember this day as the beginning of the journey returning me to earth. In fact, I think of this guy I'm following up the mountain as my lifeline. He is the one who scooped me out of the ocean of loneliness I inadvertently dove into by finally getting the nerve to divorce my affable, spacey, totally incompatible husband.

Before I met my husband, I'd dreamed of going to San Francisco, where the hippies were having love-ins; the war protesters were nailing establishment hypocrisy; and Janis Joplin, the Grateful Dead, and Jefferson Airplane were penetrating the darkness of the times, trailing psychedelic colors and my generation behind them. But short of sticking my thumb out, I didn't have any way of getting there. I wasn't foolhardy. I enrolled in college instead. I'd attended one summer session and was in the middle of my first fall semester at KU when along came this exotic guy with a plan. I hitched a ride on his volition. I know that I'm doing it again. It is not only the pace my boyfriend is setting, but the fact he is setting it that makes me want to burn holes into the back of his head.

What is this? He's stopping. He turns around, walks back to me, and with this ecstatic look on his face, takes me by the shoulders. "Isn't this, isn't this . . ." He tightens his jaw theatrically. *"Err-grrr!"* Apparently lacking a sufficiently exalted descriptor, he leans me back for a passionate kiss, then steadies me as I begin to topple under my unbalanced load.

"Yes! It's . . . fantastic!" I pretend to share his enthusiasm over this brutal climb through a dark forest just as I pretend to enjoy the frenetic, Coltrane-style jazz he drags me to most weekends. The one positive thing—the strain on my lungs prevents my craving a cigarette. I've been struggling to quit smoking since my divorce. Not the best of timing, I realize.

Begrudgingly, I do allow that this seeming death march will probably have a payoff, like when we cross the Golden Gate Bridge and go to the beaches in Marin County, where we run barefoot. He has a philosophy for exertion outdoors, as he does for almost everything. Holding fingers to thumb in a teacherly circle and his pinkie in the air, he has explained to me that most people are "herd animals" who lack independent spirits and will not walk, let alone run, far. All you have to do to escape the crowd is put out a little effort. The same goes for moods. You have to power through them. Be physical, and the endorphins will kick in, elevating your spirits. Go even if it's raining. Usually the sun comes out and you will have the beach all to yourself. At the very least, the effort in the face of opposition will win a revelation of some kind.

We got up at five a.m. this morning, had our cappuccino at six, arrived at the trailhead by nine, and the sun is now at its zenith, so he's been keeping up this grueling pace for three hours, most of that time in the trees. They were gloomy to walk through. I hated not being able to see far, but now that we're getting above the timberline, the mid-July heat weighs on me and makes my pack feel twice as heavy. Admittedly, the vistas are terrific—gray granite slopes with waterfalls cascading over them, and now a solitary clump of tall trees, the last of their kind, leaning skyward like exclamation points. "Look at those amazing pine trees," I call out, hoping he will stop to appreciate them.

He turns his head but doesn't even slow down. "They're lodgepoles."

Thank you and fuck you too, know-it-all. The strap of my canteen is pinned under my pack and I can't lift it high enough to get a drink. But damned if I'm going to ask him to stop. The muscles in my thighs ache, yet I continue to punish them, straining now through a boulder field, each step so high above the last one, I can barely lift myself onto it. "Just put one foot in front of the other," he's told me before. Well, I'll do that one hundred times, then I'm stopping whether he does or not.

One jerk. Two jerk. Three jerk. Four prick. I ration the pejoratives, afraid I'll run out before I get to a hundred. Five prick. Six pri—

His neat hiking shoes and straight-legged jeans are planted on the step above me. The toes are pointing toward me, not away. "How ya doin'?" he asks, with real concern, like a coach who has suddenly realized his drill is on the verge of murdering his pupil.

I'm almost woozy enough to pass out. I wish I would. That would teach him. "Great!" I say as convincingly as I can muster, but hearing the hollow ring in my voice, revert to sarcasm. "How are you doing?"

He laughs. "Don't worry. This is the final assault."

My fists clench at the enticing images that word conjures. He waves his hand at a vertical wall of rock to our left. Only now do I see that the path turns here, to go straight up it. "You've got to be kidding."

He frees my canteen for me. "Here," he says, pouring water into me as if I were a plant. Or a child. He takes my hat off, pushes my hair off my sweaty forehead, jambs the hat back on with two hands, pats my shoulder as if placating a tiger. "It will be worth it, Juleney. You'll see. I promise."

"Thanks," I say, liking that he at least acknowledges my anger. I picture the campsite we will build on the shoreline of the lake. Tomorrow morning we will sleep in together in the comfort of sun-dappled nylon and plush down. I remind myself that I have good reason to be optimistic. He's proven his theory to me many times. When we go to the ocean and those magical endorphins heighten my awareness, something as commonplace as a sand dollar can fascinate me. Once, a pod of seals followed our progress along an otherwise empty beach, their rubbery black heads bobbing in the surf so close to us that we could see their whiskers and limpid black eyes. Another time, a couple of miles up the beach on a foggy day, we discovered a driftwood hut to shelter in. Sitting in that tepee with cold, gray sky showing between the sea-smoothed slats, the fire we'd built casting its warmth over me, I imagined a buffalo rug beneath us and the walls sheathed in hides. I speculated that if we lived mostly outdoors, the way the Indians had, we would experience the gratitude we were feeling in that moment every time we stepped inside.

My boyfriend remarked, as he often does, on how the prairie shaped my aesthetics and my imagination. He thinks of the plains as a pure and open place, an outer representation of my inner nature. He puts me on this pedestal and I know he'd be appalled at the impure thoughts coursing through me right now, but when he says things like that, I feel almost as proud of my Kansas roots as when I was a kid singing "Home on the Range," the state song. It was written only about seventy miles from where I grew up, I liked informing him. He grew up among New York intellectuals, went to an Ivy League school, and has a successful career. Yet he says that sparks fly between us because we are "equals but opposites." Being admired by a man with such lofty credentials and who has such a correspondingly high opinion of his own worth gives me a higher opinion of mine. His thinking I am his equal makes me aware of my potential and fuels my lonely weekdays, which I spend at my bookkeeping job as the only employee of an accountant.

My boyfriend scales the virtual cliff before us, then stops on what I hope, for God's sake, is the crest. "Eureka!" he shouts.

I grab on to boulders to keep from losing my balance and climb. My eyes, as always, are aimed toward him, but the sun blinds me. As he reaches down, all I can see is his dark silhouette outlined by blue sky. He pulls me up beside him. We stand on the edge of what he tells me is a cirque, a silver-gray cup of granite filled with glacier melt as clear as the air. A few trees grow on the shoreline protected by this wall of granite, and in their shade on the water, we can see the undersides of boulders and the sandy bottom. My boyfriend beams a dare at me, then slaloms down the gravelly path, tossing his pack, his hat, his shirt. He is putting on a show, but I can't take my eyes off the water.

It beckons glasslike, receptive. The world's purest element in its purest form. Seemingly innocent, yet I suspect it is so cold that a prolonged immersion in it could kill. Every cell in my body and every neuron in my heat-addled brain thirst for that immersion.

I make my way down the path faster than feels safe, skidding over talus, banging my hip on a boulder, and almost falling more than once. I drop my pack on the pine duff along the shoreline, then my boots, socks, and jeans. An unusually dark boulder with mica sparkles in it calls to me, but it's almost too hot to touch. So I dip my hat into the startling cold water, scooping it onto the rock, then lower myself into the now wet and warm shallow depression down the boulder's center. I hang my arm off the edge, and, trailing my fingers through the water, begin a slow, delectable flirtation. The high-altitude sun presses my back as with a dry iron, while below me, riffles slap rock. Glare refracts off the water, dappling my arm and flashing hypnotically on my retinas.

I am irradiated, intoxicated. I rise to my feet, pull my now wet shirt and underwear off and try not to notice where my boyfriend is or whether he notices me. I don't care about his shouts of cold and pleasure or the splashes he makes cavorting. This is about me and you, I think toward the lake. Not me and him. Go, I urge myself. Go! Go!

I've done something really, really stupid, like jumping off the Golden Gate Bridge. The lake is liquid ice, the cold so shocking I panic at first. Echoes of my scream circle the jagged peaks. So do those of my boyfriend's "yee-haw!" His example and approval help me resist the urge to splash ashore. It only takes a half minute or so and I'm willingly giving myself to the water and it is giving itself to me, driving me into my body the way good sex does, only better, the climax unending. I am nothing but sensation, all of it glorious. I dive back under. I've never swum naked in broad daylight and I love the water's silken feel on my skin. I love watching my hands move underwater, as if I were a creature who evolved in this medium. Drifting like a fetus in a womb of laced sunlight, I ponder the startling clarity and whiteness of my hands and feet.

But I'm beginning to feel this strange, hot sensation high in my stomach, as if a burner has ignited inside me. This cannot be good. Because my brain has lost all sense and thrown me into this predicament, my body is resorting to metabolic triage, my blood abandoning my limbs and rushing to save my vital organs. I climb out and, shivering, lie down on my boulder. Soon the sun's high heat penetrates me, lifting and nullifying the lake's deep cold. Enlivened, awakened, I savor all to which I've been reborn—the rasping call and obsidian sheen of a raven slicing the depthless blue above me, the tickle of my arm's sun-bleached hairs as I drag my lips over them, breathing my skin's smell. The fragrance doesn't come only from the lake, but from granite, ozone, and pine.

I DID A LOT OF THINGS DURING the six years I lived in the city after my first divorce. The love-hate relationship with my boyfriend lasted for two of them. I took an eclectic smattering of courses—accounting, computing, Spanish, Eastern philosophy. I made new friends, became part owner of a picture-framing business and the volunteer director of a filmmakers' organization. I grew more confident and ambitious, eventually winning a grant and producing my own film. But nothing I did affected me so powerfully as that first dive into a mountain lake. I couldn't get enough of the scent of water and wilderness on my skin.

In November, four months after our trip to the Desolation Wilderness, the smells of wormwood and sage folded themselves into that bouquet. To avoid awkward Thanksgivings with our respective ex-partners and the friends we had in common with them, my boyfriend and I fled south through hundreds of miles of empty grasslands, stopped for a bleak turkey buffet in Bakersfield, then crossed the Sierras by way of Lake Isabella. Winding into Death Valley from the Panamint Mountains, we saw our planet laid breathtakingly bare. The pink gold of sunset gilded the sand dunes, alkali plains, saltwater ponds, and labyrinthine canyons. Although we rolled down the narrow highway as fast as we could in my little Honda, the planet rolled faster. Glancing over our shoulders, we watched helplessly as the Panamints heaved upward, consuming the sun.

We took the only spot left in the official dunes campground—a bare patch of gravel beside snoring, elephantine RVs. It was a lot colder out than we'd hoped it would be, but it seemed ludicrous to erect a tent there. We threw a few supplies into our day packs, tossed our canteens and sleeping bags over our shoulders, and against park regulations, headed for the objects of our fascination. As we walked, a nearly full harvest moon overtook the eastern Amargosa Range, spilling orange light onto the dunes' flanks.

We climbed the nearest dune, plunged down the back side, trudged upward again. All evidence of the day's tourists gradually disappeared, the snaking ridgelines becoming sharply distinct undulating spines, unmarred by footprints other than the ones we left behind us as the moon's orange glow faded to white. I had never seen anything more sensuous than the milky-white skin of the earth lapped in moonlight.

We bedded down in a hollow between dunes, zipping our bags together and pulling the drawstrings so tight all we had to breathe out of was a small hole. Even then, the cold woke us early. We put on every stitch of clothing we'd brought, draped our sleeping bags over our shoulders as shawls, and climbed to the peak of the nearest dune.

Pink dawn light illuminated the entire valley, a few lustrous clouds floated above us, and as we watched, a sheet of sunlight inched operatically down the face of the Panamint Range toward the valley and us. "Wow," I said.

"Yeah. Wow," said my boyfriend. He hadn't been to the desert before either. I liked discovering it together. For once, he wasn't the expert.

When the sunlight reached us, warming the top of my head, then my shoulders and thighs, it felt like an all-encompassing caress.

If we kept our backs to the distant campground, it was easy to imagine ourselves the only humans on the planet. So we did that, following the ridgelines away from all signs of civilization. By midmorning, the sun was beating down on us. I needed to put some sunscreen on my arms and face and, grateful that I'd brought a pair of shorts, took off my boots and socks, then my jeans. How wonderful to feel the sand on my bare feet, especially during November.

Mark Twain got it right when he said the coldest winter he ever spent was a summer in San Francisco. Except for my trips home to Kansas and camping trips with my boyfriend that summer, I hadn't felt truly warm in eight long years. I pulled my shorts on, but couldn't bring myself to put my feet back into my boots. Instead, I sat down and dragged my toes through the sand, savoring the contrast between the sun's heat on the surface and the night's chill beneath it. I made rainbow arcs in the sand, then tried to erase them with my hand. Failing, I lay down.

How quiet it is, I thought. There was no traffic or other human-generated noises to filter out. I'd always thought of the desert as a wasteland, eerie and alien. I hadn't been prepared for this softness or the stunning beauty. I felt at home here. I stuffed my jeans into my pack and, carrying my boots, climbed upward again.

All this climbing took effort, but I was now a complete convert. As on the lakeshore after my cold swim, I felt enlivened, awakened—not just in body but in mind. I wanted to visit every mountain range that surrounded us, to see into each dark, distant crevasse.

The desert wasn't alien. We were. The only humans for miles, we'd sprung up clothed, with Gore-Tex day packs, wearing boots and shielded behind polarized sunglasses, as if the light on our own planet was too bright for our eyes, the ground too harsh for our feet. In fact, with crumpled brown mountain ranges as boundaries, the Death Valley dunes seemed as safe and finite as a cradle. Shadows hugged the southern convex sides of the steepest hollows. We wandered—cool to hot, up and over, light to shade.

With the dune's curving tan walls as a backdrop and a blue limitless ceiling overhead, every plant we saw might have been a statue in an otherwise empty gallery. Blades of rice grass, swayed easily by the slightest breeze, had traced circles around themselves in the sand. Wind had exposed the roots of mesquite bushes, making them look convoluted and sinister. We skirted the valleys they grew in but were drawn to the shade of one plump specimen. I got out my knife and opened a can of tuna. Leaning on my elbow to drain the juice, I noticed tiny tracks leading under the bush. I crouched down to investigate and came face-to-face with a lizard. He swallowed, thin white shutters lowering over his eyes.

• • •

HAVING SPENT THE NIGHT AND MORNING DRENCHED in transfixing beauty, neither of us could stomach the thought of erecting our tent in the campground, so we gassed up and headed for more remote desert. After leaving Death Valley on a gravel road, we saw no other vehicles for the rest of the day. The only evidence of human habitation was a weathered-gray abandoned cabin perched all by itself on a smooth mountain slope. Intrigued, we hiked up to it and toed through broken glass and chunks of aqua plaster to look out a window onto an infinity of sandy-brown soil, uniformly small and equidistant sagebrush, and blue sky. The window frame had no glass in it, so nothing stood between us and the vibrant desert. Staring at the unlimited space fanned out before me, I felt magnified and ethereal, yet grounded, as if the house were my body and the window my eye sockets.

I'd forgotten how enlivening it could feel, seeing clearly and far. Aridity frees light. It also unleashes grandeur. The earth here wasn't cloaked in forest, nor draped in green. Green was pastoral, peaceful, mild. Desert beauty was "sublime" in the way that the romantic poets had used the word—not peaceful dales but rugged mountain faces, not reassuring but daunting nature, the earth's skin and haunches, its spines and angles arching prehistorically in sunlight.

2

AFTER THAT TRIP TO DEATH VALLEY, I WENT DESERT CAMPING EVERY CHANCE I GOT. My zealotry now exceeded my boyfriend's, but I didn't let that stop me. If he wouldn't go, I invited other friends to join me. If they declined, I went by myself. Most of the desert belonged to the federal Bureau of Land Management, or BLM. I could camp anywhere I wanted, the more remote, the better. Although I sometimes had to share the scant shade of a Joshua or piñon pine tree with a cow, never once during that period did I sleep in a developed campground. This was one of the things I loved most and which still amazes my nonwestern friends when we go camping today.

Still, I did choose campsites carefully—not for proximity to other people, as there usually were no others, but for the ability to see head-lights approaching from far away. Seeking beauty, adventure, and mean-ing in the wilderness is a time-honored American tradition, but I was undertaking the quest in the body of a woman. I had to take precautions. After stopping at a small-town gas station or café, my eyes strayed in-stinctively to my rearview mirror. If anyone followed me for long, I slowed down so they would have to pass. I bought a little .22 pistol and kept it beside me at night, reaching out often to assure myself it was there.

Although I was frightened and lonely at times, I found it increas-ingly more difficult to stay home. In the desert, I had discovered the West of my imagination, my childhood canyon infinitely magnified. I went there for inspiration and insight. When I returned home and stepped back into my city life, the more authentic Julene stayed behind. I daydreamed about that shack my boyfriend and I had visited. Just remembering it, I could feel the landscape's profundity seeping into me. I thought I could write in such a place, and a writer is what I'd decided I wanted to be. I had enough money from selling my house that, if I was thrifty, I could live for two years without needing a job. I'd seen other abandoned cabins in my travels. Gradually, an idea took hold. What if I could find out who owned one of those places and they let me fix it up and live in it?

To realize that dream would require a vehicle that could go any-where. I traded my little Honda in on a boxy oxidized-red Toyota Land Cruiser. My best friend, Beatrice, who was both an artist and a carpen-ter, installed a false wood floor in the back of it for me. The floor had two hinged doors into compartments big enough for a week's worth of food and clothes. Onto the outside of the Cruiser, another friend and I fastened mounts for gas and water cans, and onto the front bumper, a locking army surplus ammo box for storing tools that same friend had taught me to use.

I went down to the U.S. Geological Survey office in San Francisco and bought topographic maps of every western desert, from eastern Washington all the way to the Chihuahuan in New Mexico and the Anza Borrego in Southern California. The maps were beautifully detailed, with symbols for everything from windmills to mines. A solid-black square meant an occupied dwelling, while a hollow square meant a vacant structure. A miner's shack perhaps, or a failed homesteader's cabin. Sometimes the squares had little tadpole-shaped squiggles beside them, indicating springs. Most of these oases belonged to ranchers. But there were some squiggles that had no squares beside them, or only hollow squares.

Those hollow squares beside squiggles became my prime destinations. Whenever I got within a few miles of one, I didn't need the map anymore. On a mountain where all else was pale and muted, there would appear a splash of dark green. Many of those jeep trails were so steep that, driving up them, I could see only sky over the Cruiser's hood. But the reward for taking such treacherous roads, through hundred degree heat without an air conditioner, were these miraculous glens of trees, sedges, rushes, wildflowers, butterflies, and birds. I would take off my clothes, sink into a bath-sized pool, and look down at the valley I'd come from—as broad as San Francisco Bay, ringed in craggy mountains, with no dwelling or other human in sight. There was no beauty so complete, none so sensually intense and satisfying. Here, together, were the two elements I craved most. Water in the desert.

My fantasy of a home in the desert fueled my travels for two years. I saw many possible candidates in that time but none so perfect as the little rock house in the middle of what, today, is the Mojave National Preserve. A hundred miles south of Death Valley, the 1.6 million-acre wilderness, although unique and deserving, had not yet received Park Service protection. It was still just BLM land. A generous ranching couple owned the private inholding. They consented to my living there for as long as I liked. In exchange for my fixing up the house, they even promised to give me a couple of horses.

Never mind that the place had been sitting vacant for years or that it needed a new roof and all new windows and doors. Its beauty trumped those minor drawbacks. The World War I veteran who'd homesteaded the Rock Springs section had built the cabin from large yellow-granite stones he'd quarried from the Gold Mountains—one of four ranges that rose above Cedar Canyon Road. The house sat on a hill on that washboard-gravel thoroughfare, halfway between Cima, a little railroad town where nine people lived, and a phone booth that stood all by itself at the other end. This was before cell phones, so the pay phone would be my only link to the outside world. The ranchers who owned the rock house warned me that there would be days when I drove ten miles to make a call and the phone would be out of order, but I viewed this as just another minor disadvantage.

Sweet and inviting, humble yet commanding a view of a cordillera that fell away into blue distance, ridge on ridge, the flat-roofed, rectangular cabin reminded me of the Hopi dwellings I'd seen in Arizona. Like those houses, it fit into rather than reigned over its landscape. If anything dominated on that hill above Cedar Canyon Road, it was the big juniper tree beside the house, its branches hurled eastward by the prevailing wind. The natural vegetation was more beautiful than any intentional garden. Yucca and bunchgrasses. Hundreds of wildflowers and blooming forbs. Blue sage, purple sage. Shoulder-high pancake prickly pear and beavertail cactuses, their heart-shaped pads crowned in fuchsia blooms.

On a boulder-strewn hill behind the cabin, pink barrel cactuses fended off would-be munchers with whorls of bright-pink spines, and in the gorge between that hill and the cabin, water trickled. The pools were too tiny to immerse myself in, but a mile upstream stood a windmill beside a six-foot-tall stock-water storage tank where I could go swimming! Well, dunking anyway. Neither the water from the windmill nor from the spring was potable, so I would have to haul my drinking and cooking water from my nearest neighbor's house, two miles away. Again, a minor drawback.

Recalling my first several months at the rock house, I see myself wearing faded jeans and a ragged white cowboy shirt and driving Dorf, my white 1959 Ford pickup, down a wide, sandy wash. I'm returning from a dilapidated mining shack where I pried up the weathered tongue-in-groove floorboards with a crowbar. The plan is to nail the boards over the cracked linoleum in my cabin. Then I will drive ninety-five miles into Las Vegas, where I'll rent a drum sander and, since I have no electricity, a generator. After sanding down the boards, I plan to cover them in polyurethane.

I'm steering the pickup with one hand, the way my father used to steer his pickups, while he absentmindedly stared at some field or another. My elbow is resting on the windowsill just as his used to do. It's October, the air starting to turn crisp. The leaves on the cottonwoods near the windmill flutter like millions of yellow butterflies, and the rabbit brush is in full bright-yellow bloom, scattering pollen onto Dorf's dash as we squeeze past. I don't care that the rabbit brush is scraping Dorf's already scratched and dented sides.

I call my pickup Dorf because someone who owned him before me switched the "F" and "D" on the hood. I'd found him in a used car lot in Needles, on the California-Arizona border, my unlucky town. Just after I bought him, I was driving home when I heard an unmistakable noise. A few years before that, I'd been approaching Needles in my Cruiser when my passenger and I heard that very same clanking sound coming from the engine compartment. We lost all power and rolled to a stop on the interstate's shoulder, flinching as the engine continued to gurgle, hiss, and steam. The Cruiser had thrown a rod bearing. A local mechanic charged fifteen hundred dollars to rebuild the engine. I couldn't afford spending that much again.

In Dorf's case, I would have to do the work myself, especially since he was just my beater work truck. When I'd begun exploring the desert, it had seemed necessary to learn some basics about engine repair. Otherwise, if I were stranded during one of my forays, I might have to walk more miles than I'd walked in all of the years of my life combined. The friend who had taught me the essentials came for a visit shortly after Dorf broke down. He helped me free the engine and winch it out of the truck, then, before leaving, reminded me of the main precepts. You have to throw yourself into mechanical work and not hold back. Don't worry about getting greasy. You can buy this product in an orange bottle that removes grease. If you aren't strong enough to loosen a bolt, use a cheater bar—a length of pipe that fits over the end of the wrench and gives you leverage. And a company called Chilton's puts out a manual for every American vehicle ever made. The instructions are easy to follow and accompanied by pictures. When in doubt, ask the parts guys at the Napa store in Needles.

I looked at Dorf's engine, dangling by chains from the beams of the old roofless carport attached to the rock house. Truly, learning the rudiments of engine maintenance had reminded me of sewing, which my mother began teaching me when I was only seven or eight. Both were just mechanical processes, involving skill with tools and parts that you fit together. I'd done my own oil changes and tune-ups for years now and had performed a number of minor repairs on the Cruiser. I could do this. And with some additional advice and tools borrowed from the same neighbor who had lent me the use of his well, I did.

Compare this woman with the girl who got married just so a man would take her where she wanted to go. Compare her with the young woman who resentfully climbed that trail in the Desolation Wilderness behind a man who was not, in fact, forcing her to do anything. Not since I'd been a little girl running around the farm, dragging ladders that weighed twice as much as I did up barn stairs to see into pigeons' nests or busting quartz nuggets with my father's sledgehammer to ponder the shiny crystals inside, had I been filled with more volition. For the first time since that childhood, I was at home in my body in a place that felt like home. Because I'd had to rewin that centeredness, I was not likely to lose it ever again.

There was just one problem.

Now I'm stuck with myself, answerable to myself, and the future is nothing more than more of myself. That's what I wrote in one of the countless spiral notebooks I filled by kerosene lantern light. In satisfying my yearning for wild land, I had reopened myself to the loneliness I felt after my divorce. Like any animal who had strayed from its bevy, brood, flock, or clan, I yearned for my own kind.

I recalled the warning look in the eyes of the ranchers who owned the rock house when they'd said that the pay phone didn't always work. Years later, in 1997, that phone booth would become famous when a desert wanderer's account of it spread through print news stories and over the Internet. People from far away would journey there in order to camp beside it and answer the calls that poured in, from random places around the world. But for me, "the phone in the middle of nowhere" was not a quirky anomaly or just a camp place to camp. Predictably, I now realized, I had become as addicted to it as I was to the cigarettes I was constantly trying to quit.

Most often I called my friend Beatrice in San Francisco, the one who had built storage compartments into the Cruiser for me. She'd done me more favors than I would ever be able to repay. She'd helped me move to the rock house, even though it had been January and cold weather was not her thing. When it began to snow, she had intrepidly dug a long four-by-four out of the remains of the caved-in barn. Using my sledgehammer, she'd whacked the support into place under my buckling roof to keep the weight of the new snow from collapsing it completely. Before leaving me to fend for myself, she'd drawn plans for the outhouse I would later build.

Talking to Beatrice restored my spirits when I was feeling alone. But sometimes, as I'd been warned, I put my money into the phone and got nothing, not even a live hum. The receiver sounding as dead as a rock, I would slam it into its cradle, start the Cruiser, and head in the other direction, driving right past the turn to the rock house.

"Just need a carton of milk," I would say to Irene, who ran the Cima store and adjoining post office with her rancher husband. I always did my best not to eye the red-and-white, rectangular packages on the shelf behind the counter.

Irene would give me a kindly look. Most of her clientele were lonely desert rats. "Your timing couldn't be better. Truck just left us ten half gallons. So how're you? Keeping busy up at the rock house?"

Whether it was her chitchat or her husband, Bob's diatribes against the BLM, those conversations entered my veins and soothed my nerves like Valium. Sometimes I even managed to resist saying, as if it were an afterthought, "Oh, and give me one of those packs of Marlboros too."

Irene and Bob's kindness normalized my loneliness. They conveyed acceptance, an understanding that the state of mind was not a weakness to be overcome. You couldn't get accustomed to it or get through it, emerging tougher on the other side. It was as real as hunger and grew out of a similar but emotional need for nourishment. They were in the business of satisfying the physical need with the staples they sold— American cheese, Wonder Bread, ketchup, tins of Spam and tuna—and the emotional need with free conversation.

"Are you ready for the dance?" Irene asked one day as I lingered in the post office after buying a book of stamps.

I gave her a questioning look.

"Didn't you hear? It's gonna be at the general store in Goffs." Goffs, twelve miles south of the pay phone, was the big nearby town, population twenty-seven. "They're thinking of having them from now on. On the first Saturday of every month."

"Guess what," I said during my next call to Beatrice.

"Maybe you'll meet a man there," she said.

"Yeah, right. Like that's going to happen." Imagine! Men's voices. Men's eyes. Hands that had the potential of crossing intimate boundaries.

Beatrice was more practical and less idealistic than I was. Like Irene and Bob, she normalized my longing for companionship. I'd moved to the desert thinking I could prove I didn't really need anyone else, including men. Men especially. They were like cigarettes. I thought of all the packs I'd crumpled and thrown out my Cruiser window on my way home from Cima, after smoking just one. I hated litterers, but that was the only way I could keep myself from having another—unless

I was able to find them when I drove back later and walked up and down the road, peering beneath bushes and risking being bitten by a Mojave green, whose venom was worse than any other rattlesnake's.

IT FELT STRANGE DRIVING THE CRUISER IN dainty shoes and a dress. The parking lot was overflowing with vehicles, so I parked behind the Goffs Bar and General Store, freshened my lipstick in the rearview mirror, got out, stopped beside the propane tank to remove a rock from my sandal, then continued walking with fateful determination toward my destiny.

I had no idea the place could hold so many people, most of them strangers. There must have been twenty couples bouncing to George Strait's "All My Ex's Live in Texas." I scanned the crowd, looking for Connie, who owned the store with her husband. I'd stopped in to fill my gas tank the week before and had confided that I didn't know how to dance western swing. "Don't worry. Come on down," she'd told me. "The cowboys will teach ya. It's part of their code to dance with every woman. Don't matter if you're twelve or eighty."

I was hardly in the door when one of the Overson brothers—in a crisp, white, pearly-snapped shirt and a black string tie, his face beer reddened—began proving that cowboy dictum. He didn't bother asking. He just grabbed me and, with confident, muscle-taut guidance he'd perfected riding horses and roping calves on his ranch, reeled me around the floor.

Soon I was dancing and drinking with the best of them, having a much better time than I'd imagined possible. But I was also disappointed that most of the men wore wedding rings. Of the two who didn't, one had a scar where his left ear should have been, and the other had tobacco stains in a yellow-white beard. Then a guy in a classy sports jacket and jeans that fit just right appeared beside me. "Want to?" He didn't hold me any closer than the other men had, yet the dance was more intimate, his movements more suggestive, like notes played on a slide guitar rather than the banjo twang I'd bounced to with the others.

The broad-shouldered, narrow-hipped, hazel-eyed charmer cowboyed for the ranchers who owned my cabin. "So you live up at the rock house," he said. "I've heard all about you."

"What'd you hear? No one knows me well enough to tell you much."

"That there's this looker up there and she has a truck she fixed up herself."

"His name is Dorf."

"Think you could work on my truck when I get one? I've never been much of a mechanic."

"I don't know. What's going to be wrong with it?"

"Probably everything. I tend to go for the glitter. Just show me chrome and big tires, and I'm a goner."

He sent me away from him, spun me half around, then pulled me in so my back was to his front. For an instant we danced as if to rhythm and blues, not Merle Haggard. Turning me again to face him, he seemed to check himself. I could tell he'd felt it too.

He introduced himself as Stefan. I didn't learn until much later that this, like much else he claimed to be and to have done, was an embellishment. His real name was just Stephen. Steve.

My relationship with the man who would become Jake's dad was the classic tale of the responsible woman who falls in love with an irresponsible man. This was the observation of an equally irresponsible but older and more seasoned cowboy friend of his, who tried to warn me that "you can't change a man." But I was certain that I could sand off all of Stefan's rough edges. Hadn't I refurbished the rock house and rebuilt Dorf's engine? I thought I could fix anything.

Within the year he quit drinking and I married him. Soon after, I became pregnant. And soon after that he came home nonchalantly toting a six pack. He lost jobs, we went through my money, and we had a couple of blowout fights that got physical. I resorted to looking for safety, security, and shelter in the only place I knew I could find it.

3

WE ARRIVED IN MY PARENTS' GOODLAND DRIVEWAY IN THE STYLE OF THE BEVERLY HILLBILLIES, THE BED OF OUR PICKUP PILED HIGH, OUR DOGS RIDING ON THE LOAD, AND MY HORSES TOWED ALONG BEHIND. If anyone had told me that I would end up back in Kansas, I would have been horrified. I'd had nightmares about this while living in the rock house. I dreamed that I would wake up and, like some reverse Dorothy, discover that I wasn't in the rugged, fanged, and taloned desert but in a weedy yard next to a broken-down old trailer house on my father's farm. Crushing despair would greet the realization.

It was early July, and my brothers had come home also, to help with the harvest. The morning after our arrival, Stefan went to the farm with them and my father. He was to work there until we figured out our next step. At least that was the stated plan. At noon my mother and I brought dinner out to the men, just as we used to do at harvest time when we lived in the country. We dined under a scraggly elm in the farmyard.

"Oh!" my mother gasped. "Those damned dirty bugs!" She swiped at a grasshopper that had hopped onto the blanket under us. It hopped onto my lap. A beat too fast to conceal my disgust, I picked the bug up and flung it into the mowed weeds.

Stefan said, "Didja hear about the American farmer who visited this sheep rancher in the outback of Australia?"

No one answered. From this I deduced he'd been telling jokes all morning. He didn't understand that this wasn't a leisurely dinner. In the Mojave, cowboys were more aware of the figure they cut, whether loping a horse or telling a joke, than of getting their jobs done. Farming was serious business. It wasn't for show. The men intended to eat and jump back into the trucks, not lollygag all afternoon telling jokes. Everyone but him had noticed the scalloped clouds in the west and knew that by nightfall those clouds might produce a full-blown storm. Rain would stop the combines. Dad's custom cutters, who moved north as the crop ripened and had other farmers waiting in Nebraska, would start getting antsy. If it hailed, they might as well move on. There would be nothing left to cut.

The joke went on and on. "Then the American sees this kangaroo. 'Whoa! What is that?' 'What?' says the Aussie. 'You mean you don't have grasshoppers in America?'"

Bruce looked away. Clark smiled faintly. Dad took a bite out of his dinner roll and grimly chewed. A tempest raged behind Dad's eyes at harvest time, clouds or no clouds. He certainly didn't have the patience to be entertained.

I was embarrassed. While Clark and my parents had come to our wedding in the Mojave and had given Stefan the benefit of the doubt, our current circumstances didn't testify too well on his, or my, behalf. And my brothers and I rarely came home at the same time. This should have been a celebratory occasion. I sat beside Bruce, whose admiration I longed for no less than I had as a child, when he resented me for usurping his role as the youngest. Across from me sat Clark. When I was twelve, he had let me stand on his feet so he could better teach me the jitterbug. And when I was little, he would tie me in knots until I said, "Click click," releasing the lock. I wished it were that easy now. Click click and voilà! I would escape this mortifying moment.

If not for three nights ago on the trip here, when we'd camped in the Utah desert; if not for Stefan having kicked his dog, Bear, in the ribs for getting underfoot when we were putting up the tent; if not for the dog's yelp echoing in my ears, I might have roused a laugh in support of my husband. But I was preoccupied, as I'd been ever since that incident, adding two plus two. If Bear and I were on the receiving end of his violent impulses, it could happen to our baby. Seeing that sweet, mild-mannered dog punished so severely, my chest had begun draining of the last remnants of love. Ever since, it had been filling with the embalming fluid of resolve.

That night we lay together in the darkness of the basement bedroom my mother had assigned us. Stefan complained that I hadn't upheld him among my family.

"What do you mean I didn't 'uphold' you?"

He pinned me beneath him and struck me with his open hand. It was almost a play slap, and I saw right through it. He was intentionally breaking the promise he'd made not to lay a hand on me ever again so he would have an excuse to go get a drink. "Do you want me to leave now?" he asked.

"Yes, please. Now."

In less than five minutes, he was gone, bar hopping to Denver in our pickup, a newer Ford that I'd cosigned on. I went through the house's ashtrays, looking for the butts of Bruce's and our cigarettes. Finding one with a half inch left, I lit it and took two puffs of burning filter, then crushed it in the empty driveway. I'd smoked for seventeen years and had been trying to quit for the last five. But in that clarifying moment, with Jake on his way into my life, I understood that my priorities must change. I would not let Stefan come back, and I would not smoke another cigarette.

Unable to make my feet descend the stairs to the basement bedroom we'd shared, I slept on the living-room couch. As humiliating as my predicament was, lying there at the center of the home I'd instinctively run to was a comfort. In the morning, I heard my mother starting the coffeepot and stirring batter for pancakes, a ritual when we kids visited. Then she noticed me. I'd lain awake most of the night dreading the question she was about to ask.

"Julie?" she said, with such innocent concern I couldn't bear to open my eyes. "Why are you here? Where's Stefan?"

As CLARK PASSED ME THE PANCAKES, I dropped my napkin on the floor so that, picking it up, I could wipe away tears. "Want some cholesterol for those?" he asked when I resurfaced. He was offering me a yellow brick on a saucer. Since having a heart attack a few years before, at forty, he'd reinvented himself as a triathlete and lectured us all frequently on risks in our diets.

Mom said, "That's not butter. That's margarine." After a visit to Dad's cardiologist, where she'd learned that Dad's heart was working at only 25 percent capacity, she'd performed this remarkable feat for a farmwoman. Gone were the fried chicken, pork chops, and steak. Gone the mashed potatoes and gravy. Her recipe file had filled with low-fat and low-sodium dishes.

"Should get some butter," Bruce said. "Growing babies need fat."

"So do old men," Dad said. "She's starving me to death."

Instead of judgment, my family offered ordinariness. Stefan was probably sleeping off a hangover in Denver, expecting that as soon as he apologized, I would let him come back. That was the pattern he'd grown up with, the pattern from his own previous relationships, and he'd probably assumed it would be our pattern.

When the first call came, his empty apologies were like being exposed to a viral disease I'd already had and was now immune to. I hung up. But the calls kept coming. He was staying in Denver at a cousin's house, and his promises began to ring more sincerely.

I now understood why I had come home. If I were anywhere else, I would have been tempted. At night, I hugged my pillow, pretending it was him. I wanted our life back, the one we'd had before his drinking had undermined it. I recalled the square dances we had gone to every week—I in a bright-pink, full-skirted traditional outfit complete with bric-a-brac, he in his turquoise cowboy shirt with white piping and his white hat. What fun we had being teased by everyone. Not about our clashing outfits, although they certainly did clash, but for the bloom that love had put on our faces. Since returning to Kansas, I'd had an ultrasound. That Stefan would never be an acting father to the son I'd conceived with him was too brutal a truth to absorb.

But I was not going to insult my parents' generosity by continuing on a ridiculous, even dangerous, path. We Bairs were not melodramatic people. We were emotionally contained and sensible, what my parents would call decent people. Stefan, they now knew, was not decent.

My longing lost its heat when, after weeks of my resistance, Stefan showed his true colors by shouting insults at me. Shaken by his vitriol, I hung up the phone, pulled on my dignity like an apron, and returned to the kitchen to help Mom. Finally, he returned to California in the truck, leaving it up to me to make the payments.

• • •

Stuck. Whenever I recall how I felt that first summer home, I see myself standing in my father's tail-water pit, my tummy stretching the bright stripes of the swimming suit I'd bought to impress Stefan shortly after we met. The tail-water pit was a topographic feature that hadn't existed in my childhood—a bulldozed, rectangular pond that collected runoff from Dad's flood-irrigated fields.

Dad kept it stocked with bullheads and channel catfish. He stood holding a cane pole over the water, his grin communicating that I was making a fool of myself. Thanks to the diet Mom had imposed on him, he was at a healthy weight for the first time in my memory. But it pained me to see how much he'd aged. What hair he had left had gone from the gray I last remembered to almost white, and folds of skin hung at the front of his once thick neck. Instead of overalls, he now wore dark-blue baggy jeans, and instead of his gray work hat, a Farmers' Co-op cap shaded his face. But the same gold teeth bejeweled his smile. The same hulking, somewhat stooped shoulders and frog's back, together with the beaked hat, created a profile reminiscent of his huge four-wheel-drive tractor, the chartreuse-green Versatile. Because his land was flat and treeless, I could still see the tractor where I'd parked it, a half mile away on the summer fallow I'd finished cultivating that morning.

I had no money and no health insurance and was determined not to accept any more help than I was already getting from my parents unless I earned it. Each morning I rode out to the farm with Dad and drove tractors for pay. At least I could hold my head up about that. When I was a kid I'd begged him to let me drive tractors. Anyone could tell that was the most important work on the farm, and I'd wanted to be as important as my brothers. My mother had put her foot down. *No daughter of mine is going to bake out there in the sun like a man!* But a lot had changed since then. The tractors all had cabs now with air-conditioning, my brothers had both refused to pick up the farming mantle, and I had acquired enough confidence and skills in the desert to finally be a boy on my father's farm.

Make that a pregnant boy.

Before my feet became so mired in the clay bottom that I would have to ask Dad to pull me out with a rope, I pushed off and swam a few tentative strokes. A white pickup appeared on the gravel road, swerving as the driver braked, then sped back up, causing a cloud of dust and road sand to rain onto the water. I paddled to the shore, if you could call the mud bank a shore, grabbed a willow branch and pulled myself out.

"Feel refreshed?" Dad asked.

I slapped a fly off my clay-streaked, sticky thigh. "God, no." The water had been tepid and full of silt, and the afternoon felt more sweltering than before. Having left my sandals where I'd gotten in, I picked my way barefoot through the weeds. "Ouch! Damn!" Wobbling on one foot, I lifted the other and yanked a goat-head sticker from my heel.

"You almost had old man Noelstrom and his pickup in there with you. He's probably never seen a naked woman outside Sears and Roebucks."

"I'm not 'naked,' Dad. And neither are the women in catalogues. They have underwear on."

He gave me that *I-guess-you're-telling-me* look.

"You should have seen me in the Mojave," I added. "I did swim naked there." I wasn't concentrating on our exchange but was mourning the end of my swimming life. It was over. Although I might be able to immerse myself in clean, cold water if I used the loader tractor and moved that stock tank I'd noticed in the implement lot into the farmyard.

"Je-sus Christ," Dad said. With a flick of his hand, he dropped his pole in the knee-high kocia weeds and stomped off toward his pickup.

I hopped after him, tugging my sandal straps over my heels. "What?" I said, climbing in as he turned the key in the ignition. He always started the engine and began driving before his passengers could even get their doors closed.

"Don't try that here! You'll get arrested."

"Dad," I said, "the tank where I swam in the Mojave was in the middle of absolutely nowhere. It's not like here."

"That it is not." His voice rang with the same finality of the pronouncements he'd made in my childhood. Feeling like a child brought up short by a spanking, I stared silently out my window at the long shadow the truck cast in the ditch and kept my arms folded across my swimsuit's bulging stripes.

He drove right past the farmstead. Apparently, our workday was over. Acutely aware of my exposed upper thighs, on which strands of sun-bleached pubic hair were yet another indication of my recent craven past, I grabbed my jeans from the floor and struggled to pull them on over my damp skin.

Closing my eyes, I pictured the sun shimmering in the leaves of the grandfather cottonwood that towered over the stock-water storage tank I'd swum in every summer afternoon when I lived at the rock house. Beside it the windmill was probably spinning right now. Were I there, I would be standing on Dorf's hood, performing my ablutions. First I would dip my head in. My scalp burning with cold, I would shampoo my hair and rinse onto the ground using the old aluminum sauce pan I kept there for the purpose. After washing, I would dive in. I loved that first thrill. Once my body had unclenched and acclimated, I would float on my back in the silken water, my arms spread, and stare up into the cottonwood's branches, where a pair of tanagers—their bodies yellow, the male's head fire orange—flitted back and forth, bringing food to the nestlings.

Imprinted on my memory were the conical peaks of the Pinto Mountains, dappled in juniper. They and the craggy sandstone pinnacles of the New York range beyond them spoke the layered language of geology. To float in that valley had been to float on the sea of time. Daily I revolved, my arms and legs extended like clock dials, at the center of everything, water and desert, the water being the desert's most profound expression of itself. The antithesis without which desert could not exist, the joy that made its barren beauty habitable.

Now, riding in the pickup. My father driving. Immersions in water on hot days, whether in cold groundwater pumped into that tank or in mountain lakes filled to their granite brims with snowmelt, were the closest I had ever come to ecstasy. Yet were I to describe those swims to my father, all he would see was a naked woman, his daughter.

How had the largeness of my desert life been reduced, so suddenly, to the smallness of this one? Never mind. I knew how. But having brought myself to this pass didn't make it any easier to take. Looking out my window, I saw bare dirt and stubble on the wheat fields, and rows of corn and soybeans made green by irrigation. What grass our pioneer ancestors hadn't broken out by my childhood, Dad and his neighbors had plowed since. To his eye, each new quarter section of pasture ground turned to grain production was an improvement. It meant more money in the bank for someone. Only land that could be farmed was beautiful.

That was what angered him about me. I wasn't as domesticated as his land. It disgusted me that I'd wound up back here, under my father's protection, infantilized. I wasn't his little girl anymore, ever seeking his approval or whatever bone of equality with my brothers he might toss my way. I'd made my own life, and now I'd thrown that life away. I would be leaving here as soon as I could.

The truck slowed as Dad gazed at a neighbor's summer fallow. It seemed he'd forgotten our quarrel. You could put disputes behind you, I guessed, if you were the uncontested boss of your world.

"Brr," I said. I reached over and turned the fan down. Dad didn't seem to notice. A meadowlark's call pierced the closed windowpane so sharply I imagined it carving scrollwork in the glass. I am going to find my own place, I thought. I knew it wouldn't be anything like my desert house, but there might be some haven with a modicum of wilderness nearby. I envisioned an old frame house surrounded by pasture, perhaps on the way up to Bonny Dam, just over the Colorado border. Eventually, in a year or two, I would make my way back to the Mojave. I might get the caretaker's job at the Granite Mountain ranch where Stefan and I had lived for a while. That ranch had since been sold to the University of California, for a desert research center.

Then a vision flitted through my mind of a small child amid rattlesnakes and scorpions, and another of unwanted male visitors driving into that child's and its mother's remote yard. It was one thing to put myself in danger but quite another to put a child in harm's way. I couldn't reconcile my passion for the desert with the new facts of my life. I felt like Gulliver, waking up tied to the ground with those Lilliputian facts swarming all over me.

The pickup began to veer toward the ditch. "Dad?" He crept along, studying a neighbor's field.

"Dad!"

He corrected his steering just before we drifted into the ditch. "Darrel's full of weeds," he said.

Not Darrel's field, I thought, but Darrel.

"His son shot himself," my father added. "He hasn't been the same since."

"Not many people would be after something like that."

"No, but the weeds keep growing."

Such pragmatism had ruined this landscape in the first place. It ignored the heart's knowledge, devalued its needs. I turned to the few remaining pasturelands as my only hope. Occasionally on my drives I would see a small white farmhouse surrounded by buffalo grass. I believed that I could live in such a place. At least I could see a short distance over land that enchanted rather than assaulted the eye—the quiet, the mild blues and greens, the reliable sunshine, and the all-embracing sky. Although I knew I would be lonely in such a place, and although loneliness had rolled me flat and pulverized me in the desert before I met Stefan, at least I would be an independent spirit, a free adult.

My parents thought the idea was preposterous. They suggested I rent a place in town. To me, that would be a worse fate than the farm.

So when I couldn't find a rental on a remote scrap of prairie, I reentered the nightmare I'd had in the desert, of waking up on my father's farm. Only this time I wasn't dreaming.

My uncle Johnny wasn't dreaming either. He had returned to Kansas too, and was working for Dad. He had lost the money from selling the land he'd inherited by investing in city real estate. "Let what happened to Johnny be a lesson," Dad warned me. "Hang on to your land!" I assured him that I would, and I meant it. No matter how much I treasured the desert or how little I wanted to be stuck back home, I wasn't so spoiled as not to be grateful for the secure foundation that Dad and his land put under me.

Johnny, with his shock of brown hair and blue eyes, was the handsomest and the youngest of my uncles, and in some ways the kindest. When he could be spared from more pressing work, he helped me refurbish the two-story, barn-shaped house where Mom and Dad had lived before they took over the Carlson farm. Since then, the house had provided little more than crude shelter for hired men and their families. Johnny and I removed cracked plaster, sheet-rocked the walls, and laid new linoleum in the kitchen. I hung new light fixtures, built a vanity for the bathroom sink, glued vinyl over the walls above the tub, painted everything and, employing the wiles that only a returning daughter possesses, got Dad to buy me the carpeting I wanted.

"Solid colors show dirt," he argued.

"Where'd you figure that out? You've never used a vacuum cleaner in your whole life."

"Well, you'll be using yours plenty. I can guarantee you that."

I knew he was right, but so what? I would willingly vacuum every day if I could have the rose-colored carpets I remembered so fondly from fifties living rooms. If I had to live on the farm, then I would do my damndest to recreate the ambience of my childhood—when Kansas had last been my true home. In the kitchen I hung wallpaper with a strawberry pattern. Over the counters, I glued red Formica to match.

I moved into the house in November, three months before Jake was due. Today I recall only the nights during that winter hibernation. I see enclosed overlit and underfurnished space. I hear the loud furnace that, because there was no basement, we'd installed in my bedroom closet. The carpet's barren plush undermined its rosy optimism, reminding me that I was not a family knee-deep in its own reassuring history and therefore content even if the rug was threadbare.

I hear the whirr of my thrift-store sewing machine as I raced to cover the windows. The house's lights reflected in the black panes, magnifying my isolation. When I turned the lights off, I looked onto an empty farmyard where a mercury-vapor light, designed to come on at sunset, illuminated Quonsets and the corrugated-tin fence Dad had built to protect his sheep from north winds. He'd sold his sheep a decade before—too much work for a man his age. So I didn't even have their baaing to keep me company. Across the farmyard, a trailer housed a hired man and his family. But I had nothing in common with them, and it would have been awkward inserting myself into their nights even if I did. A few other blue yard lights floated in the distance, marking farmsteads where no one lived anymore. Only tractors and their implements dwelled on those places, awaiting the return of spring and their owners.

In my house, the furnace's blowers mixing new smells with old, I stood before the mirror, draping sleeper jammies I'd made over my shoulder and trying to imagine the heft of a baby. I hadn't held many infants in my life, and I didn't know what to expect. When I studied the blurry ultrasound picture, I couldn't decide which white smudges might be Jake. I loved the idea of him enough to cut those jammie patterns out of cuddly, soft velour and painstakingly stitch the pieces together, even though it was beginning to be uncomfortable to sit. But only as my belly expanded and he began to kick did I truly understand he was real. Even then, I could not foresee how much he would change my life.

4

He announced his imminent arrival one January afternoon when I'd gone into town to do errands and had stopped at the car wash to spray frozen mud out of the wheel wells of Dad's biggest pickup. At first I thought the spray wand had a leak, then I realized that the warm water seeping down the insides of my legs was not coming from the wand. Jake wasn't due for another month. I instantly regretted driving that stiff-clutched, stubborn nag of a truck to town. Had manhandling it caused this to happen? Or all the pounding I'd been doing last week as I hammered together shelves for the porch?

I'd heard rumors that even moderately premature babies had died in the Goodland hospital. Suddenly my maternal instincts were strong and fierce. I insisted on Flight for Life. Amazingly, the hospital complied. Paramedics strapped me onto a gurney, loaded me on a plane, and allowed Mom to board too. They stuck electrodes onto my chest and belly and turned out the lights. Our two green heartbeats blipped on the screen as a hundred miles of farms, then another hundred of yellow Colorado prairie rolled under us. In Denver they transferred me to a helicopter and Mom to a taxi. The helicopter landed on the roof of St. Luke's, and next thing I knew I was lying in a softly lit hospital room with oak wainscoting and yellow wallpaper. Soon after, my mother was beside me. I was a little embarrassed by all the attention I was receiving but also deeply relieved. Jake would have every chance of being born safely.

In the vacuum left by the husband I'd exiled, Mom held my hand through my pains, wiping my forehead with the washcloth the nurse provided. How soothing her hands felt, how reassuring her grasp! Now that she had a legitimate reason to show physical affection, the reserve that had overtaken her once I was too big to hold in her lap anymore vanished. We were in a cocoon together, enacting a ritual, mother to daughter, that predated our own sterile culture by all of human time.

"Oh, look at the little guy," Mom said, her voice quaking with joy as the nurse handed Jake into her arms. She laid him on my chest. He weighed only four pounds, thirteen ounces. Because he was tiny and because I viewed him through a new mother's fearful eyes, he had mortality written all over him. Or ephemerality, the implicit likelihood that he would fade into his mysterious origins.

I recall that fear whenever I look at the overexposed photograph taken at the hospital within hours of his birth. His edges bleed to glaring white, as if he were a visitation, a possibility, not an actual presence. He wears a little peaked knit cap like a Tibetan's, and his tiny fingers splay like the rays of a star. He looks out of the picture at me sideways, his features seemingly Oriental, his eyes deep black pools.

I'd never felt so invested before. In my living, his living. "Isn't it amazing how you love them?" another new mother said to me as we sat in the day room, nursing. How, I wondered, had I carried so much power so darkly within me?

No longer did I lie awake plotting my return to the desert. I was too busy taking care of Jake. His fussing woke me several times each night. I would stumble over to his crib, lift him out, nurse him if that's what he wanted, or change his diaper. But usually he didn't need those things. Maybe he had colic. Whatever the cause, only one thing could give him peace. I would stuff him in the chest pouch and walk loops through the kitchen, living room, and bedroom, counting the rounds. He usually succumbed at about one hundred laps. His contentment would then fill me like cream in a glass pitcher—the round-bellied kind that wanted nothing more than to be filled with just that substance. After a tortuous hour, wishing for my own bed, I couldn't tear myself away from him. I would collapse in my recliner and sleep with him.

It took four months for the fretful nights to end. Meanwhile, spring arrived.

I was toting Jake on my hip one evening, headed for the burn barrel carrying a bag of trash, when beauty stopped me in my tracks. I was arrested not only by the sky's fanfare and glory but by the serenity it draped over the farmstead. All the men had driven away in their pickups.

Regardless of what the deed of ownership says, a place most belongs to the people who remain after everyone else goes home. Jake and I were those people. I liked the feeling. Up until that moment I had gone through the motions, fixing up the house as if it would be our home for years to come, but I hadn't felt that I could truly abide there.

I hadn't stood outside without shivering since I moved in. Now the earth was warming up, damp and fertile. I pulled the musky smell into my lungs, held it. Took another swig, and another. I went inside, got Jake's baby swing, and set it up near the flower bed that some hired man's wife had planted.

The bed had not been cared for in years, but now that the soil had thawed, it was loose and moist. The ease with which the weeds released their hold satisfied me so much I forgot about the time. When I finally stopped, Jake had long since gone to sleep. I leaned down to lift him, but his plump bowlegs brought the swing's chair with them and he awoke.

I rotated in the surround of dusk, letting him gaze at the last powder of mauve in the west, the sheen of abalone in the east. The sky was one part of western Kansas that farming hadn't messed up. In the daytime, rarely overcast, it radiated the most genuine sky blue imaginable. At this quiet hour, with darkness lowering over the fields, I could almost forget that the grass that once stretched, infinite green under infinite blue all the way to the circular horizon, had been plowed. Was it possible that with Jake in my arms, an unfarmed sky would be enough?

His mouth hung open as his black eyes absorbed the wonder. "Nighttime coming," I explained. "Look! Venus! Pretty soon there's going to be a star party."

When I was a kid, Dad had held me up under the sky exactly like this, filling my head with the big questions: *Astronomers say the stars go on forever. How could that be? They have to end somewhere. But if they do end, what comes after? Nothing? How can there be nothing? There has to be something. And how did it all start? The Christians say that God made the universe. Well then, who made God?*

"And see that one," I said. Jake fixated on my finger as I tried to point out another star bobble, perhaps Mars. Just then, the mercury-vapor "security" light blinked on.

I turned Jake away from me and thrust him skyward. He let out a peal of squeaky-hinged giggles, his frog legs paddling sideways. "See that light, Jake? Someday I'm going to get you a BB gun. First thing I want you to do? Shoot that thing out!"

5

THE NEXT MORNING THE MUD-PORCH DOOR SLAMMED AND THE GLASS IN THE KITCHEN DOOR RATTLED. I looked up from tipping a spoonful of Cream of Wheat into Jake's mouth.

There Dad stood. Unannounced, uninvited, light streaming around him through the east windows. He was wearing his field hat, its brim wrinkled by many washings. His cheeks jowly. His old shoulders clothed in a thin, blue, short-sleeved work shirt. His jeans bunched at his waist.

Cocking his head at Jake, he made a big smile full of silver and gold crooked teeth. Jake's mouth opened wide on vacant gums, cereal dripping down his chin. He beat his hands at his sides. "Oooh, ooh," Dad said. "It's good to see you too, Jake!"

I said, "Why doesn't it ever occur to you to knock?"

He hunched his shoulders and flinched at my reprimand, then pulled out a chair. "Got a spot of coffee for your old man? How's he eating?"

"Great," I said, pouring. "He's eating great."

"Good," he said. "Keep on feeding him that wheat cereal and he'll make a good farmer someday. I thought you would've taken him to the sitter's by now."

"I'm going to take him, but as I told you, I can't leave him with her all day. I can't keep expressing that much milk, for one thing."

"You should never have gotten started on that business."

That business was breast-feeding. "Don't you get it?" I said. "I told you I could work mornings, but not afternoons."

"That so?"

I detected a whiff of insult. Did he think I was lazy? Was that it? Had he treated Bruce and Clark this way? After sacrificing their childhoods to field work, they had abandoned him and the farm so they could have lives, complete with weekends and vacations.

He stood up—headed for the bathroom, I assumed. Instead, he opened the silverware drawer. I dashed to intercept him before he got to the freezer. "A teaspoon of ice cream isn't going to kill me," he complained.

"Yes, it will." The diet Mom had him on was working. His cholesterol had gone down with each blood test.

"Well, all right, damn it. You women just want to get another harvest out of me."

"Poor guy. You're just surrounded, aren't you?"

At thirty-five, I was reliving my brother's childhoods and, I hated to admit, feeling what was probably the same mix of emotions. I remembered how they used to follow him out the door after summer breakfasts—begrudgingly on the surface, pridefully beneath.

I pulled on my oldest pair of jeans and a tan work shirt I'd torn the sleeves out of and drove ten miles up the road to an even flatter irrigated operation. This farm belonged to an ambitious, humorous couple who had two great girls but clearly wished they also had a son. I trusted this woman to babysit Jake, but I wanted Jake to be one of us, not one of them. I couldn't explain this concern to my father, who thought that rearing children was women's work, so any woman could do it.

A good tractor driver, on the other hand, was a rare commodity. Back at the farm, I stuffed my hair up under my cap and shoved my pliers in my pocket. "Only until noon," I reminded him on the way out to the field. Even that was too long. My breasts were already beginning to fill. By noon they would be hard and sore. Thinking of the relief that would come as I nursed Jake caused my nipples to twinge. Nothing had prepared me for the instinctive nature of this animal love I was in. Alarms sounded inside me every second we were apart. I grabbed my water jug off the seat.

"Remember, cultivating's a slow job. You'll pile dirt up on the corn if you drive too fast."

"I know, okay? You told me five times." As usual, I'd had to sit scrunched up beside him on the arm of the tractor seat while he demonstrated for far more rounds than necessary. Then I'd felt his eyes watching my every move, just as I could feel them doing now. I pulled the engine and hydraulic dipsticks, put them back, and climbed up on the front tire to unscrew the radiator cap. "Always checking up on me," I grumbled, but when I looked over my shoulder, dust hung in the air where his pickup had sat idling a minute before.

Finally. God. Good riddance. It was easy, cultivating. Slow, sure, but satisfying to look behind me and see the ground perfectly worked between straight seams of untouched corn. It gave me this neat, all-is-well-with-the-world feeling. I could understand what made Dad's farming heart tick. I liked making things orderly too. It was the way I felt after vacuuming my carpet, seeing a clean swath—no dog hair, no clumps of dirt at least for a little while. Dad had been right about the color though.

I put my hand under my breast, lifted it, gauging its weight, let it down gently, did the same with the other one. Get realistic, I thought. You are here for Jake. Nothing else matters that much. His grandparents are here. He's loved here by more people than he would be anyplace else. We'll have more financial security here than if I decided to teach. I'd been taking secondary ed correspondence courses ever since coming home but wasn't sure how or if I'd ever get a degree.

I was coming to the end of the field and would have to turn soon. Turns had scared me at first, with so many things to remember all at the same time. Gear down, reduce speed, pull the hydraulic lever to lift the implement out of the ground, hit the turn brake. This stopped the back wheel on the turn side from revolving so the tractor could pivot, but you didn't want to go too far around or you'd wind up redoing rows. Straighten out, push the hydraulic lever forward, gear up, throttle up. I had turning down so well now, though, that it was practically automatic.

It wouldn't be that bad, I thought. I could get away for vacations in the winter. Maybe they would let me have the rock house to stay in on those trips. Say Dad gave me a fourth of the profits. That would be fair. This crop could make two hundred bushels to the acre. That's two hundred times—

How come the turn brake isn't working? I pressed harder and spun the wheel more to the left, but the tractor still didn't whip around. I was overshooting the next rows that I needed to be in. I would have to back up.

Stop. Put it in reverse. Check to make sure the hydraulic lever is back. What? Please tell me I didn't. Please?

"GOD, DAD. I'M SORRY. I DON'T KNOW what I was thinking." I knew exactly what I'd been thinking. I'd been computing how wealthy this life I didn't deserve and would probably never be good at was going to make me.

His eyes passed over me as if I were a fence post. The only objects of interest to him were the bent shanks on the cultivator. Iron is not made to take turns when it is buried in four inches of dirt. Dad didn't take hard turns very well either. Now he would have to readjust his calculations. He'd been pushing me to finish cultivating so he could sow pintos with this tractor. I steeled myself for what was bound to be one of those classic dressing downs that Bruce had told me about. But amazingly, Dad didn't cuss at all. All he said was, "Well, now you'll learn to weld."

Back at the house, I called the sitter, who said she had enough of my milk stored to get Jake through until midafternoon. Then I pumped my breasts so she'd have plenty for the next morning, and to relieve the pain. The process was messy and slow and always frustrated me, failing to yield as much as I thought it should.

I threw together a peanut butter sandwich and ate it as I headed for the shop Quonset. Dad must have eaten lunch in his pickup. I could hear his sledgehammer clanging on steel. This wasn't welding, really. He was just using the torch to heat the iron so it could be pounded straight. Broken equipment could be fixed. I'd learned this simple, comforting truth in the desert. And now the shop smells of argon, hot metal, and greasy dust had a settling effect on me despite my guilt.

"What can I do?"

"Go take another one off and bring it to me."

I did my best to redeem myself, lying on my back on hard ground to reach the least accessible bolts, applying the wrench and ratchet with skill it would have made me proud to demonstrate, if only the circumstances were different. When two o'clock rolled around and we still weren't finished, Dad could see I was getting nervous.

"You don't have to break your behind puttin' 'em back on until the morning," he said. "The pintos can wait another day."

"I guess I'll just go get Jake then."

He assented with a slight tuck of his chin. Either he had learned his lesson the hard way when his sons defected, or age had softened him—or he actually did understand I had something more important to worry about. Every day, with every lesson, he'd been conveying to me the same values he had to Bruce and Clark: *Kill all weeds at first sight. Get in the field now, while you can. I don't care if it's Sunday and the weatherman says it won't rain. Assume it will rain. Before you know it those weeds will be a foot tall.* But he was doing it with less rigidity. If you've got a baby to feed, okay, goddamn it, go.

"Okay, goddamn it, have it your way," he said after we'd argued for a month over what kinds of trees to plant in the new windbreak. He liked seeing the place come to life and must have figured he owed me a little consideration for my effort putting in a garden and lawn. Although Beatrice had done most of the hard work on the lawn. She'd come for a visit to meet Jake and had wound up, as she always did, helping me. Decades of hired men and their wives had parked their cars right outside the front door, and the tiller bucked and bumped through the hard ground. But Beatrice had kept it tracking straight.

For the windbreak, Dad had wanted me to choose either junipers or the new variety of elms immune to disease. I wanted both—and lilacs, Russian olives, and sandhill plums.

Okay, goddamn it. But he drew the line when I argued for planting them randomly like in a real forest. I might have suggested we put them in the ground upside down. They had to be planted in rows.

"You don't understand!" I said. "I'm trying to make a home here. My home. You live in town. Why does everything you do have to be in a straight line?"

If there was one expression that made Dad Dad, it was this one. Eyes mischievously alight. A smile stretched across his face with double parentheses on it. His old heart kept going well beyond what should have been its limits for two reasons—the chance to plant and harvest a new crop, and the entertainment value he got when other people were acting like idiots.

The three hundred sprigs from the Soil Conservation Service arrived in June. The two men working for Dad at the time helped me plant them. We'd already tilled the ground. Now we had to dig the holes, in straight, separate rows the way Dad insisted. That I hadn't been able to convince him of my forest idea ate at me, but there is immense hopefulness in planting trees. I was having fun.

I asked one of the hands to go find a garden hose. He threw the posthole diggers down and stomped off. Had I done something to make him angry? I worked my way down the row, planting seedlings, until I ran out of holes and had to start digging them myself. Where in the heck was he? I wondered. It must have been a hundred degrees out. I wiped the sweat from my forehead, then sensed someone behind me. How long had he been standing there? Without a word, he dropped the hose on the ground and took back the diggers.

At noon, I retrieved Jake from the trailer across the drive, where he'd spent the morning with that same hired man's daughter. He had sticky Popsicle juice all over him, so I put him on the front step, took his clothes and diaper off, and turned on the hose. Jake grabbed it and tried to drink out of it, the water running down his front.

Dad stood behind me, holding the lunchbox Mom had packed for him that morning. "Look at the little devil," he said. "He likes it."

"He's a water baby like his mama. It'll be nice when the grass gets established. We can do this on the lawn."

Dad said, "Too bad you planted fescue. I like a bluegrass lawn."

"Growing bluegrass in this climate makes about as much sense as growing corn. But oh," I added, "You do grow corn."

Dad's eyebrows shot up. And his lips took on their inverted U. "That friend of yours, Beatrice," he said, "manhandling that tiller? I don't know about her."

This again. He'd already told me he suspected she was a lesbian. I wrapped Jake in the towel and picked him up. Inside, I grabbed a diaper and went into the living room. One nice thing about motherhood, you always had some task you could use to avoid unwanted conversations. But not for long. Dad's hands, wet from washing in the mud-porch sink, dripped onto the carpet beside me. "I *said* I don't know about that Beatrice."

Apparently, he was hell-bent on badmouthing my best friend whether I bit or not. With all the sarcasm I could muster, I said, "What don't you know about Beatrice, Dad?"

"Gawd! I came out here and there she was, strutting around the house in her nightie at eleven o'clock in the morning."

"It was a flannel nightgown, Dad. It was Sunday. What were you doing out here then anyway?"

"And when I took her for a combine ride, it was Oh Harold this, Oh Harold that, blinking those big eyes at me. She practically sat on my lap. A guy could have had her right there."

I let my jaw drop. "You could have what?! Don't flatter yourself."

In the kitchen, Dad took his sandwich out and began chewing in a workmanlike manner. Mom made a good sandwich, he often allowed, but it wasn't like eating a hot dinner. "I'll tell you one other thing," he said now. "I had a talk with your friend Larry."

"What about?" Larry was the hired man who'd stomped off that morning. It seemed everyone was my friend today.

"He almost quit on me, said he wasn't going to take orders from a woman."

This news hit hard. Until today, Larry had never let on he didn't like me. I'd been so innocent, thinking that I could be accepted among men here. "So what did you tell him?"

"I will tell you what I told him," Dad said, enunciating every word. He picked up his iced-tea jug, took a long drink, put the jug down. All for effect, I knew. "I told him, quit then, or get your ass back out there. She's your boss today."

Above the table I'd hung a picture of the Virgin Mary. Her exposed heart was encircled by a crown, had fire coming out of the top of it, and shot rays in all directions. Don't ask me why I'd chosen that image. Maybe because as a new mother I found Mary exquisitely beautiful. Or was it for some frivolous decorative purpose? The heart's shape and color did mirror the strawberries in my wallpaper. Or maybe I put it there to irritate Dad. He hated all religious iconography, even if it was something camp like this and he knew I was in no danger of converting to his least favorite brand of Christianity. I do know now why I remember that image, though. It was because my heart felt as jubilant as Mary's looked.

She's your boss today. Sexism was alive and well in Kansas. Larry had proven it and so had Dad, calling Beatrice a lesbian one day, implying she was a harlot the next. But as Harold's daughter, I got special dispensation. I might have been six again and he'd employed his old trick, slipping an ace into my hand when we were playing rummy.

WITHIN TWO WEEKS, WEEDS THREATENED TO SUFFOCATE the seedlings. Dad had me hook his smallest set of spring teeth to our smallest tractor. With the random planting I'd wanted, we couldn't have hoed an acre of trees without sacrificing several days, not to mention our backs. With rows, we could drive between them. For close weeding, we could weave the rototiller in and out. And drip tubing kinked when you tried to bend it. You couldn't lay it in tight curlicues to water trees planted randomly.

"You see," Dad said. "Your old man knows a thing or two. Half of your forest would have died."

By the time I was ten, he would hold his cards until he had a complete rummy, and then he would go out leaving me stuck with all the discards he'd snookered me into thinking I could safely pick up. He didn't have to coddle me anymore. He'd invested me in the game so much that all defeat did was make me want to play another hand.

So it was now. After messing up the cultivator and learning how wrong I'd been about the trees, I reminded myself to consider my father's long experience before mouthing off next time. But being the uncontested boss for that one day of tree planting had also filled me with heady power. I realized that not only did I have tools at my disposal, I also had men. I could choose my fantasy. A sidewalk? Sure. After the next rainstorm, while we waited for the fields to dry out, the forms were built and the concrete poured. A fence so that Jake wouldn't toddle out in front of a wheat truck? Done.

It had been almost twenty years since there had been immediate family on the farm. Seeing the way Dad undertook and enthused about these improvements, it occurred to me that the move to town in the sixties might have been as disorienting for him as it had been for me. Of course, no one acknowledged the shock at the time. I'd been excited about the move, thinking it would add to my family's status and make me more popular at school. The new house was more luxurious than our old one, and it was airtight, meaning Mom and I didn't have to dust nearly as often. Instead of landing on cold, pine boards in the morning, my feet now sank into a thick, royal-blue carpet. That room was fit for a princess—with knotty pine walls, western furniture, and my own sink. But the new brick house was also empty of history. Even if the farmhouse had been surrounded by weathered outbuildings, it had been gracious and grand. And it had enough prairie around it to remind us of our land's former grandeur. Instead of pasture hills, the new house had a weed-free, chemically green lawn as level as my brother Clark's butch-cut hair in his graduation picture.

That's what I'd been doing when I moved to the desert, I realized—

not only seeking to live surrounded by natural beauty again but also trying to get back the gritty, real life of my childhood. I'd once had dozens of pets, ranging from crows and cottontails to calves and colts. Yet Mom had wanted nothing, not even a housecat, to mar the new house's perfection. Our dogs and cats, along with my horses and Dad's sheep, were moved to this farm. And Dad had begun commuting here, like a suburbanite going to any job.

Even if he'd never breathed a word of complaint, I suspected that after a lifetime of no separation between home and work, it felt alienating to leave his family in the morning. He wasn't able to cool down in his own house at midday anymore or eat the noon meal at his own table or take an afternoon nap in his own easy chair. Or watch his children and grandchildren grow into the only life that made sense to him.

But now he had Jake and me. And we had him. The possibilities of the paradise we could make together seemed endless. A swimming pool? Possibly. I'd learned that with the loader tractor, we could dig a hole as deep as we wanted. That's how the in-ground silos had gotten there. And we'd proven we could pour concrete. A hydroponic greenhouse? A herd of bison? Maybe someday, but I knew better than to mention those things yet.

Dad had his own ideas. "What you need is a sow."

"Do I?"

"There's good money in pigs." Within a week, I had a pregnant sow. Then it was thirteen piglets and pulling the afterbirth out of their noses and keeping them warm with heat lamps and shoveling the stinkiest shit I'd ever smelled.

6

HUMBLED AFTER BENDING THE CULTIVATOR SHANKS, I BECAME A MODEL APPRENTICE. I got so good that the following spring Dad rewarded me with the most prestigious job, planting corn. Corn rows had to be straight so that they could be cultivated and then furrowed for irrigation without the implements tearing out any of the crop. A marker extended from the edge of the planter, making a groove in the ground to follow on the next round. I had to keep the chrome arrow on the John Deere's hood centered perfectly in that groove.

Every so often I stopped the tractor and opened the cab door onto the day's mounting heat, climbed down the ladder, and circled the idling mammoth as Dad had told me to do, making sure the hydraulic hoses were still connected and that no weeds were balling up in the blades that opened the ground ahead of the seed spouts. I manually turned the planting gears, then checked beneath each spout for the pink, chemically dusted kernels that spilled out. I looked in the planter boxes and made sure the seed levels were even. When they got low, I called Dad on the two-way. "I'm out of seed."

"So fill it."

"No."

"Jesus Christ. Okay then. I'll send Larry out."

I refused to open the sacks and pour the seed. I didn't want to breathe the pink dust. The one time I did come in contact with the insecticide, it stung my skin. Trying to wash it off, I poured all the water in my field jug over my arms. I'd looked up to see the amused look on my father's face. "Think about it," I said. "If it kills the corn borer and cutworms, it can kill you."

"Hasn't yet."

"Who knows? Maybe that's what happened to the other seventy-five percent of your heart."

That was the only thing I refused to do. Work with chemicals. The so-called Green Revolution had arrived in my absence, brought about by chemical fertilizers and pesticides with macho names like Roundup, Lasso, Prowl, Bladex, Lance, and Bicep.

I'd read *Silent Spring* and knew that while the chemicals were cowboying weeds into submission and magnificently boosting our yields, they were also leaching into our groundwater and our bloodstreams.

Poisons developed to kill enemies and clear forests so enemies couldn't hide in them were now being used to make war on unwanted vegetation and insects in our fields. The compounds all had carbon in them, the chemical basis of life. They could interact with our cells and cause damage in us just as they could in the life forms they were intended to destroy. We couldn't depend on the government to protect us. Regulations were few and lax. As with everything, you had to use your own brain, and my brain sensed danger whenever I smelled a farm chemical as readily as it did when I heard a rattlesnake buzz.

"Don't do that there!" I shouted the first time Dad pulled his spray rig up to my garden spigot, which happened to be less than twenty feet from the well that brought water into my house.

Disgruntled, his shoulders hunched, he climbed back into the tractor cab and drove to the other side of the yard. "Is this far enough for ya, Miss Prissypants?" he said as I dragged the hose over to him.

He was mixing Treflan, a chemical he used on his pinto beans. The orange liquid splashed above his protective gloves and onto his arms. When he sprayed Treflan in the field, it turned the ground that same sickly yellow orange. "Just drink it why don't you?" I said, then it occurred to me that I possibly was drinking it.

I insisted that we have my house's well water sampled. Concerned that he might be poisoning his grandson, Dad agreed. The test came out okay, but going through the process heightened his consciousness a little. Mom helped too, saying she was worried about what Jake might get into when he started roving about the farmstead on his own. Dad gathered all the cans, some bulging as if about to explode; jugs, some lying on their sides beside syrupy puddles they'd leaked; and sacks, some torn open and spilling lethal powder, and locked them into a little trailer house that had once been sleeping quarters for his sheepherder.

But even with this precaution, exposure to chemicals was unavoidable on the farm. In my childhood, Dad had put temporary electric fences up on his wheat stubble so that his sheep could eat the weeds and volunteer wheat, fertilizing the ground as they grazed. Instead of sheep, he now had big brawny tractors that pulled five hundred-gallon tanks of ammonium nitrate fertilizer and forty-foot implements with V-shaped blades that undercut the stubble, killing weeds at the same time they infused the fertilizer into the soil. While applying ammonia fertilizer, he had to wear goggles and be careful not to breathe any of the gas. It could blind him or burn his lungs.

When I drove out to the field to give him a lift back to the farmstead, he would stand with the pickup's passenger door ajar, playing peekaboo with Jake, while ammonia mist hovered in the wake of his last tractor round.

"God, shut the door! The ground smells like cat piss."

"Small price to pay for fifty-bushel wheat," he would say, dropping his iced-tea jug in Jake's lap as he climbed into the pickup. Jake would giggle and hug the thermos, the dust on it smearing his shirt.

WHEN I WASN'T TRAINING A JOHN DEERE'S chrome arrow on some fence post or distant patch of weeds, I was one of my father's "floodmen." He would eventually convert to center-pivot sprinklers, but when I lived there, we were still irrigating mostly out of huge pipes laid along the tops of the fields. Each summer morning and evening I would belt Jake into his car seat in the blue Chevy pickup Dad had bought me for both farm and personal use and drive out to the corn.

As I knocked the floodgates open, the water would gush out in beautiful arcs and with such force that if I tried to slice my hand through it, my arm would be thrown back, almost dislocating my shoulder. To direct the water into the furrows, I placed "socks"—tubes of woven plastic mounted on wire hoops—over gates in the pipe.

Having lived in the Mojave, I quickly adjusted to working in hot sun, and the work led to sensuous exhaustion at each day's end. *In Main Street*, I wrote in my journal, *Sinclair Lewis calls the look of the land at sunset 'fulfilled.' True of the land's creatures too. Work and my past here make me one of these.*

But life in the desert had also sensitized me to the value of water.

Because the rock house had no well, I had borrowed a tank from my neighbor. Whenever the tank ran out, I would hook the Cruiser up to the flatbed trailer it rested on, drive the two miles to his house, and refill from his carefully conserved windmill supply. I have since learned that Americans, on average, use between eighty and one hundred gallons of water each day. I made that five hundred-gallon tank last for more than a month.

Imbued with the respect water demands where it is not readily accessible, I greeted the appearance of so much of it coming out of the ground in our desertlike heat as surreal. Why didn't all High Plains farmers—who had surely grown up conserving water just as my mother had, her father making her drink all she poured into the tin cup that hung on their windmill—not mistrust such bounty?

I had not yet seen any of the maps that would later trouble me. No brown blots where the aquifer had been exhausted. All I had to go on was a gut feeling. I knew we couldn't draw that much water from the ground and expect it to keep flowing forever. What would we do when we ran out? What would the next several thousand years of High Plains inhabitants do for water?

As I lay in my bed at night, the backs of my lids strobing with images of all the rows of corn I'd driven past that day and of silver water snaking down each furrow, the incessant growl of the pumps plagued my conscience. The big truck engines, converted to run on natural gas and mounted on concrete pads at the edges of the fields, seldom stopped, even at night.

The water didn't belong to the farmers, although most of them seemed to think it did. The state allowed us to use it, but only up to the limits of the rights granted to us. Many farmers, however, didn't even bother to fill out forms reporting how much water they used. Dad was apparently among them. One day over dinner he fished a letter out of his lunchbox and handed it to me. It was from the Kansas Water Office, informing him that from now on, farmers would be fined for not reporting.

We didn't know how much water we'd pumped that year. The Water Office hadn't made us install meters yet, so the only way to figure it out was by using the bills that the utility company sent for each engine. Dividing the total gas usage by an estimate of how much the engines used in one hour, we could estimate the number of hours we'd pumped, then multiply by the engines' pumping rates. Dad said he'd tried to do all this himself, but he couldn't get his "ol' noggin to do the numbers."

I can still see the utility bills scattered over my kitchen table. I remember how confusing it was to discover that two of the wells shared a gas meter. But mostly I remember my shock when I totaled the numbers. We'd pumped 139 million gallons that season. Even though we irrigated more than seven hundred acres at the time, half of that amount went onto our eighty-acre cornfield. That was more than four thousand gallons of water for every bushel of corn we'd harvested.

Hoping to prove that irrigated corn wasn't really profitable, I suggested I do a spreadsheet computing the cost of labor, fuel, depreciation, chemicals, seed, property taxes, everything. "Go ahead," Dad said. "Compute your heart out."

The conclusion I reached: We barely broke even on corn—until I factored in the subsidy checks, which put us ten thousand dollars in the black.

"Are you satisfied?" Dad asked.

"No. They're paying us to throw away water. And it's so irrational. The only reason people out here grow corn is because of the subsidies. But there's a corn surplus. The more we grow, the lower the price, so the more subsidies they have to give us. It's a vicious circle."

That might be true, he allowed. But if the government paid midwestern corn farmers to the east of us to grow corn, it wouldn't be fair to draw a line down the middle of the country and "separate our poor, dry old plains asses from those lucky so and so's who get rain."

I sighed.

"Don't despair," Dad said. "Big Daddy will put the plug in before it's too late."

By Big Daddy, he meant the government. He had faith in this. It was the government's job to look out for the general good, preventing any serious harm individuals might cause in the pursuit of private gain. In his lifetime he'd seen the feds bust trusts, protect unions, and protect the environment with clean air and water laws. The Farm Program dictated many of his practices. In return for his subsidy checks, he had to leave a certain amount of organic matter on the surface. He'd been required to terrace his hillier land. The Soil Conservation Service, set up in FDR's presidency, enforced these measures to prevent our topsoil from abandoning itself to water erosion, or the wind from picking it up and dropping it on Oklahoma, as it had done during the Dust Bowl. Big Daddy always had his hand in, and he would certainly reach in and do something before the water was all gone.

In the meantime, my daddy would raise his brows, cock his head at me, and smile with overstated cheer. "Until then, I got mine!"

How had we managed to farm before we had access to all that water? The same way we still farmed on our dry land. We employed the art my grandfathers and other plains farmers had developed by hit and miss. The first hits had been the wet years during the early half of the 1880s, when settlement boosters claimed that the rain had indeed followed the plows westward as they'd predicted it would. Farmers heartily embraced the rhetoric even if many agronomists warned that the science was extremely dubious.

The misses had been the dry years, culminating in the worst drought ever, in the Dirty Thirties. The thirties were called that because when the wind blew, which was practically all the time, the air filled with topsoil that had been tilled to a powder. My mother told stories of dirt blizzards so thick that they couldn't see the barn from the house. After those storms, they resorted to using scoop shovels for dustpans. Through those tremendous trials and errors, farmers figured out that to grow wheat on the plains, they would have to let half their fields lie dormant each year, leaving stubble on the surface to prevent erosion and to allow enough moisture to accumulate to support the next crop. To keep weeds from taking over the field, they undercut the stubble with sweeps, the implement we now used in combination with ammonia fertilizer. When, after a year of dormancy, the stubble had to be removed to make way for a new crop, the two-way disk came into play. It piled dirt up in opposing directions, thwarting the wind.

My father still farmed more than a thousand acres of dryland winter wheat. After making as clean and well packed a seedbed as Farm Program conservation rules allowed, he planted in September, placing the seeds deep enough to rest in damp soil but shallow enough so the sprouts could reach the surface. If he was lucky, snow would come and keep the crop moist. "Drip, drip, drip!" he would say, playing the air like a piano with his thick fingers, his eyes shining with delight over nature's built-in irrigation system. If there was no snow on the ground when January winds began to rage, he was quick on the draw with an implement called a chisel, which tore gashes in the ground perpendicular to the wind. The ridges this left prevented the fields from blowing.

When Dad had done all he could to ensure success, he prayed. No matter how irreligious he claimed to be, that's what he'd been doing in my childhood when he stood on the balcony of our old farmhouse summer nights, scrutinizing the sky. Seeing a thunderhead approach over the western windbreak, his face would swell with hope the way the ground seemed to swell in advance of a rain. To me, he had looked kinglike, standing on the ramparts of the house my grandfather had built. But like every farmer who invested his family's future in the interplay of soil, seed, and weather, he was no king. He was merely a supplicant, completely subject to the sky's whims.

Now that I was back, I couldn't get enough of watching my burly, arthritic father kneeling behind his wheat drill, flicking dirt out of a furrow with his pliers handle to make sure he was planting at the right depth. He had this uncanny knack for uncovering the kernels. "Ooh, ooh, there she is," he would say. "Now you try."

For the life of me, I couldn't find a single one. But I liked crouching beside him and being given the chance to learn. Even with our big equipment, everything came down to kneeling in the dirt. The action went back ten thousand years to when wheat was first domesticated in the deserts of Mesopotamia. At least in this particular instance, nature's and my father's dictates were one. You must plant in moist soil. You confirm your success by uncovering the seed and checking.

"Look at that. Julie," Dad said in August, proud of the corn I'd planted in April. Fully tasseled, it stood six feet tall, a solid green wall, every plant a uniform height and color. But to me, the corn seemed hypergreen. It looked unnatural. What corn and sorghum we'd raised when I was a kid had survived on our scant rainfall. Without irrigation, seeds had to be planted farther apart so that they could compete for moisture. Looking at a cornfield then, I'd seen as much gray dirt between the stalks as I had emerald green.

Our old, dryland, prechemical approach had more in common with the way I'd seen Hopi Indians farm than it did with our present methods. Although the Hopi generally distrusted outsiders, I had a San Francisco friend who assisted the elders of Hotevilla, the most traditional village on the reservation, with their causes. This was in my desert exploration period. My friend didn't own a car, and when he told me he'd received an urgent call from James, the village spokesperson, I had offered to drive him to Arizona in my Cruiser.

The Hopi, who traced their lineage in the desert southwest to AD 600, were still farming the way they always had. James took us to his field, where I watched him drop to his knees, that universal posture of farmers. He pressed holes into the mounded earth with his planting stick, then dropped corn kernels into them one by one.

He and his family stored their harvested corn inside their house. At night, stacks of the burgundy and indigo ears gleamed in the lantern light as we crowded around the family's small, painted wooden table. We ate posole, piki bread, and pinto beans. After supper, James and my friend worked together composing a newsletter. James hoped the newsletter would garner support from *Bahana*, or white people, to stop a town well that the Bureau of Indian Affairs wanted to dig and a tower it wanted to erect to store the water. The Hotevilla elders were willing to lay down their lives in this battle. They'd done it before, preventing the BIA from bringing electricity to the village by lying down in front of bulldozers. If that well went in, James explained, people would waste water. Their spring would dry out—an unthinkable tragedy, as it would make it impossible for them to live there any longer.

Could two cultures be any different? I now wondered. We were taking federal money to mine water and would do so until the unlikely day that same government made us stop. The Hopi had been trying to prevent the government from giving them a well in the first place.

"It's an attack on the values that have been teached to us by the elders for thousands of years," said James, who spoke English with a gentle accent. Hearing him speak Hopi with his wife and children, I realized for the first, mind-bending time in my life that I was a foreigner on this continent. In their low-lying, flat-roofed house made of adobe and rock fragments, James and his family lived seamlessly with the wild desert around them. According to Hopi legend, humanity failed to appreciate and therefore destroyed three previous worlds. The Hopi had been given the desert this fourth time around and were grateful for the privations of the arid climate. It reminded them to stay within their limits and avoid making the same fatal mistakes.

Not to say that the Hopi were less provincial than any other tribe, including ours. When my friend introduced me to a group of the village elders, I was as naively reverent of them as any white, twenty-eight-year-old Carlos Castañeda aficionado would have been. A man in his nineties who was revered by everyone motioned me to his side. Had the old man seen something in me that promised I would be especially receptive to his wisdom? No. Apparently he'd misinterpreted my interest in him as flirtation. He grabbed my hand and pulled it toward him with surprising force, like an old crab creakily dragging carrion toward its mouth, except his destination turned out to be the fly of his khaki pants. So much for my dream of becoming the first woman ever allowed into a kiva. As he pressed my palm into his crotch, I jerked free. The old guy must have thought he "could have had" me right there.

Some things, I guessed, were the same everywhere. But other things were so different it was hard to believe that the Hopi and we were members of the same species. James's village was formed in 1906, the same year that my Carlson grandparents traded the Texas land they'd homesteaded for Kansas land—as my mother liked to say, "sight unseen." A chart graphing Hotevilla's and our progress would have diverged rapidly from that year forward regardless of what you measured. Standard of living, as defined by our culture, up, up, up for us. Horizontal for them. Crop yields up, up, up for us. Horizontal for them. Groundwater reserves down, down, down for us. Horizontal for them. Biological diversity of the plants and animals we shared our land with down, down, down for us. Horizontal for them.

That was the main difference between the Hopi and us. They were okay with horizontal. We were not.

7

I T TOOK ME A YEAR AND A HALF, BUT I FINALLY GOT MY OPPORTUNITY TO RESTORE NIGHT TO OUR FARM. An electrician came out to raise the wire between the shop and old sheep barn so that Dad's new seed drill could pass beneath it when folded up for transport. Surreptitiously, I had him install a switch on the light pole. He said no one had ever asked him to do that before.

Because it had rained recently, the pump engines weren't running the night I turned off the mercury-vapor light. The darkness, therefore, was doubly sweet. Starlight glazed the road somewhat, but I couldn't gauge the distance between my eyes and the ground. Each step I took felt like an act of faith. Remembering how juniper, yucca, and cactus had billowed out at me like ghosts during my nighttime walks in the Mojave, I tried on my wilderness mind-set. Imagining the blackness around me as unfarmed prairie filled me with a sense of limitless possibility.

"The strangest thing," said the new hired man's wife the following morning. They lived across the drive in a new double-wide that Dad had entrusted me to order for them. "Did you notice that the yard light went out last night?"

I told her that I'd turned it off and that I hoped to keep it off from now on. "Won't it be nice to step outside at night whenever you want to and look at the stars?"

She stared at me as if I'd lapsed into a foreign language. "I wish you wouldn't turn it off," she finally said. "That light's for see-cure-i-ty." She drew the word out in the explanatory way you might use with a small child.

This was the same hired man's wife who had invited me to a Tupperware party. I'd sat with my legs folded demurely in the circle of women who were as careful not to say anything they couldn't live down as the women in my mother's ladies' club had always been. In most rural communities, you keep your private business private and you don't express any views that might upset or alienate your neighbors. It hadn't been like that in the Mojave. Once I'd gotten together with Stefan and began circulating more, I discovered that people there argued about politics and gossiped openly. You had to be pretty free-spirited, I guessed, to live in the Mojave.

But in Kansas, women carefully tiptoed around one another. All we talked about at that party were our gardens, the weather, and our parents' health. I took a slip of paper from the bowl handed around, to see if it had my birthday month written on it, in which case I would get to take home a free lemon-squeezing contraption. I competed to see how many words I could make from "Tupperware."

"Weep" came first to mind. Probably a reason for that. Did the other women bluff their way through those gatherings, pretending to be entertained by the small talk, while boiling inside with ideas and unspoken needs for true connection roiled within them? How did they keep from exploding?

For the double-wide, I'd ordered a fireplace, a pretty built-in hutch, and oak trim—niceties that Dad had balked at. "Because you're cheap," I'd said. "Jesus, Dad, give them something to make it homey." He forked over the cash because this new man was young and smart and experienced—promising management material. Dad's heart was not getting any stronger. He would not be able to run the farm forever. So I left the yard light on after the hired man's wife asked me to. Dad needed a manager more than I needed darkness, especially now that I had been having traitorous thoughts again.

"Ah-ah-ah." Each summer night, the baby sounds Jake made as he lay in his crib playing with his toes kept rhythm with the *"grr-rr-rr"* of the pulsating pump engines. I would sing the lullaby I'd written for him.

> *Jake's a little cowboy, yes he is.*
> *Someday he'll ride a horse named Biz.*
> *Biz'll be a red horse, big and strong.*
> *He'll be Jake's best friend all day long.*

Maybe at harvest time I would go out to the field and choose an ear of corn to lay beside him, as James had told me the Hopi did, so that the Corn Mother might protect the little one. There would be no need to search for a perfect ear. They were all perfect. Would that fact render my gesture meaningless? Or worse, bestow a curse instead of a blessing? I knew what gave those ears their look of perfection. Sometimes a menacing chemical odor wafted in through my windows, as if carried on the engines' growl. I would scurry through the house, slamming the windows shut, then stand over Jake's crib, as helpless as if bombs were dropping.

I wished I could give Jake a childhood like mine. I wanted him to know how to grow vegetables; understand where meat came from; hold snakes as they wrapped around his arms; be tickled by the toenails of lizards, salamanders, and box turtles; hand raise birds, mice, ground squirrels, and cottontails; slop hogs; pluck chickens. My brother Bruce liked to point out that I'd never milked a cow, which was true. In fact, all I'd done on a regular basis was ride the big wooden barn gate, spooking the cow, causing her to kick over the pail and step on Bruce's toes. But Clark had shown me how to milk a few times and I knew the warm, scaly feel of Rosebud's teats in my fist and how to pull them alternately, causing the milk to flow.

I wanted Jake to have that sensory grounding, to be of a place in a real way, integrated with the other creatures that lived there. But not even the ditches were safe for wildlife anymore. If Dad didn't mow them or scatter poisoned bait in them to kill grasshoppers, the county sprayed them to kill weeds. The sheep were long gone. Jake would never be asked to climb into the barn rafters above the giant gunny sacks Dad hung at shearing time and jump into them to compress the wool. He wouldn't emerge with lanoline coating his skin or be, for reasons such as that, entwined with other-than-human life on a cellular level. He would never know the sound of a thousand ewes and twelve hundred lambs milling in the corrals, their *baas* as divergent as human voices— some high, some low, some scratchy, some clear—a chorus of comfort when he might otherwise feel alone. And I certainly wasn't going to marry a farmer and give him any siblings to play with.

Light cast by the mercury-vapor bulb seeped in around the drawn curtains—sickly blue, as if contaminated by the chemicals that hovered in the air. In desert darkness, I had experienced danger of the enlivening kind, not this danger of the deadening kind. What would happen to my heart, to my mind, to Jake's and my bodies, if I chose to stay on?

From my journal: *Sinclair Lewis uses the verb "enfeeble" to describe what loneliness does. What a perfect word for the almost physical diminishment loneliness causes.*

8

I HAD ACCUMULATED EIGHTEEN CREDITS IN THE CORRESPONDENCE COURSES I'D BEEN TAKING IN AN EFFORT TO RETRIEVE MY EDUCATION, THE MOST THAT THE UNIVERSITY OF IOWA WOULD ACCEPT IN TRANSFER. I promised Dad that I would come home and help him farm every summer, that my return to school wouldn't change things too much.

At least I can say that I did come home the first summer, then the next. Each time, the smell of mothballs, dead mice, and the Rodex that had killed them greeted me as I opened the farmhouse door. I had read that naphthalene, the active ingredient in mothballs, had been linked to brain damage in infants. God knew what other damage the chemical caused, but no matter how much I insisted that the hired man not use poisons in my house, he did it anyway. Like his wife, who couldn't comprehend why I would prefer stars to mercury-vapor light, he couldn't understand why anyone would rather swat moths or trap mice when the pests could be vanquished with perfectly good chemicals. I opened all the windows, scrubbed every surface, and while the house aired out, slept at Mom and Dad's house in town. Once resettled, I embarked on another summer walking up and down the pipes and knocking gates open, bleeding the Ogallala of her life-giving power.

At each summer's end, I packed up Jake and our dog, Rex, and drove the eight hundred miles back to Iowa. I would get about halfway across Kansas before I hit the hundredth meridian, the approximate longitudinal line separating east from west, wet from dry. As the Rocky Mountain rain shadow dissipated, the land got greener, the skies diminished in both height and breadth, and I saw the sun less often. I felt like a child going inside after recess. No pale vistas. No vaulting, translucent blue. As hills and cornfields multiplied, my sun-dependent, distance-dependent soul shriveled to a nubbin of yearning.

Corn and soybeans, those sisters in the standard crop rotation, grew everywhere I looked—in glades between trees, on hillsides, and along the many mud-brown rivers and creeks. Farmers didn't have to irrigate. The sky did that for them. And I'd spent my summer helping my father turn the Great American Desert, as the explorer Stuart Long had dubbed the plains, into a midwestern farmer's paradise. It made no sense. In school, I'd discovered the western writer Wallace Stegner, who'd confirmed for me what I'd discovered on my first trip to Death Valley. Aridity was the West's defining feature. Without it there would be no famously western aesthetic. Trees would conceal rugged contours and diminish distances. A midwestern farmer's paradise was a westerner's hell.

How to get back? That would become the theme of everything I wrote in my Iowa writing courses and of everything I have written since. How to be the person I'd become in San Francisco and the Mojave yet also access, for Jake and me, a life interconnected with our family and land? After Dad's eventual death, how would I manage to honor his first precept, the one most essential to my understanding of who I was? *Hang on to your land!* I hadn't thought through the eventual consequences of my leaving, but my unconscious bit into this problem and wouldn't let it go.

In August, a year and a half after I'd moved to Iowa and as I was preparing to enter graduate school, Bruce called to tell me that Clark had been killed in a bicycling accident in California. This was my first adult encounter with death. Clark had left home for college when I was only nine, but I had always been his beloved little sister. For weeks after the funeral, I walked around in a leaden haze by day and dreamed of him by night.

In a dream that would replay in my memory for years afterward, he was lying on top of an implement being pulled up the hill by an open-air tractor driven by Dad. I knew it was Dad even from the back, because of the way he sat the tractor—not with panache, the way a showy cowboy sits a horse, but with the acceptance of mud. His shoulders were curved downward in his wool-lined denim jacket, his brimmed field hat square above his thick neck.

The implement was a seed drill. Not the new, forty-foot-wide set that I'd used when planting wheat but one of the old, narrow sets that Dad and my brothers planted with in my childhood. It had a long flat lid over the bins containing the seed. Clark lay on his back atop the lid. Instead of falling off as the drill angled up the hill, he remained frozen, his arms crossed like one of those Egyptian funerary statues that were found in the pyramids, buried with the pharaohs. Under his arms lay Jake, also on his back and facing the sky.

I knew in my heart that the dream was about our inescapable

destiny as Dad's progeny, and children of that land. I was in the process of breaking away from the farm and Dad, but none of us could ever really do that. It didn't matter what our occupations were. There would always be that superior occupation, the one that we were supposed to be practicing and still were practicing deep in our psyches.

When I went through the things that Mom and Bruce had brought from Clark's condo in Chico, California, where he'd taught chemistry in a junior college, I chose as my memento his tin Future Farmers of America sign. An eagle perched atop a circle of golden corn kernels, holding a sheaf of wheat in one talon.

A FUTURE
FARMER

LIVES

HERE

CLARK L. BAIR

I looked at that sign and recalled Clark in his blue corduroy Future Farmers of America jacket, with that same emblem on his chest. He wore the jacket without the least bit of irony, fully intending to excel at the occupation. A teenage perfectionist, he'd followed the chrome arrows across our father's fields with purpose as sure and straight as the rows of wheat he planted. But he worked hard and excelled at everything, especially science and math.

When he graduated as valedictorian from high school, he made it clear he was finished with farming. Feeling that he was never good enough for Dad, whether he slaved his heart out or not, had embittered him. Yet he'd kept this sign. I knew how fraught his choice must have been, between science and city friends and sophistication on the one hand, and approval in our father's huge willful heart on the other. I'd been a future farmer too.

9

I N ONE PICTURE OF JAKE FROM THE SUMMER HE WAS THREE, HE'S SMEARED HEAD TO FOOT IN MUD. That was the day I'd been so focused on rototilling weeds from around the trees that I hadn't noticed him wandering toward the lagoon, a low, boggy spot in the surrounding field. I ran to extract him, a half-buried frog. At four, he stands shoulder deep in wheat, his hair wet and recently combed, wearing a wide-striped, old-fashioned shirt I'd bought because it reminded me of the ones my mother dressed my brothers in when they were little. Beside that picture in my album, I placed a shot of Dad in the same field, examining a seed head for ripeness. It is impossible to look at those two pictures and not think about succession, a way of life continuing through the generations.

But after Jake turned five, there are no more pictures of him on the farm. That was the third summer after we'd moved to Iowa. In May, I had a scholarship to attend a writers' conference in Utah. After the conference, I planned to pick up Beatrice from the airport in Denver and go camping in the Colorado Rockies. I longed to see the earth's jutting bones again, not just its outline beneath crops. I had to return to Iowa by the second week of June. I'd been offered a summer teaching assistantship. It was an honor, and better pay than I earned on the farm. I stopped in Kansas only for a brief visit.

The young man whom Dad had pegged as management material had quit. His family didn't enjoy living so far from town. That was okay. Dad wasn't that happy with him anyway. The guy hadn't been willing to make the sacrifices. Sundays he went to church regardless of what the crops needed, and his wife was always "running up and down the road" to town. Dad hired a new man. The Oddball, he called him.

Over supper during the first night of my visit, Dad said, "The Oddball told me he can remember being born. Well, if that isn't a crock."

"Are you going to fire him for that?" I asked.

"If I've gotta pry him out of bed in the morning, I might as well can him and go on without."

"It would kill you to do all that work by yourself," Mom said.

As I ladled her lean hamburger stew into my bowl, Dad's eyes, as menacing as the sky before a hailstorm, moved onto me. "Want to earn eighty dollars?" he asked.

"Why? What do you want?" I should have said no, I thought. It was the kind of question you asked a teenager.

He tore a dinner roll in half and slathered it with margarine. "Go out and do those girls' eighty. I'll pay you a dollar per acre." The Errington "girls" had gotten Dad to farm their wheat ground for them by "wiggling their pretty asses," he normally would have said, adding that of course their asses were about ten feet wide and wiggled naturally. But not tonight.

"I'd like to help, Dad, but what would Jake do? He can't sit on the tractor with me all day. I'm worried he's getting a cold."

"Jasmin can take care of him."

"No, I can't. I have a hair appointment, and then I have club in the afternoon." Mom and Dad had an understanding. She'd earned her right to refuse. If he wasn't willing to sell the place or rent it out, well then, that didn't mean she had to work herself to death too.

All through the next day I replayed the conversation. Did he really need my help? "Grandpa needs us," I could have told Jake. "Bring Kermit the Frog and he can help too." So what if Jake fidgeted and cried, having to ride on the ledge behind my seat in the tractor cab all day? Even if his cold got worse, even if it led to the inevitable ear infection and the trip to the hospital emergency room for an antibiotic and I missed going to Utah. After all that Dad had done for me, didn't he deserve my help?

But besides the Oddball, he had also hired a neighbor man. Surely with the two men he had enough help to get the Erringtons' and his own field work done. I suspected that he just wanted to see me out there.

I remembered that dream image of Clark lying statuelike, holding Jake frozen in that same posture, pinned under his uncle's arms. They hadn't rolled off, even though the top of the seed drill had been flat and narrow. It looked as if they were permanently affixed and had no choice but to lie there and be pulled up the hill by Dad. But nothing visible held them in place. That's how I felt now, as if breaking invisible ties. Refusing Dad was like denying the very structure of my universe.

I had looked up the Egyptian figures the dream reminded me of. *Shawabti*. The figures represented "deceased persons and were intended to do agricultural work in place of those persons in the afterlife."

"Like little clones," the article had said. Little replicas.

The wonders of the subconscious! Agricultural work, no less. The replicas were entrusted with "sowing the fields, filling the water-courses with water, and bringing the sands of the east to the west."

I was not sure what the sands were needed for, but I knew all about sowing and filling water-courses. "I am here and will come whenever you bid me," the clones pledged to their masters.

Well, I will not come, I vowed. I am going to have my own life.

DAD RETURNED FROM THE FARM THAT EVENING as I stood at the kitchen sink, tipping a teaspoon of Tylenol into Jake's mouth.

"I'm getting medicine because I've got a sick head," Jake told him.

Dad looked beat, dust collected in his frown lines and the crevices around his eyes, but this didn't prevent him from putting on a cheery face for his grandson. He leaned down and gave Jake's forehead a loud kiss. "Did that help?"

Jake closed his eyes, taking a reading, then opened them. "No," he said, unable to hide his smile.

"No? It helped your mom when she was little."

How could I have spent the whole day steeling myself against this man? As always, he'd proven larger than I was.

But over a supper of baked chicken, he said, out of the blue and with obvious derision, "Camping."

"You want to talk about this, Dad?" I struggled to keep my voice even. "If I'm such a huge disappointment?"

"You're not a disappointment," Mom said. "It's just a busy time of year."

Dad gnawed the cartilage off the end of a leg bone. "Eating everything but the saltshaker," Mom usually observed, but no one was willing to make jokes in this climate. Dad dropped the bone onto his plate, scooted his chair back, and went into the living room.

Wordlessly, Mom and I did the dishes, then I took Jake downstairs to play with his barn animals. I helped him hook together little sections of white fence, much more idyllic than the corrugated-tin fencing on our real farm. Inside his corral, Jake placed "three sheep like Grandpa used to have. See Mom? And our horsies." For turf, the animals had Mom's loud, sixties-print, chartreuse carpet to graze. One of the horses whinnied and reared. "Oops," Jake said. "Broke the fence."

While mending the damage caused by the unruly white mare, I heard footfall on the stairs. Then he was standing behind me. "You want to talk about it. Well then."

Chilled by the resentment I glimpsed in his eyes, I sat down beside him in one of the cast-off basement recliners.

He launched his first volley. "You could relieve the situation here a lot, but you're not gonna."

"I've got a kid to take care of, Dad. He's getting sick, and we have to leave in two days. I have my work too."

"Oh sure. Running up and down the road. Camping. I tell you, you're not getting another nickel or dime out of me unless you get up off your ass in the morning and help out."

The insult came at me like a broad board. It wasn't as if I hadn't seen his anger before. It was just that he'd reserved it for my brothers. "I'm not asking for any money," I said.

"Sure. Not until you need it."

So that was how he saw me? A freeloader, as he called my aunts and uncles when his father had given them "handouts." I vowed to live on my student loans and my assistantship and not give him the satisfaction of asking for anything ever again. Not ever!

"What you need to do," Dad added, "is stay here this summer and learn how to take over this farm."

"I've learned a little," I said.

"A little. Not enough."

So this was the other side of it—what it really felt like being in direct line of our sun's rays. Those rays could scorch as easily as they could warm. It was a wonder Clark hadn't torn that Future Farmers sign and stomped on it.

Jake jumped the white mare over the fence and trotted her up Dad's chair and onto his arm, but Dad didn't even look at him. All innocence, Jake had no idea what was in store for him if he ever got the full attention of his grandpa.

"What about me?" Dad said. "I need some quality time. I've been working at this for seventy years. What about me?"

He had a right to ask that, I knew. But a son or daughter with ideas and dreams is an irresistible force, and even though my father was the immovable object, I would go over, around, or through him. Whatever it took. "I wish I could help, Dad. It's just that I need to have my own life. Bruce has his own life. So did Clark. He wasn't such a failure was he?"

I watched him chew on that, his old body a container for a lifetime of stress. "Clark was a good teacher." His voice was a little softer.

"He was his own man too. No one told him what to teach, how to plan his lessons. We want to make you happy, Dad, but we can't always do that and make ourselves happy too."

Another person's pain is often invisible if you let it be, if you have a stake in not seeing it. But when I next looked at my father, tears were etching trails down his cheeks. This I couldn't ignore. "Dad?"

He didn't say anything. I placed my hand on his. He looked straight ahead and made no move to accept or acknowledge my touch. In my whole life, I'd seen only one tear fall from his eyes, at Clark's funeral. He'd reached up and wiped it off his cheek with his knuckle.

I owed it to him to understand, not by issuing any more statements of arrogant sympathy but by breathing the same air he did. When I did this, when I aligned myself with my father's heart, I felt the earth shifting below me. He was my underlayment, the source of almost everything I took for granted, always stalwart and so certain of himself, I'd never considered it possible that he might give way.

10

ONE MAY NIGHT FOUR YEARS AFTER I'D MOVED TO LARAMIE, AND SEVEN YEARS AFTER THAT FINAL DEFECTION, I GOT A CALL FROM MY MOTHER. Dad was so weak that he hadn't been able to make it to bed by himself. She'd had to call the neighbor over to help her with him. I made arrangements for a friend to watch Jake and get him to school, then rushed down there, arriving in the early morning.

The first task that greeted me was helping Dad from his easy chair to the bathroom. Mom and I had to brace him from both sides, guiding him down the hall and through the door. We backed him up to the toilet and I left them in there together. But Mom called out for me when he was through. I kept my eyes averted as I struggled to pull up his boxers.

Later I would be ashamed of my embarrassment. This had been my father dying, crouching, all his weight on my free arm and my mother's bad shoulder. His hands, which had obeyed his will in a lifetime of manual labor, were too weak to fasten the snap.

Mom called the doctor, who said he would send an ambulance. "Thank goodness for Ron," Dad said. For almost his whole life, he'd complained about the laziness or ineptitude of the men he'd hired, but he had finally found a man able to take over the daily operations. Ron and his wife, Nila, had been living on the farm by then for six years.

He turned to me. "Cook me something to eat." I scrambled an egg, nuked a cheese-filled hotdog, and lacquered a slice of toast with the good margarine, not the watery kind that Mom normally gave him. There wasn't much point in being careful about cholesterol anymore, I was prepared to say if she objected. He was lifting his first forkful to his mouth when the doorbell rang.

Three blue-smocked paramedics rolled a gurney into the room. A rude invasion, it seemed to me. He should be allowed to leave his own house on his own feet. "He can walk with a little help," I said.

The tallest attendant motioned for me to move aside. "We need some room here."

Ordinary locals, the medics wore scrubs and outdated shoes with thick Vibram soles. They pulled out blood-pressure cuffs and stethoscopes, but they had no tricks in their bags to reverse the toll age was taking on my father's heart, or that this moment was taking on my mother's and mine. We looked on, our lips set and our lungs drawing shallow, reluctant breaths of the changed air.

The tall attendant took the readings without commenting on them, then signaled the other two. They lifted my father from the recliner, laid him down, tightened straps over him. I reached out and wiped a speck of egg from his chin, squeezed his white-socked foot as they wheeled him out the door, then, with my mother, watched through the kitchen window.

As the medics bustled around him, Dad stared straight ahead toward the garage. There was the aspect of a trapped animal in his gaze, fear and reckoning blending in his brown eyes. It had always been his body that made the first impression—his hunched shoulders; arms that bent a little even when they dangled, muscle strung; and his round shape. His bald head. His determination. This last quality was so much a part of him that it seemed a physical feature. At least it animated everything physical about him. Now he was down to his eyes, puzzling it out, grizzled brows slightly knit, his gaze focusing inward. He knew he was up against something that he held no sway over.

The attendants opened the ambulance doors, emblazoned with two identical snakes and staffs, then dropped the gurney's accordion, chrome rear legs first. My father might have been a pharaoh, his attendants carrying him prone up the stairs of the Sphinx. His wind-scuffed, sun-worn face seemed geologic and I wondered how they could lift so much rock.

IN PAST CRISES, THE AMBULANCE HAD TAKEN him all the way to Denver. The heart doctor would adjust his meds and it would be, as Dad joked, like starting an old tractor engine on a cold morning with a burst of ether sprayed in the carburetor. But this time he wasn't sent to Denver. The doctor didn't seem to think that was necessary. What the doctor was really telling us, we realized later, was that there would be no point. This old workhorse had plowed his last field.

One week later, a long funeral procession snaked through Goodland, paying honor to a man who had lived righteously by the true local religion. Not Christianity but production agriculture, which bowed only to getting crops into the field and getting them out the moment the weather allowed, and to grain mounting in the elevators on the south end of town so that when your family buried you in the north end, they would not have to suffer the deprivations you once suffered. Traditionally, the religion demanded at least one son who would carry on. But the world had changed enough now that a daughter would have done.

At the cemetery, we immediate family were ushered under the awning and given chairs. It was a windy Memorial Day weekend, and around us, petals of artificial blooms fluttered at other gravesites. Everything was artificial. The Astroturf that surrounded the incision they'd made in the earth to accept my father. The embalming fluid in his veins. The manner of burial. I didn't like thinking how effective the brushed-metal casket and the vault around it would be, preventing him from decaying into the ground.

I wanted to see the casket lowered. I wanted to toss dirt on top of it and hear the minister say, "Dust unto dust." But it was now customary to lower the caskets later, said my mother. Why? I wondered. So that the family isn't traumatized? We were already traumatized. If it was closure we needed, like all the experts on "death and dying" said, then give it to us. Let us spade in the dirt and seal the wound.

III
WARD AND JULENE

Time and again I discover that I have not completely let go of the notion that salvation will come to me in the form of a man.

—SIGRID NUNEZ, *A Feather on the Breath of God*

1

FROM MY JOURNAL, A CONVERSATION JAKE AND I HAD WHEN HE WAS FIVE:

Mom, will you ever marry another dad?
Maybe someday, Jake. Would you like that?
Yes because I want a dad really bad, and the only one I have is in California.
Well I understand your wanting one, Jake, and I'll try, but they are hard to come by.
Because you have to go to a ball? Like in Cinderella?
No, Jake. That's just a fairy tale.

I was not an earnest seeker of a husband for me and a father for Jake. I couldn't spare the time from my teaching job and from raising him to look for one. And I couldn't let our happiness depend on some man I may or may not find who may or may not turn out to be compatible with both of us.

Yet from his earliest babyhood, Jake seemed eager to bond with any man of a likely father's age. When Bruce jiggled him on his knee or Clark held him, Jake stared up at his uncles with idolatrous wonder. At age one and a half, when a male friend from California visited us on the farm, Jake begged to be carried on his shoulders again and again.

Then at two, looking through my photo album, Jake saw a picture of one of my friend's daughters being playfully dangled from her father's hands. "Sage's Daddy?" Jake asked.

"Yes, Jake."

"Where's my daddy?"

I'd been steeling myself for this question but hadn't expected it to come so soon. As casually as I could, I told him that his father was in California. I didn't know exactly where.

The cruel irony of a missing parent is that the absence shapes the child at least as strongly as the participating parent does. My son's heart formed around that shadowy figure he dreamed of meeting one day. His dad was out there somewhere, carrying around Jake's identity. It was truer than the one he got from me because his father was male, like him, and his father's name corresponded to the second, more fundamental half of Jake's hyphenated last name. My son obsessed on the lack in his life, asking about Stefan often. I could only show him pictures and assure him that the man he saw branding calves and riding horses across the desert was a good man. He just had some problems that made it impossible for him to be with us.

If he couldn't have his own father, Jake must have reasoned, maybe he could pick one up somewhere. At the cooperative day care, he would try to fend off his best friend so that he, instead, could be taken home by the boy's father. When the UPS man brought a package to the door and spoke kindly to him for a moment, Jake would suggest I marry that guy.

After a long wait, I was able to get him a big brother through the Big Brother/Big Sister organization, but when we moved to Laramie, we had to go back on the waiting list, and the Iowa brother failed to stay in touch.

The open craving went on for years, with Jake falling in love with every male teacher he had and each of my male friends. A mother not only feels her child's pain, it magnifies in her. Each of his pleas for a father was a goad to find him one. And I tried—reconnecting with an old California boyfriend after moving to Laramie. The one and only reason? He was good with Jake. Anyone could have predicted where that would lead.

At twelve Jake began to realize that his yearning caused me pain. If there was one thing he couldn't stand, it was witnessing the suffering of others. "I don't need a dad, Mom," he insisted when I apologized to him for not being able to supply him with a father. "You're enough."

After another long wait, Laramie's Big Brothers/Big Sisters organization found a new brother for him, but this guy lasted less than a year.

What was so special about men anyway? I reasoned. What could they give him that I could not? I could teach him "male" chores like carpentry, plumbing, and engine repair. But Jake fought me when I showed him how to do things. I couldn't imagine my brothers resisting my father in that way. They had no choice but to conform to the work ethic. True, Dad had worked them too hard, succeeding only in robbing himself of farming sons. But there was also such a thing as working kids too little. If Jake had a real dad, as I'd had, not his ne'er-do-well father, and not the substitutes I'd tried to get for him, maybe he wouldn't be having so much trouble now in school—or so went my thoughts as alone, I wrestled with our daily challenges.

In the fall of his junior year, Jake refused to go back to the regular high school and was now enrolled in Laramie's alternative school. Even though his teachers demanded little of him, his attendance was poor. He put me in mind of Bartleby in the famous short story of that name by Herman Melville. "I prefer not to," Bartleby said whenever his boss asked him to do anything. "I prefer not to," Jake also seemed to be saying. Like Bartleby, Jake followed his own inscrutable lights.

Into this thicket of worry and regret stepped Ward, an iconic man's man who, despite his obvious self-sufficiency, emanated a willingness to belong and be belonged to. On Christmas Eve, he abided with us in the glow of my mother's fake tree. Jake and I always arrived on the twenty-fourth, while Bruce and his family showed up on the twenty-fifth, excruciatingly late, in Jake's opinion. He wanted to open presents on predawn Christmas morning, as he was convinced every kid in

America except for him got to do. Images of perfect holidays and perfect families played in both our imaginations. On most holidays, I feared that Jake would sense my despair and be infected by it. But on this Christmas I didn't have to pretend. I experienced holiday bliss, not because my family behaved according to fantasy, but because I had my own man now, and he did.

His presence beside me on the couch made Mom's house seem aligned and balanced, as it used to feel when Dad sat in his easy chair with Mom beside him in hers. Diane, a girlfriend from Laramie en route to a temporary nursing job in eastern Kansas, had stopped to spend the holiday with us. Ward suggested a board game, and I dug the old Pictionary box out of the basement closet.

"What do you think, Jake?" Ward said. "You want to partner up against these gals?"

I noted a brightening of Jake's dark eyes, a perceptible upward tilt to his lips. He settled into team-ship with Ward the way I'd seen him settle into barber chairs as a child, the mirror reflecting his pride in his temporary male milieu. My son was finally getting the attention he needed from a man, and Ward made his regard for me apparent too. I couldn't have been happier. As Diane, who knew Jake well, observed the magic unfolding, her cheeks puckered around her barely contained smile. My mother laughed louder than she had in years. All of us—Mom, Jake, and I, and even Diane—lit up like a string of lights restored by the replacement of one missing bulb.

Ward went home, and the next morning Bruce and his clan de-scended on the house, bringing with them their ongoing battles and obsessions. My brother and his family were in their own solar system, Jake and I visible within it only when the holidays drew us into their orbit. Now we had our star too. It radiated across the plains from Ward's house. The others sensed the magnetism, the weight of that star.

"Will Ward be coming to dinner?" asked my sister-in-law, Kris.

"No, he's spending Christmas with his own family."

"I suppose he has a pretty nice spread," Bruce said.

"Not really. You know, an old house, the kind that Dad would've hated. No farmland. No irrigation." I paused. "But he pastures his horses and cattle on the Smoky."

The Smoky had been one of Bruce's favorite haunts as a teenager. "Sounds pretty sweet," he said.

"Yeah, it does," Jake said.

After he'd opened what he thought was his last present, I went to the hall closet and retrieved my father's .22 rifle. I unzipped the sleeve from the gun, revealing its walnut stock. I'd promised Jake that he could have his grandfather's gun when he turned seventeen, which was in just two weeks.

"Wow, Mom. Thanks!" He received the rifle as if it were a precious artifact.

I said, "You can bring it with you when you come over to Ward's tomorrow. He promised to take you shooting."

"Now be careful," Mom said. "There are safety rules you need to learn."

"I learned 'em," Jake said. "Mom taught me. I got my first BB gun when I was eight."

"That rifle is no BB gun," Bruce said.

DIANE DROVE ME OVER TO WARD'S THAT night as planned. Jake would bring my car in the morning, and she would continue east to her nursing job. She slept in the guest room and had coffee with us in the morning. Then Ward and I walked her out to her car.

She thanked Ward and complimented him on his place.

"Well," Ward said, "it may not be much, but it's almost paid for. Five more years and I'll be a debt-free man with a dowry."

Diane winked at me as those words trickled warmly through my chest. I imagined a neighbor seeing our wedding picture in the *Handshake*, and saying to his wife, "Well I'll be damned if some gal didn't finally tackle ol' Allbright!" People would want to call me Mrs. Allbright. Would I be the first woman in the region who kept her own last name?

Ward said good-bye and headed to the barn to finish his morning chores. Diane smiled up at me from the driver's seat. "He's a keeper."

"You really think so?"

"Oh, Julene, are you kidding? It's obvious."

"I know this is schmaltzy, but it's almost as if we were made for each other."

She smiled. "Your job is to keep him thinking that way."

"Not to keep myself thinking that way? I mean, it could all go poof. What if I don't like the way he dances?"

Diane laughed and started her engine. "You're gone on him and you know it."

After she left, I put a note on the door for Jake, and Ward and I drove down to the pasture to grain the mares. Returning, I was disappointed to see no Subaru in the front yard.

"That's all right," Ward said. "We have plenty to do while we wait."

I revised the note, and, the weather being good, we saddled a couple of horses for a ride down the bluff and along the Smoky.

Ward gave me Joe, a docile buckskin. I kept trying to get him to step out, but he just plodded along. As I looked down at his short neck, he reminded me more of a mule than a horse. Riding him made me wish I'd brought Henry, one of the horses that the owners of the rock house had given me. I'd sold the mare, but I'd kept Henry, now pastured at a friend's place near Laramie. He was a tall, energetic, raw-boned gelding with long legs and a true sorrel coat. At twenty-two, he still walked faster than most horses trotted. He held his head high on his long neck, stuck his tail out, and liked to move. These were not characteristics cowboys looked for in a horse. They liked them built closer to the ground, with more quick turning ability, and they liked them less hot. "I have enough trouble wrapping a rope around a steer without pulling on leather and wrestling with my horse," Ward explained.

Back home, still no Subaru. We made sandwiches from the leftover Christmas ham Ward's mother had sent home with him. While eating, I got up every so often to look out the window over the sink.

"Don't worry, Mom," Ward said. "He just slept late. He'll make it pretty soon."

I envisioned Jake standing at the Walmart ammunition counter, the Christmas gift card my mother had given him pulsing in his wallet. What if he'd gone shooting on his own instead of waiting until Ward could take him out, as we'd agreed?

I tidied up the counter as slowly as possible so I could continue looking out the window without seeming to. Finally, I couldn't stand it any longer. I called Mom. She said he'd left more than an hour ago. It took me less than an hour to drive to Ward's. If Jake didn't show up in the next few minutes, I wouldn't be fit company. I would have to excuse myself and go sit in a corner of the barn.

Spider barked, sounding my reprieve.

"Here's our boy," Ward said.

Jake stepped from my car wearing his black motorcycle jacket over one of his dirty white T-shirts. Not what I'd hoped for. "How was the drive?" I asked.

"Oka-ay. How was yours?" he said, daring me to say more.

Ward peered through the car's back window. "What've you got there?"

"Oh man, wait till you see." Jake opened the door and took out the gun. He flipped it past our chins without obeying the barrel-down rule.

Ward accepted the gun from Jake and turned it in one hand, examining it. He pulled back and returned the bolt, nodded, put the stock to his shoulder, aimed at the weather vane on the barn, pulled the trigger. The gun clicked. Had this been his tactful way of determining that it was empty? Again with one hand and in one smooth motion, he circled the gun in an arc away from us and back to the ground. He gave the rifle to its owner. "Now that's a work of art, Jake. They don't make 'em like that anymore. Must be worth a thousand dollars."

"No kidding?" Jake said.

"Really?" I said. I'd recognized only the rifle's sentimental value. It had been the first gun I'd shot. When I was ten, Dad had set up cans along the pit silo and beamed his gold-toothed smile over every one I hit. It had also been the gun he'd used to kill the jackrabbit when I was six, before I understood what hunting was. Sent to fetch the rabbit, I'd carried it next to my chest like it was a kitten, the blood dripping down my shirt. I hadn't gone in for hunting much after that.

"Want to shoot it?" Ward asked.

"Could we?"

Ward grabbed his own rifle from the mud porch, where a shotgun also leaned openly in the corner.

I watched the tail end of the flatbed pickup containing my men disappear down the road, then went upstairs, where I could keep watch for their return from the high windows. Sitting in the big armchair that Ward and I liked to snuggle in before bed, I tried to read the book I'd brought about the Sand Creek Massacre, which had taken place only about fifty miles the other side of the Colorado border. It was much better known than the massacre that had happened at Cheyenne Hole because many more Indians had been killed—137 Arapaho and Cheyenne. "The worst blow ever struck at any tribe in the whole plains region," according to George Bent, the half-white, half-Cheyenne author, who had been wounded in the book's attack. "And this blow fell upon friendly Indians." But I couldn't concentrate. I got up, wandered through the upstairs, then the downstairs, then went outside and talked to the horses.

Back inside, I lay down on the couch. Ward and I had been up late, making love after Diane had gone to bed, and we'd gotten up early. I really did need a nap, but when I closed my eyes, the house seemed to hold its breath, waiting with me the way it must have waited with Ward's aunt for the return of her men. I thought of all the blood that had been spilled and all the wrong done winning the land for us. I thought of the rabbit's blood, which had stained my shirt when I was six. What did I want Jake to learn by owning a rifle? What was I trying to share with him exactly?

Farm boys hunted with their fathers while still in diapers. His grandfather would have taught Jake to shoot if I had raised him on the farm. The heritage was male. I had no way to hand it to him. I was just a mom who didn't share the interest and was always worrying and was therefore not to be taken seriously. Now Ward was out there, sharing in the joy of the sport and lending weight to the rules I'd tried to impart. I loved that this was happening.

But the house was lonely. I didn't much like the feel of it without Ward there. I remembered how lonely I'd been during Jake's toddlerhood, when the only invitation I received, other than for dinners in town with Mom and Dad, had been to that one Tupperware party.

If I moved here, would Ward's many connections extend to me? How about to Jake? Would he want to learn to ride and rope? He was, after all, the son of a cowboy. Would he grab at the chance as if it were his birthright?

I WAS IN THE KITCHEN LOOKING THROUGH the pitiful contents of Ward's refrigerator when they burst in. Only an hour had passed since they'd left, but it had felt like five. I could smell the outdoors on their jackets, even Jake's black leather one, which he'd painted in psychedelic swirls. The tobacco odor it normally harbored had dissipated in the crisp air.

"How'd it go?" I asked.

"Great!" Jake said.

"Great for you," Ward said with mock resentment. "You whupped my ass!"

"We slid rocks across the ice," Jake said.

"And shot them on the go?" I asked, incredulous.

"Yes! You should have been there, Mom."

One morning with Ward, and my son had a new, positive self-image to turn over in his memory for years to come—hitting the rocks adeptly with his grandfather's rifle, the bullets' impact deflecting them into the yellow grass on the bank.

That night we ate in Colby, the nearest "big" town, then went to see *The Fellowship of the Ring*, the first of the movies based on the Tolkien trilogy. What were supposed to be thrills only bored me. Ward, whose life in nature granted him immunity to special effects, said that he thought the movie had been "all Tabasco, no meat." But as we walked to the car, we pretended to be as wowed by the film as Jake had been.

"Mom, do you think we could stop at a store?" Jake asked as we pulled out of the multiplex lot. Even a Kansas town of four thousand had a multiplex. "I need to get a pack of smokes."

As much as I hated his smoking, I remembered what that addiction was like. It would be terrible going through withdrawal while trying to cope with this new situation. "Okay," I said.

Ward pulled up to the curb outside Walmart's fluorescence. "I'm sorry, Mom," Jake said. "But can you get them for me? I can't buy them here myself."

It was wrong, but what could I do? I went in and bought his brand, Marlboros. "Here you go," I said, getting back into the car. "I can't believe I'm doing this, though. Feeding your addiction."

Ward flicked my thigh. "Cut it out," he said.

My ego bounced off those words like a pinball hit by a flipper. The only man who had ever dared command me in such a way had been Jake's dad, and it hadn't gone down well then. I wanted to call Ward on it but not with Jake sitting in the backseat.

Later, lying awake in Ward's darkened bedroom, I said, "Diane says you're a keeper."

"She *does*?" he said, obviously pleased.

"Yes. And I know you are, but it was kind of shocking when you told me to cut it out tonight."

"I didn't mean to insult you, but give the kid a break. I might not have bought him the cigarettes, but I figured either buy 'em or don't."

Wouldn't it be nice, I thought, to be that certain? To always know what was right and wrong. And to make decisions with such simple clarity. This trait struck me as distinctly western, and distinctly male, part of what Jake had been missing out on all those years. And what amazed me even more—Ward seemed to be investing himself already.

He was taking a parental role. This seemed worth the trade. I would take a little high handedness from a man, especially one I was this attracted to, if it meant my son would have a father.

The next morning, while Jake was still sleeping, Ward and I left him a note and went into town to get groceries. The plan was to take him horseback riding after lunch, but when we returned, my car was gone. Apparently, he'd gone back to his grandma's. I couldn't pretend I wasn't disappointed.

"All in good time, sweetheart. Let him make his own choices."

It sounded so easy when Ward said it. A few days later I asked Jake if he liked Ward. He said, "Ward and I'll get close when you guys get married."

I wouldn't have exposed him to Ward unless I thought we were headed in that direction, but given what he'd been through, Jake's choice was wise.

2

MY TOWN WOULDN'T HAVE INTERESTED WARD IF IT HAD BEEN LINCOLN, NEBRASKA, OR LAWRENCE, KANSAS, OR ANY OTHER MIDWESTERN UNIVERSITY TOWN. But Laramie had the advantage of being a cowpuncher's paradise. He had fond memories of trips he'd taken with buddies through the area. "We were rougher and readier then, and oh brother, the good times we had at the bar!" That would have been the Buckhorn, we determined, a morbid Noah's ark of a saloon, its walls hung with the stuffed heads of every type of mammal that had ever hopped, loped, or padded through the Rocky Mountains. The mirror over the back bar at the Buck had reflected the faces of Calamity Jane and Buffalo Bill, and still sported a bullet hole left by some anonymous rowdy.

Ward practically salivated over the silver bits and spurs at the western antique store. Unwilling to let go of so much cash, he bought only an old Wyoming license plate embossed with the state's logo, a bronc-riding cowboy. But in the used-book stores, he picked up treasures on Butch Cassidy, Tom Horn, Charles Russell, and famous quarter horses.

Evenings during his visits we cooked together and marveled at our inability to sit through a meal without getting up to hug. When Jake brought his band friends over to practice in the basement, Ward descended with me into the din. Sitting on an upturned bucket, he extended his approval of Jake even to his punk-rock drumming.

On his third visit, I invited some friends over for a game of dictionary. Ward noticed that my tiny living room wouldn't seat everyone, so he brought two chairs in from the dining room. I relished seeing him play host in my home. We sat side by side in the straight-backed chairs he'd brought in. He looked relaxed, the ankle of one leg resting on the knee of the other, his soft roughout loafers undercutting the formality of his crisp blue Wranglers, pin-striped shirt, close shave, cologne, and recently clipped hair.

In the game, players attempted to dupe others into believing their made-up definitions of real but obscure words. While Ward leafed through the dictionary, searching for his word, my swimming buddy, Jonas, indicated him with his eyes and held up ten fingers.

I gave him a *really?* look.

Jonas nodded, his face alight with mimed lust. A few years ago a young man named Matthew Shepard had been savagely murdered in this town—the tragedy that had become a rallying ground for making attacks on gay men and boys hate crimes. Yet here sat Jonas, unselfconsciously gay as could be. Laramie was a university town. "Conservative and bigoted" didn't sum it up any more than "flat and farmed" summed up Kansas.

"I can't wait until this summer," Jonas said to Ward. "Julene and I will take you *swimmin'*."

Ward looked at us over his reading glasses, which he wore studiously low on his nose. "Oh no you won't. I wouldn't jump into one of those alpine ice tanks for a million bucks."

"Why not?" Jonas said. "You'll like it. Right, Julene?" His impish laugh reminded me of Tommy Smothers.

I said, "Wait until you see Lake Hattie, Ward. The water is magical." I knew he could not fail to be amazed by it. At seven thousand feet above sea level, Hattie reflected the sky, sun, and weather. Her colors shifted at the touch of wind or shadow. She was predominantly turquoise. But when clouds passed over, ultramarine patches advanced across the surface. And when I swam, always with my eyes open, the water was the color of jade underneath. In the crystalline air at that altitude, snowy peaks thirty miles distant seemed to loom directly over me. All of my senses thrilled to be surrounded by the earth's most ubiquitous elements—sky and bare green hills and clear green water.

Most people found Wyoming lakes too cold for swimming, but Jonas and I shared secret knowledge. After the initial shock, our bodies adapted to the cold, and the water exhilarated us. Everyone else stood on shore hot and miserable, their fishing poles stuck out over the water. It never occurred to them to take off their clothes and jump in.

"You'll see," Jonas said. "It's easy." In an explanatory, self-deluding tone, he told Ward how he entered the water. "First I put my toe in. Then I walk a little ways. Then I stop awhile."

"Then you sing your song," I said, unable to contain my laughter.

Jonas nodded and held his hands palm down at his waist. "When the water gets up to here, I sing my song. *Mannee, manno, mannaa.*" He'd entertained me with the song often, his voice getting higher in pitch and more frantic the farther in he waded.

"Everyone liked you so much," I said as Ward and I were getting ready for bed. He'd won the game that evening, bluffing us all with perfect imitations of dictionary language.

"And I liked them," he said. He laid his jeans on the arm of my pink wingback chair and turned back the bedcovers.

I got in beside him. "How about Jonas? Did you like him?" Ward had told me once that he didn't believe homosexuality was natural, but he wasn't going to judge anyone for it. And that's not judging? I'd thought.

"Especially Jonas. What a comedian!"

"Isn't he?" Relieved I wouldn't be fighting any political battles tonight, I wriggled closer.

"But you know," Ward said. "I feel sorry for him."

"Sorry?" I tried to keep my tone light. "Why?"

"It's clear to me that there's nothing he can do about it. He can't help how he is."

I responded carefully. "Can't help that he's gay, you mean?"

Ward nodded.

"You don't have to feel sorry for him," I said. "Jonas doesn't feel sorry for himself."

"Really?" Ward sounded surprised. "You don't think he does?"

"I'm certain he doesn't."

"That relieves me, because he's such a good person."

His receptivity to my ideas and insights amazed me sometimes. I felt as if I were a space probe that had self-launched from Kansas in the late sixties and had returned, bringing news of the universe—to a receptive audience for a change.

Ward was proving far more adaptable than I'd imagined possible. But this didn't diminish my surprise when, over the phone, he began talking about moving to Laramie. "It's the only practical solution," he said. He didn't see his ranch as an option for us. "Who would you talk to here in Plum Springs? All you'd have would be me and your computer."

He actually preferred my friends to his own in some ways. "In Laramie, people talk about ideas. At home, they talk about things. It's always bored me. I just never realized I had any options." Now he saw his way into another life. Wyoming would be good for both his horse-breeding and livestock-supply businesses. Instead of a spare mix of farmers and ranchers, hundreds of cowboys would be potential buyers of not only the bloodlines he was developing but also the roping horses he trained. So yes. He would move to Laramie because "I can and it is what you deserve."

I feared that taking Ward out of Kansas would be like trying to transplant the huge cottonwood tree we'd met beside. The roots were too formidable. All sorts of heavy equipment would be required, and when you were done, all you'd have would be a dead tree.

I wasn't even sure I would want a transplanted Ward. I didn't voice this reservation because the thought of leaving my beautiful house, the mountains, and my wilderness-loving friends frightened me. At the same time, I secretly considered the possibility. Ever since I'd met Ward, an irresistible compulsion had been rising in me. It contained the same mixture of fear and desire I felt when standing at the edge of Hattie each June, about to take my first swim of the summer.

I applied reason, although reason had nothing to do with it. In Kansas, Ward was well connected with every horse fanatic in a hundred-mile radius. His friendships would give me access to people I hadn't had as a single mother. There would be neighborhood gatherings, like the card parties my parents used to attend when we lived on the farm. Jake would have horses to ride and guns to shoot. He would have instruction from a man who was at one with his land, not some uprooted caricature of himself.

Just as Ward liked some things about Laramie better than home, there were some things about Kansas that I liked better. I would soak up the quiet especially. I loved the air. Western Kansas air had a lofty aridity to it. Sun and air and silence mingled on the plains so that the qualities were inseparable. They blended with that particular ethereal-blue sky that the land yearned toward whether it had been farmed or not. Throw in the native grass on Ward's place, and I would be home.

All I had to do was sing my song and accept the immersion gradually. Pretty soon Kansas would be my element again. And I would be loving it. *Mannee, manno, mannaa.*

3

WHEN THE FIRST WARM WEATHER ROLLED AROUND—UNUSUALLY EARLY FOR KANSAS, IN MARCH—WARD AND I SET OUT TO FIND THE JOSEPH COLLIER HOMESTEAD ON THE MIDDLE BEAVER. Collier had been Sherman County's first permanent resident. I wanted to find the exact spot, to see if there was any water left where he'd lived.

With one finger on his pickup's steering wheel and one arm on the sill of his open window, Ward drove us into the valley on a winding road, a welcome diversion from the straight section-line roads on the flat divide we'd crossed after leaving his place. He was wearing his King Ropes cap and his chocolate-brown Carhartt jacket, which set off his blond mustache and hair. On the tape deck, Lucinda Williams was singing about her own knee-buckling addiction to a man. We were both enjoying the liberating breezes of spring after a winter of long drives on snowy highways, then excruciating weeks between our visits, when the season's cold exacerbated our longing.

I inhaled the sweet smells as we passed groves of budding cottonwoods and sprinkler-irrigated hay meadows. That's one thing that would make living here nicer than living in Laramie, I thought. I wanted to wake up each spring morning to the promise in the soil. Laramie winters were too friggin' long.

As we rounded the turns, white-tail deer sprang across the meadows and disappeared into stands of mature cottonwoods. Wild turkeys trotted through tall grass. Pheasants scurried into ditches. In Collier's time, the valley must have been even richer in animal life, although there would have been one notable absence.

Collier had started coming into the area as a bone picker, one of the men who roved the prairies collecting buffalo bones. In the 1870s, the plains had been littered with those bones because the hide men, or hunters, who'd wiped out the buffalo herds had a ready market only for the hides. Vultures, wolves, coyotes, cougars, and in some cases, even grizzly bears had cleaned the bones of flesh, leaving them easy pickings for the final scavengers.

Collier alone claimed to have gathered a thousand tons of bones. I envisioned him crisscrossing the unfenced prairie from pile to pile on still mornings, his horses' harnesses creaking, the bones in his wagon clacking. Using the same trail that had served as the Indians' Ladder of Rivers, he hauled the bones to a railhead near Fort Wallace, on the Smoky. From there they were shipped east and made into all sorts of things—knife handles and combs but mainly bone black, a form of charcoal used in refining sugar. Some bones were ground up, shipped back west, and dusted onto the monarchs' own Elysian fields, as fertilizer.

My map led us onto the headquarters of a showy ranch with a big barn and several Quonsets. I didn't recognize the locally famous ranch until Ward stopped in front of a two-story limestone house with a red tile roof. I'd heard about the beautiful house from my mother, who had once attended a ladies' club meeting there.

We found the owner in the side yard, spray-painting an iron bed frame gold. "You got a little on your boot," said Ward.

The man looked up. "Well, look what the cat drug in." Ward knew all the ranchers, the dwindling number who had not succumbed to farming. This one was compensating for low beef prices by stocking his pastures with game and selling hunting rights. He'd turned the house into a bed and breakfast for the hunters. The bed frame, he explained, was destined for one of the guest rooms.

Ward stood with his arms folded and his mustachioed lip curling in a wry smile.

"Sometimes hunters bring their wives," the man explained. He wasn't sure, but he thought that his great-grandfather, who'd bought the place from Collier in the early 1900s, had torn down the homesteader's soddie when he built the barn.

When I asked, he recalled that the ponds along his family's stretch of the Beaver had been large enough to swim and fish in when he was a kid. They used to irrigate alfalfa out of the creek too but hadn't been able to do that for a long time.

"Why not?" I asked.

"Oh, I don't know," he said. "Groundwater pumping and what all. The big spring under the bridge still runs." He pointed down the road.

As we approached the body of dark water, a pair of mallards churned over the surface and waddled into the shoreline brush, where hundreds of red-winged blackbirds trilled from their perches on the powdery heads of last year's cattails. I leaned on the bridge's railing and stared down at the shiny water, stained dark by cottonwood and hackberry leaves. I'd read a beautiful definition of a spring: "a place where, without the agency of man, water flows from a rock or soil." Such appearances were a kind of grace, like the buffalo that the Indians once believed flowed perpetually from a cave hidden on the prairie. It was only human, I supposed, to think that these fonts could never dry up.

Funny, though, how all could seem right with the world as long as I stood in a beautiful place. It helped to be under love's spell. "Hello, *Homaiyohe*," I said.

"The Mighty Beaver," Ward said.

It had thrilled me to run across Cheyenne words for the creeks and rivers. The Smoky Hill River that still trickled in the valley below Ward's house was *Manoiyohe*, Bunch of Trees River. My childhood creek was *Homaiyohekis*, Cheyenne for Little Beaver. The beavers would have dammed the water that trickled from the springs, creating marshes for wildlife and allowing the water enough time to trickle down through the sands, recharging the aquifer. But the animals had disappeared long ago, trapped by fur traders in the first half of the 1800s.

Many beavers had returned, Ward now explained, but ranchers used to dynamite the dens, freeing the water for their hay meadows.

"Did you ever do that?" I asked, hoping the answer was no.

"Never did on my place. But I helped my uncle do it when I was a kid."

"Did that bother you?"

"I tried not to let it. If you want to make a living, you have to pull in your feelers sometimes, sweetheart." He squeezed my hand.

I squeezed back. I was in no position to criticize.

Blue dragonflies flitted about, their wings blurring the air. One of them landed on my forearm.

"A good omen," I said.

"Do you think?" Ward smiled indulgently, letting show his western condescension toward anything that smacked of the New Age.

But this was Old Age stuff. The Cheyenne believed that dragonflies were messengers from deep water. They called them little whirlwinds because their swarms took that shape, warning Indians of enemies and indicating which direction to travel. This insect was a lustrous mechanism, with bulbous aquamarine eyes and what looked like precious blue-green stones on its back where the wings attached. The wings were delicately veined and so clear I could see the hairs on my arm through them. One wing had a notch torn from the lower edge.

Ward raised his camera and shot the picture that he would later hang on the wall over his kitchen phone—my hair white fluff in the sunlight, and the dragonfly a strike of blueness on my glare-whitened arm.

In 1857, a military expedition had discovered the remains of a recent sun dance on the Middle Beaver, probably at this very spot. Historians believed that almost every member of the tribe had been present. "More than four thousand people," I said now. "Can you imagine?"

"There must have been a lot more water than this," Ward said. "Must have run all the way up and down the valley. Hold that pose." Grasping his camera, he left the bridge and threaded his way into the cattails.

I waited, transfixed by the warmth of the day and the clarity of the dark water in Collier's spring.

Not long after Joseph Collier built his house, wrote his granddaughter in a Sherman County family history volume, another man and his family settled in the valley. One day soldiers appeared on the road, escorting some Indians. When the Indians turned their ponies out in Collier's hayfield, the two neighbor men rode out and told them to graze their horses elsewhere. This so angered the band's chief that he grabbed the reins of Joseph's horse and jerked them. Joseph was almost thrown. *The two made a hasty retreat to the Collier home*, wrote the granddaughter. *They decided the ponies would not damage the hay land so much as they had first decided.*

The anecdote had struck me as a remarkable admission of less-than-heroic behavior in a pioneer ancestor. I sensed that the grand-daughter was on the chief's side. Was there some awareness seeping out between the lines that the meadow belonged more rightfully to him?

That chief might have been one of the many who'd defended the land from invaders, returned to it now as a prisoner. He might have been among those who'd sun danced here in 1857. If so, he'd won his rights to this rich valley with his own suffering. Braves doing the sun dance bled into the dirt, went thirsty for days, ate nothing. The medicine man would have pierced the chief's chest, strung a rawhide rope through the wounds, and tied it to a cottonwood tree that the tribe had chopped down and erected at the center of the circle with exacting ceremony. The custom was to pull back on the rope until it tore through the flesh.

Although the Cheyenne had come onto the plains from the forests around the Great Lakes, they had known what to worship here. As the writer N. Scott Momaday put it, on the plains "the sun has the certain character of a god." His Kiowa people had also adapted quickly. "After untold centuries bent and blind in the wilderness of the northern Rockies, they soon reckoned their stature by the distance they could see." We had no idea what it was like to meld with indwelling spirits, I thought. Because we were unwilling to bleed for the land, as it did for us, we were still foreigners here.

"Don't look at the camera," Ward called from his stand in the rushes.

"It doesn't help, telling me not to," I called back.

I'd wanted to visit this place to see what had made life possible here for my own people. Were it not for this and other rare surface water, there would have been no homesteaders. Settlers who didn't live near water were said to have filled barrels at places like this one and rolled them home. But as usual, it was the Indian history that excited my imagination. When I'd read that the sacred sun dance had been performed on the Middle Beaver, I'd looked up from the book and stared. Triangles in my office's southwestern-print wallpaper had floated in my vision as the marvel set in. The knowledge that the plain old dry creek my family crossed every time we went to town had hosted such a spectacle no more than twenty miles east of that crossing gave me a glimpse of the land as once wild. I would never attain the Indians' ferocious connection to the place. You did have to bleed for that, but thanks to the image the words conjured, when I thought of the past on our land, I now saw colors. Instead of gray images of windblown homesteaders, I saw dancing, heard drums and songs that praised and gave thanks for the grass and sky. I saw wild animals. I saw live water.

THROUGHOUT THE SPRING, WHENEVER I WAS ABLE to visit, Ward and I continued making rounds to all the old watering places. On an unseasonably hot Saturday in early April, we went searching for the headwaters of the Smoky Hill River and the campground of the Dog Soldiers. We stopped at Sherman State Fishing Lake, where my brother Bruce used to play hooky from farm work. I remembered his triumphant returns home, the silver tabs on his stringer flashing as he pulled sun perch, catfish, and blue gill from his bucket. Now only heat waves swam in the dry lake bed.

As we continued south through the Smoky Valley, a glimpse of blue in the distance led us to traipse across a pasture in the record heat, visions of a cool swim egging me on and giving Ward a window on my fanaticism. As we arrived at the pond, which turned out to be unappealingly muddy, the banks erupted in dark, bubblelike objects. These scuttled, like a battalion of remote-controlled robots, into the water. Turtles! We perched on a chunk of limestone and watched for them to reappear. Only once did we spot what looked like a wood chip floating on the water—the knot of a turtle's snout, taking in air.

We began hearing tiny splashing sounds. *Plip. Plip-plip.* Out of the corner of one eye, I noticed something streak through the air. Tiny frogs were leaping into the pond. The frogs stampeded like grasshoppers in dry weeds as we walked the shoreline. Finally, we spotted a shell protruding from one of the deep hoof prints cows had made in the mud.

The turtle was doing his best to be invisible, but I lifted him out and peered at his retracted beak. He kept his eyes closed in what must have been abject terror and held every protuberance in as tightly as he could, but his withdrawal had limits. I tested the claws on his yellow-speckled toes, and Ward lifted and let spring back the little pointed tail he kept curled against himself. His shell, which was darkest river green, camouflaged him. I turned him over. The smooth shields over his stomach were outlined in fire orange, dramatically brilliant in his habitat of mud and dark water. Within the outlines, brown, odd-shaped splotches evoked a series of symmetrically positioned lakes, no two shaped alike. I fancied they constituted a prehistoric map of the region when it had been wetter.

Back in the car we consulted my map and discovered that one of the Smoky's tributaries was actually called Turtle. The possibility that this was the same creek enchanted me. But we decided the pond was on Lake Creek. On one of my forays in the Goodland library, I'd run across an old newspaper story about a cowhand who'd drowned in Lake Creek in 1905. It was hard to imagine the pond ever being large enough or enticing enough to swim in. Then had come, as the owner of the ranch we'd visited on the Middle Beaver had put it, "groundwater pumping and what all." In a few more years the pond might be gone entirely. Where would the turtles go then?

WHENEVER I PULLED INTO WARD'S YARD AT night, after driving those three hundred miles from Laramie, I would glance up at his curtainless kitchen window. There waited my love, freshly shaved and showered, his arms crossed as he leaned against the counter, smiling. That he could exist so independently, that his life went on when I was away, fascinated and tantalized me. I was seeing a male version of myself in a happy context of yellow incandescence and the knowledge that family and friends populated the darkness beyond. He claimed that he needed a change, that he wanted to get off his duff, that moving to Laramie would allow him to make more of himself, but I doubted he really believed that. For him, the pond wasn't shrinking. It had stayed the same.

4

PLANNED DEPLETION." That's what the state's Ogallala Aquifer policy amounted to. I'd heard water bureaucrats cite the concept in talks, with no apparent shame. As if there were a plan, all very orderly and nothing to be concerned about. As if using up the life-giving waters of an aquifer underlying parts of eight large states could be considered sane. On the Internet, I discovered a list of observation wells, a sampling from irrigated farms that hydrologists measured annually. I plugged the township and range number of our farm into the search box and felt both excited and apprehensive when I got dozens of hits. I wasn't sure I wanted to see, in black and white, the damage that was being done to the aquifer so near to us. Going down the list, I happened onto a legal description, 07S-41W-07, that looked uncomfortably familiar.

I'd recorded those numbers and letters many times when I'd been a zealous future farmer, on maps I'd made of our farm in order to keep records of crop rotations, field operations, and chemical applications. These legals also appeared each year on the water reports I filed. Our best irrigation well was located on Section 7, Range 41 West, Township 7. We pumped it at one thousand gallons per minute, twenty-four hours per day every July and August, to water our corn and soybeans.

The damage was not conveyed so much in black print as in a solid blue line that lurched downward across a graph. The depth to water had been 180 feet when the well was dug, in 1949, the year I was born. This made it seem as if my life and that particular water were directly linked, although the place had belonged to my uncle Wilbur and aunt

Vernita then. It was their farm my parents had traded the Carlson place for in the sixties. Then Dad had the well rebored for irrigation. The depth to water was now 210 feet. Bedrock, or the bottom of the well, lay at 300 feet. In less than four decades, we'd pumped a quarter of the water from beneath that ground.

I knew I would never single-handedly put an end to irrigation, as Bruce liked to joke, but I could at least try to do my part. To write more informed articles, I would need to interview the director of our water district. He was nationally known for his zero depletion plan, the most ambitious effort ever proposed to conserve the Ogallala. I'd first read about the plan in the early nineties, in *National Geographic*, but could find no references to it in current policy news. I wanted to know what had happened to zero depletion and what, if anything, had taken its place.

Despite my experiences elsewhere, I still had a rural Kansan's unease when it came to confronting power. My father never "stuck his nose in where it didn't belong" or acted "like a big shot." He let men like our water district director run things while he kept his head down and his nose clean. But after seeing our well on the Web, I couldn't put off calling the director any longer. Because Big Daddy hadn't stepped in and stopped irrigation as my father had thought he would. And this man represented Big Daddy.

And now I didn't have my daddy to blame anymore. He'd died, leaving Bruce, Mom, and me holding the deeds and owning the invasive practices that made the land pay.

I SPENT THE NIGHT BEFORE THE INTERVIEW at Ward's house. Whenever my eyes closed for one of his deep kisses, the graph etched itself onto the darkness above the bed.

"You thinking about Jake?" Ward asked.

"No. For once." Although many memories of that well did include Jake. During the summers I worked for my father, I would stop to check the oil in the engine on my way to change the sets. Hearing its roar,

Jake would writhe and kick in his car seat and his face would redden with fear. When I reached into the heat and noise and pressed the chrome button turning the engine off, relief would settle over us both. In the renewed quiet, we would hear birds singing in the old farmstead's trees.

The candle that Ward's sister-in-law had given me for Christmas flickered as, outside, a dry spring wind churned in the budding cotton-woods, causing them to scrape the shingles. I told Ward about the graph. "It looked like a stock-market chart from 1929."

"That bad?" Ward said. "You'd think they'd need permission to publish stats from a private well."

Of course he would think that, but this wasn't the moment to begin a property-rights debate. What I'd seen on the Web had sickened me and I wanted his sympathy. I said, "Our well went down fifteen feet just since 1980, and some nearby wells went down thirty."

He said, "It isn't right, is it?"

"Thank you for seeing that."

"Everybody who's irrigating is probably showing big declines."

"Apparently not. When I called the director to set up the interview, he said it would be a mistake to conclude that things were bad every-where just based on a few wells. His numbers in the newsletter show only seven feet of average decline since 1980." I had then called a Kansas Geological Survey scientist, who said the district probably got its modest estimate by averaging in wells from low-lying, alluvial areas. To show Ward what the scientist meant, I held up my hand and wiggled my fingers, to indicate the streams.

Ward took hold of my thumb. "This'd be the Smoky."

"Right."

"And this would be the Sappa."

"Yep."

He skipped my forefinger, which would have been the Middle Bea-ver, and grabbed my ring finger. "And this would be your creek, the Little Beaver." He slid his grasp to the base of my finger and squeezed. That sensation would tantalize me for weeks to come. Had he been imagining placing a ring there? I fantasized the ceremony we would have, in the little white church in Plum Springs. I saw myself in a simple, loose-fitting satin dress the color of Wyoming lake water. His buddies would marvel that a woman had finally managed to land him, while my Laramie friends would congregate in the old hotel. It would be the greatest clash of cultures to hit Plum Springs since the Cheyenne ambushed pioneers on the Smoky Hill Trail. Maybe Jonas would catch the bouquet.

Ward let go of my finger and I dropped my hand onto my stomach. I said, "The soil in the eastern creek valleys is sandy, so rain filters down to the aquifer faster. But that recharge will never flow uphill and west into the rest of the aquifer. I'm really not looking forward to confronting the director about this."

"Don't worry," Ward said. "He probably deals with those types of questions all the time. You'll be no more trouble to him than a gnat on a bull's back."

I contemplated that for a minute. "I kind of hope you're right, and I kind of hope you're not."

There'd been a picture of our well on the Web too, with the pump in the distance and the edge of Wilbur's Quonset and just the tail end of an old pickup that belonged to my father's sister Bernice, the only one of my parents' siblings who still owned her land. She lived in Colorado and stored her equipment with us.

The place looked barren in the winter photo, the weeds around the big engine brown. But in my girlhood, Wilbur's wife, Vernita, had kept a lush yard full of vegetables and flowers. Following the calendar in *The Farmer's Almanac*, she'd planted by the moon, a practice that my scientifically minded father pooh-poohed, but he admitted he couldn't argue with the plumpness of her tomatoes and strawberries.

Vernita wore pretty print dresses, and her skin gave off the scent of bottled flowers, while Wilbur was one of those farmers for whom overalls had been invented. A big round belly, hangdog features, a rustic sense of humor. The exact opposite of his brother, my father, he'd put jokes before farming, right after playing the guitar.

A decade or so after my family acquired Wilbur and Vernita's farm, the house became the sleeping quarters for Mexicans Dad hired to hoe weeds from the sugar beets he was growing then. They had a mishap with the gas heater, and the house burned down. No one was hurt, but after the fire, only the Quonset and a small grove of fruit trees gave testament to my aunt and uncle's past there.

"Vernita was Wilbur's second wife," I told Ward. "Dad said that his first wife had a violent temper. When I drove tractors in that field, I'd see pieces of china scattered here and there and imagine Wilbur dodging plates."

"That'd be me," Ward said, "if I'd married that first girl I was engaged to. Dodging plates."

First girl? I took this as proof. He *had* been imagining slipping a ring on my finger. We lay silently for a minute. "Ward?" I said.

"Yeah."

"It was shocking seeing our well on the Web. But they have every right to measure that water and publish the findings. You can't really own water, or land, for that matter." I knew this would sound radical to Ward, and maybe that's why I'd said it. Let's have it out.

"I'll give you this, sweetheart. You always have a unique take on things."

I suspected this was not going to be as easy as convincing him that Jonas could be both happy and queer.

"You know what I think," Ward said. "This country was founded on the right to own property."

"Okay, but we don't have the right to destroy it."

"No, now. We have the right to do whatever we please. That's what owning means."

Ward had rearranged his pillow, and we were sitting up in bed. *No, now?* What made him think he could take that tone with me? "Some of the water we're draining today is recharge from ten thousand years ago, Ward. The notion that it could belong to us is pure hubris." For some reason I forgot to mention that having deeds to our land didn't mean we also owned the water. We had rights to it, but the state could reduce or rescind them.

"Hubris?" Ward said. "Now there's a writer's word."

"I mean arrogant disregard for things greater than us."

Ward play-kicked me on the side of my leg. "I know what the word means. I agree the water shouldn't be wasted. But the government can't just tell property owners what to do either. That would be communism."

"Oh right! That's what I am. A communist."

"I'm not calling you a communist, only pointing out that private property is the cornerstone of democracy. Don't think I haven't thought about this issue a lot."

"And I haven't? Who says you need capitalism to have democracy? They're apples and oranges. One's an economic system. The other is political."

"So you are a communist."

It was as if he'd struck an artesian well. I squirmed down in the bed, pulled the sheet over my head, and to distract him from the emotions I was really having, groaned and pounded my feet. Meanwhile I wiped my eyes with the sheet.

Ward laughed and squeezed my shoulder. "You know I was just joking, right?"

I didn't respond, couldn't yet. He tapped my head. "Hello?" Slowly, with one finger, he pulled the sheet off my face. He kissed my ear, my nose, my chin—a little striptease of conciliation, the bristles of his mustache tickling my neck now. "I want you."

I was defenseless whenever he said that, his voice a low rumble, like thunder. I ran my finger along the inside of his bicep, silken from armpit to elbow.

AFTER MAKING LOVE, WE WERE CONJOINED IN spirit, the tension gone, we settled into our favorite sleeping posture, cupped together, my back to his front. We'd turned the blanket down to the foot of the bed. That's how unseasonably warm it was.

Something skidded across the concrete stoop outside and banged into the fence. A horse whinnied in the corrals. I hoped the wind wouldn't break the stalks of the orphan irises in the front yard. These vestiges of his aunt's garden were almost due to bloom, a month early. Afterward, I planned to dig them up for him, then divide and replant them as my mother had done. I shouldn't bother with his poor excuse of a yard, he'd said. It was all right, I told him. I wanted to. Although I knew such actions conveyed conflicting intentions. It was beginning to seem likely that he would, indeed, move to Laramie. He'd asked me to check into land prices near town. He would need a place to pasture his horses.

"The wind blew and the shit flew and I couldn't see for a day or two," Ward recited.

I chuckled. "Uncle Wilbur used to say that!"

"Maybe the wind'll bring some rain."

I could hear a deeper harmonic in the wind. An irrigation well was running nearby. I wasn't surprised. In this drought, there wasn't enough subsurface moisture to plant corn without prewatering. Our farm manager, Ron, had told me that we might break the three hundred million gallon mark on our farm this summer.

Would I be able to hold my own the next day? I didn't have a very good track record talking to bureaucrats, not when they slung their wonky policy lingo and all their acronyms around.

Ward's voice rumbled again. "I know how strange it must have been, seeing Wilbur's place on the Web."

It was brave and good of him to return to the topic despite the dangers it now posited, and I liked the familiar way he'd said my uncle's name. "The worst thing was the graph. The line would jut up once in a while but never as high as at the beginning. You know, big down, little up, big down."

"Like those monitors they have in ICUs," Ward said.

"Yes. When the patient is dying."

5

THE WATER DISTRICT DIRECTOR TURNED OUT TO BE A TALL, LEAN, SLIGHTLY BALDING MAN IN HIS EARLY FIFTIES. He seated me across from him in one of the beige offices of the district headquarters. Nothing fancy here, just desks and files in a tin building shared with the Colby Bowl Fun Center and the Carousel Beauty Shop.

The first thing I did was almost knock over the Styrofoam cup of coffee his secretary brought me. He handed me a tissue, and I wiped off his desk and my miniature tape recorder. I am so inept at this, I thought. I turned on the recorder and asked my first question, about his background.

"I'm an outsider," he said. "A lot of people up here think I'm a little bit crazy, but that's neither here nor there. We'll keep personalities out of this and stay with the facts, and I think that'll be the safest thing for everybody."

Okay then. All he would tell me was that he was from Oklahoma and his degree was in geology. Scientific objectivity was seldom as pure as its proponents claimed. I'd hoped to learn a little about his influences. But who was I to complain? Armed with a tape recorder, an amenable expression, and an inquiring tone, I, too, was hiding behind an objective guise.

Figuring out "what the water table's doing" was the primary challenge, said the director. "That's the sixty-four-thousand-dollar question." The most difficult problem was "data variability." He handed me a graph that showed virtually no drop overall since 1980.

I began to point out that his newsletter had said the aquifer went down seven feet on average during that period, but he cut me off. "Now I don't know which database I used to get these numbers. Like I said, every time I look at this, I make another assumption."

The water level in the observation well on our land had fallen fifteen feet since 1980. I knew that we didn't irrigate at rates higher than other farmers. In fact, Ron was careful to turn the sprinklers off after rainstorms and was critical of those who didn't. He used water only when he needed to. Was this "data variability" a handy quagmire in which to lose critics of the district's minimal regulatory measures? If no one could figure out how much the water table had actually declined, then sensible controls couldn't be imposed. I wondered how the director could be the same man who'd come up with the idea of zero depletion. Had his idealism declined, as the wells had over time, depleted by the pragmatic necessity of keeping his job?

Whatever his intentions, it wasn't going to be easy for him to dampen my alarm. All I had to do was close my eyes to see the personally incriminating evidence—that plummeting line on the graph of our well. What if it were a bank account? Anyone would be upset to see their financial resources dwindling so fast. In fact, there was a direct link between irrigation and finances, for both the farmers and the local economy. But we weren't only talking about money; we were talking about life for virtually all time to come. This water had grown Aunt Vernita's garden and fruit trees. It had hydrated her, Wilbur, and their children, my cousins. If we kept pumping at current rates, they were likely to be the last humans the water would ever sustain on that particular land. Because the springs would disappear, no wildlife would survive either. Assuming a water table two hundred feet thick, which it was in many places, and less than half an inch of annual recharge, it would take at least five thousand years for the aquifer to replenish itself once it was drained in an area.

Remembering the Kansas Geological Survey scientist I'd talked to, I asked the director if he'd included any alluvial wells in his averages. Wouldn't those wells in the sandy creek valleys have risen a lot during the nineties, an exceptionally wet decade? Wouldn't they skew the averages upward? He dismissed their significance, saying that only fifteen out of three hundred wells were in alluvial areas.

Did his board have the ability to reduce farmers' water rights? I asked. It did, he said.

"What would the politics of that be?"

"Oh boy," he said, as if such action were so extreme as to be unimaginable.

"I mean, you've got a board that is mainly irrigators." A tactful misstatement. They were all irrigators. "I like the idea of local control, but you have to wonder—"

"Well, you do wonder," he conceded, "and we've been accused of being the fox guarding the henhouse, or drunks guarding the liquor store."

I laughed at the colorful imagery, eager for him to admit that the bureaucracy was rigged.

"Well," he said again. "I don't know how to answer that. If you were on this board, what kinds of decisions would you be willing to make?"

I couldn't run for the board because I didn't live in the district, but the question was still a legitimate one for a part owner of the Bair Farm, one who benefited yearly from its profits. I tried to imagine myself standing up to other rights holders and suggesting cuts. Curtailing water rights would curtail yields, reducing the size of every check farmers deposited in their bank accounts. Still, it was what I believed should happen, and the question troubled me more than I wished to let on.

Before I could compose an answer, the director said, "We basically shut down new development. We're the toughest district on tail-water control, bar none. We have promoted water-use efficiency more than any area in Kansas so far."

Was this his own defensiveness showing? When I asked him what had happened to his zero depletion plan, I began to understand that regardless of what he'd said about avoiding the personal in our discussion, his emotional investment in the plan had been huge. His official duty was to serve his board of directors. They were the ones who made the real decisions, he insisted. Yet his degree was in an earth science. Ideally, scientists sought and served only Truth.

He said, "The eligible voters of the district didn't like it as well as the board did, and the board didn't like it a lot." He still liked the idea. Zero depletion, he explained, had been "sustainable yield," that sweet spot where any water irrigators took out would be replaced by rain and snowmelt. The beauty of his plan was that it could have been "as aggressive or passive as you wanted." You could set it to go into effect over any number of years, ranging from ten to sixty.

But when I asked my burning question—how much irrigation would have to be cut back to achieve zero depletion—the timeline got longer. "Well, it happens over ninety years, well over eighty years of time." I could see why he would want to set the doomsday moment as far into the future as possible. Saying any of this to his board would have been like walking into last night's windstorm, with all the dust it carried blowing straight into his face. It amazed me that there had been a time when he was not only idealistic enough to suggest such a plan but naïve enough to believe that irrigation farmers would have gone along with it. It hurt my heart and made me miss my own idealistic youth, when I also believed that people could be persuaded to do what was right regardless of their own self-interest. What happened to those times? I wanted to believe that way again.

He said that to compute the curtailment necessary, he would first have to estimate annual recharge. I told him I understood this.

"Well," he said, "I, we, figured the long-term recharge is 150,000 acre feet a year comin' into the system."

I nodded slowly. An acre foot was 325,851 gallons, enough to bury an acre one foot deep. A football field was about an acre. Imagine glass walls around it. I later computed that to hold 150,000 acre feet of water, the walls would have to be twenty-eight miles high. The total current water rights in the district were 866,000 acre feet per year. Imagine that aquarium rising 164 miles into the sky. The director had just told me that to stabilize the Ogallala in our district, water rights would have to be cut by over 80 percent. The answer sickened me because I knew what that goal would mean to farmers.

As bad as that would be, and as impossible as it would be without citizens putting their collective foot down, I knew that even that large a cut would not be enough to save the springs. I mentioned that the Kansas Geological Survey scientist I'd talked to had said that the springs needed the natural recharge that came from precipitation. Meaning that if irrigators were allowed to use even that limited amount, the springs would still dry up eventually. How could I communicate the value of those springs, when the director was likely to dismiss my arguments as anecdotal or mere sensory data? Unscientific and subjective perceptions of sunlight on water. The diaphanous wings of dragonflies. The vibrant-orange plastron shields of turtles.

"If your end goal is no impact on stream flows," the director responded, "we'd have no water. I mean none! But if you want more than eighteen people in northwest Kansas . . ." He left it to me to conclude the obvious.

Later I would wish I'd thought to mention the four thousand Indians who, along with thousands of horses, had drunk from Big Spring during the 1857 sun dance. And what about the many native populations that had preceded the Cheyenne? How had the springs managed to sustain them and millions of bison?

Yet despite my inability to speak my heart, some invisible shift had taken place between the director and me. I'd underestimated the power of face-to-face discussion. I might have been the first person who'd ever sat across from him and asked him such earnest questions from an ecological perspective.

He now admitted that the current drought was taking a toll. "These last two years are a wake-up call. We're going back to those heavy declines again. In fact," he added, "our water table's still dropping three or four inches a year."

That didn't jibe with the optimistic graph he'd given me at the beginning of the interview. If in such a brief exchange, I could cause this well-positioned bureaucrat to increase his estimate of the water's annual decline, perhaps I had more power than I thought.

WITH HIS BREAD, WARD WIPED UP THE remains of balsamic vinegar and sesame oil I'd marinated and cooked the chicken breasts in. "Larrupin' good," he said.

"Larrupin'?"

"Cowboy talk for 'I hain't never had nothin' gooder than this,' sweetheart."

Normally his self-mockery made me laugh, but tonight I mustered only a wan smile. My failure to answer the director's question about what I would do if I served on his board still bothered me. Was it time to go public? Did I need to become an activist, a role that suited me about as well as sunshine suited a mole? Standing before an audience and announcing that we were pouring the planet's precious water down the drain of oblivion would assuage my conscience a little. But as long as my family was part of the problem, what legs would I have to stand on?

I got up and scraped my uneaten baked potato into the trash barrel, then returned to the table to gather my silverware.

"Don't bother," Ward said. "We can do dishes in the morning."

There was a spot on the oilcloth that wouldn't come up, no matter how hard I scrubbed.

"Julene," Ward said.

I sat down and tried to look at him.

"What's eating you?"

"I don't want to sell the farm, but I don't want to be a party to this anymore either. Ron isn't getting any younger or healthier. We're going to have to make a decision soon."

"Selling would be the worst thing you could do. Your dad would haunt you all the way to your grave."

"And beyond, if there is a beyond. I don't know how I could live with myself. But I can't live with this either."

I fought the urge to get up from the table. I wasn't one to leave dishes, but I would have preferred leaving this conversation. Tracing the squares in the yellow-plaid tablecloth, I said, "I just wish he'd never gotten started irrigating. I wish he'd stuck with wheat. And sheep, or cattle, like he was raising near the end. There wouldn't be nearly as much money to spread around, but I don't think I'd be contemplating selling now either. Isn't that ironic?"

Ward dropped his big hand over mine and bunched our fingers together in one fist. "I could help if you wanted."

I looked at him. "You mean help turn it back to wheat?"

"I could grow wheat in my sleep. Practically did when I was a kid, working for my dad and uncle. But whatever you want. I'm willing to do anything you guys need."

Anything you guys need. Those were sweet words, kind and well meant. I suspected, however, that they were not well considered. Ward's smile had a beatific quality to it that would surely wear off once he realized the mistake he was making.

But I said nothing. I wasn't thinking of what might or might not be good for Ward. I was thinking of my big reunification plan between Julene's divided selves.

6

STOPPING AT MOM'S ON MY WAY HOME AFTER THAT VISIT, I DISCOVERED Bruce's road hog taking up three quarters of the driveway. I needed to try my new idea on him, but I hadn't expected to see him that very day.

He was in the dining room, turning the pages on the check register and taking pictures of each. Mom had been paying the farm's bills and keeping the books ever since she and Dad got married. She wasn't going to relinquish the task now, although Bruce had told me it would make his job a lot easier if vendors just sent him the bills and he paid and recorded them electronically.

"But how can I complain?" he asked. The books were Mom's one thing. Habituated by a lifetime deferring to Dad, she now left all the important decisions to Bruce and me. The arrangement involved a pecking order, though. When Bruce had suggested that I become the family's investment guru, I had seized the role. Ever the youngest, it was great having sole responsibility for something here at home. I'd read books and studied, then began transferring Mom and Dad's CDs into a conservative mix of stocks and bonds. Bruce managed the farm. That was the division of labor. Understood. Until, perhaps, now.

"Orph!" I said, bending to pet Bruce's giant black dog. Part Newfoundland, part anybody's guess, Orph accompanied Bruce on all of his solitary trips to Goodland. I buried my nose in his fur, inhaled his doggy scent. "What a nice old guy."

"Abby says he has a three-ounce brain, all devoted to niceness."

Bruce's daughter had inherited his humor gene. I laughed on cue, stood up.

"Where's Mom?"

"Who knows? Hair appointment. Isn't that always where she is?"

"Or over at the church with her ladies' circle, quilting."

"Oh yeah, quilting. Or at the grocery store. Or the doctor's."

"So I've been thinking about the farm."

"Yes?" Bruce said in that tremulous voice of his. "What's new? So have I." He closed the register and zipped his camera back into its case.

"We could farm it ourselves if we grew only wheat. If we didn't irrigate, we wouldn't have to worry about finding a new manager or renter."

"You can farm it if you want," Bruce said. "I'm too old to bust my ass pounding steel." That would be the truth of it, I knew. Dad spent half his life in the shop Quonset, pounding on implement parts. All farming was hard work. Even when I was thirty-five, driving air-conditioned tractors, I'd gone home exhausted at day's end. But Ward was strong the way Dad had been strong. That same stocky build.

"Ward and I could do it together," I said.

"As long as it's not my ass."

Over one hump, and so easily, at least for now. I knew Bruce wouldn't just hand over the keys to the farm. There would be a lot of proving up to do. "I thought we might do it organically."

"That's the way we used to farm until we played out the land," Bruce said. It was true. Our grandfathers and Dad, when we were kids, had gotten good crops because of the fertility that had accumulated in the prairie sod since the Pleistocene. "We'd be lucky to get five bushels to the acre without fertilizer now," Bruce added. "And if you grow organic wheat, you've got to have organic fertilizer."

"A Colorado farmer I read about is using kelp," I said.

"Kelp," Bruce huffed. "From where?"

"The Gulf of Mexico."

"It would cost a fortune to ship. And what about the saline content? Anything from the ocean is going to be full of salt."

"Maybe. I mean, I don't know how we'd do it, yet. But will you send me your spreadsheet on our current inputs? So I can do some estimates?"

"I'll send you anything you want," Bruce said. He picked up his farm hat, a straw pith helmet. Above his grizzled beard, and with his hair sticking out around his ears, the hat made him look like an eccentric scientist on safari. "You staying or leaving?"

The conversation was over, I guessed. "Leaving, unless Mom comes home soon. I've got to get to Laramie and make sure Jake does his homework tonight."

"So you lock up Fort Knox." Dad's old joke. All three doors to Mom's house and the two in the garage had to be locked at all times. If she came home and found one left unlocked, she would go on a tirade. "Did the farmhouse even have a key?" I asked her once. I couldn't remember it having one. But all she had to do to defend her security obsession was mention the time a few years ago when "that disgusting trash" blew into Goodland off the interstate and broke into old Addie Newton's house and raped her. "What would two strapping young men want with an old hag like Addie or me?" Mom had asked. "It's barbaric!" The crime had shocked me too, deeply. But it shocked me almost as much hearing Mom mention herself in the same sentence as the raped Mrs. Newton and the two strapping young men.

Bruce had already gone into the living room and grabbed his guitar, which went everywhere he did. He was waiting in the entry for Orph, but the dog's toenails skittered on the linoleum as he tried to rise. I straddled him and gave him a boost, as I did for Mom when she had trouble getting up from her easy chair. That was another thing Bruce and I should be talking about. Probably time for assisted living. How were we going to orchestrate *that*?

Orph's slinking gait, as he lumbered across the kitchen on ill-strung hips, then out the door with his helmeted master, reminded me of Simba, the regal lion. Bruce always left me standing somewhere, wanting more engagement than he was prepared to provide. I'd envied his wives and girlfriends for his presence in their lives. I'd even envied his kids. But this was the first time I'd ever envied his dog.

DREAMING ALONG WITH ME OVER THE PHONE, Ward said, "This is what I've always wanted." I pictured him in his upstairs easy chair, one boot resting on the rope trunk that served as a coffee table. "We'll be going through life together, pulling each other's loads." All those other relationships that hadn't worked out made sense to him now.

My past failures, too, were beginning to make more sense in light of this new development. I had never believed in romantic destiny, but our circumstances seemed beyond providential. Following the dry Little Beaver across the prairie that day we'd first met, I'd felt as if I were tracing the lines of my family's origins in the land. Not more than fifty feet from the water I'd needed to find, to assure myself that we had not yet thoroughly destroyed what we once professed to cherish, I'd found Ward. Now we were preparing to do right by my family's land and the water together.

I would be skating along like this, then a line from one of Ward's early e-mails would pop into memory. *What is going to happen when we wake up?* If anything was going to wake up a cowboy, it would be driving a tractor.

But how was I to know what was right for Ward? Maybe he needed to make a genuine sacrifice for love. A lasting relationship demanded some self-denial, and maybe he faulted himself for never having been able to rise to the challenge.

He continued to insist that moving to Kansas would be disastrous for me. He would still come my way, to Wyoming. We would drive to Kansas as needed, to plant, cultivate, fertilize, harvest, etcetera. He would sell his cattle, and pasture his horses on rented land near Laramie and on our farm. He confessed that he'd been fantasizing about my father's old sheep barn ever since he'd first laid eyes on it. It would make a perfect indoor riding arena in the winter. His own place had no such amenity.

Jake was part of our plans too. True, his problems had worsened in the last few months, but he was still young and receptive to good influences. With Ward's tutelage and a big tractor to drive, he might straighten out and start taking school and the concept of work in general more seriously.

Bruce sent me an Excel worksheet listing everything it took to grow dryland winter wheat—the cost of fuel, the rate our tractors consumed it by the hour, the number of hours in each field operation—and equally exacting particulars for every other expense imaginable. Crop insurance, property taxes, maintenance, custom cutters, and the one thing I hoped we'd be able to do without—chemicals.

In the years since I'd worked on the farm, we'd been gradually switching over to a new method called no-till farming. In our case, Bruce said, it would more appropriately be called low-till. This meant that we killed weeds in our stubble fields with chemicals instead of undercutting them with sweeps, and we cultivated less often in advance of planting. Low-till left stubble on the field longer, preventing wind and water erosion and preserving moisture in the soil. Bruce said that ever since the drought had begun two years before, the new method had been the only reason we'd had decent crops. "Go out there and dig. See for yourself." He promised I would find damp soil in our low-till fields and no moisture in those where we still farmed the old way.

Every farm magazine I picked up in my mother's house sang the praises of no-till. None mentioned the risk to streams and aquifers posed by additional chemicals, much less aesthetics. Only immediate profits counted. But I hated the dead, gray look of our wheat stubble after it had been sprayed. It used to glitter gold for months after harvest. Gold was a color I associated with the fall, when pheasants, jackrabbits, kit foxes, and killdeer had found cover in the fields beneath a banner-blue satin sky, but their numbers had diminished drastically since this new chemical approach had come along. The drabness reminded me of postapocalyptic movies in which a future poisoned world was drained of color and light.

I had no idea how I could wean our farm off chemicals. A few farmers in Montana and the one in Colorado I'd told Bruce about were raising organic wheat on a large scale. But to be realistic, Ward and I would certainly not be able to grow organic wheat in our sleep. The less harmful and invasive methods were more labor-intensive. We would have to rededicate our lives. Splitting our time between Laramie and Kansas would prove impossible.

Then I ran the numbers. Raising only dryland wheat with the conventional approach would support Ward and me, but it wouldn't support Bruce or allow either of us to continue putting aside profits to secure our kids' future. Neither would the organic approach, even if I factored in the current premium on organic wheat, which was selling for three times what conventional wheat sold for. Fertilizer costs would be higher, and there might be times when we had to hire manual labor to hoe weeds we couldn't spray. And to market our grain, we would have to ship out of state. The undertaking might have been more profitable than conventional wheat even with those extra costs and demands, but the more I considered what would be entailed, the more I understood how major the sacrifice would be. I was not actually prepared to give up my writing for the endeavor. It would certainly not be fair to ask Ward to give up any of his business interests.

"That's really too bad," Ward said when I told him that the financial projections hadn't worked out. But he didn't offer to pore over the numbers himself to see if he might get a different read. And I could hear the relief in his voice.

TRUTH WAS, I DID LOVE THIS MAN. Although he claimed to be readying himself for a move to Laramie, I couldn't help thinking that it would be as disastrous for him as he believed moving to Kansas would be for me. But I thought our love would deepen and mature over time until we were able to cross this seemingly impassable mountain as if it were a little hill. It didn't really matter that we had to live separately right now; I was happier than I'd been in years.

In the meantime, I allowed myself to imagine spending longer and longer periods in Kansas after Jake graduated. I imagined not only making Ward's house my part-time home, but I also saw myself driving over to Goodland often to see Mom. I didn't want her to live her last years alone, then die with no immediate family nearby.

Ward was not going to save our farm. But he might make it possible for me to have a life while I did. If I lived there during the growing season, I could learn to drive the new tractors. Then I could help Bruce fill the labor gap if Ron's health failed during the summer when we needed him most. I could maybe get Ron and Bruce to let me experiment on the dryland corners of our irrigated fields. These extended beyond the circles the pivot sprinklers traveled, and tended to be planted as an afterthought anyway. I imagined experimenting with more dryland crops such as commercial sunflowers or canola. Or teff, an Ethiopian cereal grain that some farmers had been trying.

I should have told Ward that my mind had started going in the Kansas direction and that it didn't seem to be turning back. But these ideas were amorphous balloons, rising in my thoughts at night as I lay in bed. Like those splotches that float in the darkness right before going to sleep, they were gradually forming into decipherable images and then into dreams.

I didn't sense any need to rush those imaginings into words or share them with Ward. But I didn't realize he was sitting up in his easy chair on those very same nights, unable to sleep.

Not, that is, until I returned home after another visit and called him.

He tried to speak, cleared his throat, began to say something again, cleared his throat again. "I'm sorry," he managed. "I seem to have lost my voice."

"Ward, if there's anything you need to tell me, if this isn't working out, then just say it."

"No, no, it's not you, it's only . . . I can't seem to speak right now."

The next day, my inbox dinged.

I would do anything in my power to reassure you that I'll always love you.

I grasped at that reassurance because I couldn't allow myself to acknowledge what I suspected. That he was anguishing. That he was suffering. When will I ever learn? he must have been asking himself.

Yet again he'd made promises to a woman that he would not be able to keep.

7

IN JUNE, JAKE WENT TO HIS SUMMER JOB FOR A TOTAL OF TWO DAYS BEFORE DECIDING HE'D RATHER DRIVE AROUND TOWN WITH HIS FRIENDS. I withdrew his driving privileges, then did as I'd threatened I would and enrolled him in a mountain wilderness camp, where he would hike all day and receive therapy. Informed of this, he stormed out of the house, shouting, "Good-bye forever!"

I took up the position that had become all too common over the last year, hanging limply in the woven chair strung from the spruce tree in my backyard, Jake's beagle, Regina, in my lap and the one beer I allowed myself each evening dangling from my hand. Had my mother ever sat up worrying like this? I wondered. I couldn't remember giving her much grief. If I did, though, or if my brothers did, she had Dad sitting up beside her. I was grateful that tonight I would have Ward.

He arrived right on time, accompanied by the familiar clanging noise that had heralded his arrival in my life the previous August. He'd hauled Digit, his favorite horse, up with him. In the morning, we planned to go riding in the mountains. This had been a shared dream, one that I hoped would multiply into many rides in the future.

Jake's reaction to the wilderness camp, Ward assured me, only proved he needed the help I was getting for him. He was lucky to have a mother who cared as much as I did. And surprisingly, it wasn't difficult to sleep that night with Ward beside me.

In the morning, I opened the door to Jake's bedroom. Heaped stale clothing covered the bed, but no teenager slept in it. "Don't let him ruin your day," Ward said. "He'll come home. It's still early."

We were backing out of the drive when I spotted Jake walking up the block. I went to meet him on the porch. He was pale and tearful, his shoulders hunched in his black motorcycle jacket. Since Christmas, when he'd worn it to go shooting with Ward, he'd individualized the jacket further, painting the bones of a rib cage and spine on the back. Down the arms still twisted ribbons of cheerful turquoise and yellow that I wanted to think were more indicative of my son's spirit. He had to make himself ugly. He had to shave his hair, give himself safety-pin and ballpoint-ink tattoos and wear stinky, tattered clothes in order to test the world's and my love to its limits.

I'd been searching for the right conciliatory words. A lot hung in the balance and I was afraid I wouldn't find them. But I saw from his defeated manner that I'd already won.

"I feel like you hate me," he said, his eyes straying onto the pickup, where Ward sat in silhouette under his cowboy hat. "Like you just don't want me around anymore."

I squeezed his arm through the rumpled leather. "It's not about him," I said. "If that's what you think. I'm trying to keep you from ruining your life, Jake. I worry about you every minute."

Even if his arms hung limply as I hugged him, I sensed a lapse in his anger, a slight lift of the anguish on his face. For the moment he seemed to trust my guidance. At camp he would be required to speak his pain and hike trails not of his own choosing. I intuited that part of him knew he needed to examine himself in the clear, undistorted mirror that the counselors would hold up for him.

"I felt so sorry for him," Ward said. "Hurting so bad. I just wanted to go up there and hug him with you."

Why didn't you? I thought, but contented myself with his having had the impulse.

We picked up our horses from my friend's ranch outside of Laramie, where I pastured Henry, and took them to a trail leading up Sheep Mountain that a wild cowgirl friend had introduced me to. She and I had loped our horses through the aspens and pines. It had been an exciting ride and I wanted Ward to enjoy the same thrill. But he didn't seem his usual self. "Go on ahead," he told me and proceeded at a walk.

At the top we dismounted and tied our horses to a tree so I could show him the view. Lake Hattie lay at our feet, a blue eye reflecting clouds and the mountain. "Isn't the valley beautiful from up here?" I said.

"Not to me," Ward replied.

"What's not to like?"

"I don't know. Too . . . desolate or something."

His reaction baffled me. Wasn't this the kind of wide-open western territory that cowboys were supposed to love?

"HOW'RE YOU DOING?" HE ASKED THAT NIGHT in bed.

"I'm worried," I admitted. If he asked, I would begin with Jake. Would he come home from camp restored to himself, bright of spirit and potential, or as an even more defiant rebel? In which direction was I pushing him? I hoped there would be an opening for me to add, "I'm worried about us too." But Ward made no response and soon went to sleep.

Waking at seven to an empty bed, I went to look out my office window. The spot where his truck had been was empty. I'd scarcely recorded this absence when he reappeared, his stock trailer in tow, his horse darkening the space between the rails. I met him in the front hall.

He placed his hands on my hips. "How are you?" he asked, the way he always did, emphasizing the "you."

"All right. Except I woke up and you weren't there."

"I want to go back to bed with you now. I woke about six like always.

Thought I might as well go get Digit." My friends' ranch, where he'd stabled Digit, was fifteen miles from town. We'd planned to go there together after breakfast.

Ward trailed me up the stairs, our fingers interlaced. We lay down on the bed, but I sensed that he was marking time. He feigned contentment as I nuzzled up to him. He still had his long-sleeved blue Levi's shirt stuffed into his belted jeans. He was a stuffed man, his feelings buried deep inside the stuffing, under wraps. An uncooperative guy doll.

By eight he'd drunk his coffee, refused breakfast, and suffered through a tour of my summer garden. He kissed me good-bye and left.

I WAS SITTING IN THE TALL DIRECTOR'S chair in my kitchen, spilling the tears I'd held in while he was preparing to leave, when I heard the front door open, then footsteps in the hall.

I dabbed my eyes with the dish towel, fixed a smile. He was thudding through the living room. The dining room. In seconds he would wrap me in his arms. He would say, "I just couldn't leave without one more kiss." Or maybe I would find out what had been troubling him.

He entered the kitchen, glanced at me. "Forgot my hat," he said. He picked it up from the counter, dropped it on his head, and left again.

I greeted his call, later that night, with an accusation. "Things just got too dicey for you here, didn't they?"

Ward denied this, saying he had to get home earlier than usual so that he could shoe a couple of horses before the jackpot roping that week.

"I need you to take part in my life, Ward, not just disappear when things get a little rough."

He said he was there for Jake and me every step of the way. I told him that wasn't what it felt like. He'd been receding from me for some time now, like a prairie dog digging down into his burrow. Would he please just come out and tell me what was going on?

"Nothing's wrong, sweetheart. I swear."

"I don't buy that for one minute, Ward."

"Okay," he said hesitantly. "I didn't want to say anything until I was sure, but I just can't see myself moving to Laramie."

Was that all he was worried about? I shared what I'd been thinking. We could keep seeing each other one weekend a month, and after Jake graduated, I could come down to his house for longer periods. Eventually I would move there.

"That won't work," he said, his voice stepping down in pitch on each word.

"What do you mean? Why not?"

"It's just not practical, Julene. That's all I'm trying to explain here. You're an idealist. I'm a realist. That's the difference between you and me."

Not fair! He'd been the big romancer from the beginning, using all that corny language, saying I was "the one."

"This is bigger than us, Ward. Remember when you said that?"

"It *is* bigger than us. We can't make it work."

"How dare you turn that around on me!"

He hung up.

GETTING JAKE TO THE WILDERNESS CAMP WAS like stuffing a cat into a cardboard box, and when he came back, he said he couldn't put up with my rules anymore and announced he was leaving home. He wrote me a kind letter, telling me that he understood why I'd made the rules and realized he should have obeyed them, but he was practically grown up now and if he could survive in the wilderness, then Laramie would be no challenge at all. Talk about a plan that had backfired! *I will not disapoynt you, Mom. I promise. Stand back and watch me sore!* He was an immature seventeen and nowhere near ready to survive on his own, but I put on a brave face and kissed him good-bye on the front porch, reminding him he would be welcome back anytime and to please come on Sundays, for dinner.

When I came inside after saying good-bye to him, Beatrice was waiting for me, her expression grave and empathetic. She had come to see me through the final throes of the breakup with Ward and to lend support with Jake. She was his godmother and had known him since he was a baby.

"May God watch over him," she said, in her somber, low-pitched voice. Also a mother, she knew it was unthinkable what I'd just had to do. She put her arms around me and as I crumpled within them, followed me down, onto the floor.

JAKE AND HIS GIRLFRIEND STARTED FLOPPING AT a house in the worst part of our poor neighborhood. The house had a dirt yard and black curtains so thoroughly drawn that not one lumen of light could pass through them. The man who rented the house was rumored to be a meth addict. Mornings, when the principal called to tell me that Jake and his girlfriend hadn't made it to school, I went over there and banged on the blackened windows until Jake exploded out the front door. "What? Jesus Christ, Mom!" Then "Oh." They'd forgotten about school.

I consulted a psychotherapist, telling her I would stop at nothing to get my son out of the danger he was in. Together we devised a plan. I lured Jake home by allowing his girlfriend to move into my basement with him, then proceeded to finesse them both through high school one day at a time. This went against the advice I'd received from the wilderness-camp director, who took the tough-love, "he has to save himself and won't do that until he hits bottom" approach. But methamphetamine addiction was not a bottom I was willing to let my son reach.

Meanwhile, Ward kept calling me sporadically, stirring flames in the embers by saying he missed me and still loved me, then dousing the flames with the insistence that our relationship was impractical and we had no future.

Finally, in response to my demands for an explanation for his about-face, he sent a letter.

*You want to ride and camp in the wilderness. I want
to ride checking my own fences. When day ends, you want
to sleep under the stars. I want to sleep in the bunkhouse.
You worry about the environment. I worry about making
a living. I believe work should be its own reward. I don't
care about the masses, I care about me!*

What else did I need to know? How much more directly could he
have put it? I told him he shouldn't call me anymore "unless something
changes there," a request he honored a little too readily. I thought I
could starve him back to his senses. But of course it was I who starved.

My inability to let Ward go reveals to me now that my indoctrina-
tion as a woman in a patriarchal culture ran deeper than I'd ever realized. "When are you going to find another dad for me, Mom?" Jake had
asked me often in his early childhood. "When are you going to marry
me a farmer?" Dad had asked, only half joking. It seemed that the sole
means I had of contributing to the happiness of these two people I
loved most in the world was to use my feminine appeal to gain the real
prize. A father for Jake, a farmer for Dad. That's why the time I'd spent
helping Dad during Jake's toddlerhood had seemed so healing. I had
proven I could be that farmer if I wanted to, and Dad had even accepted
that I could. I rejected all those sexist implications, asserted my own
truths, became equal in my own right, but look at me now.

"He just couldn't do it, Bair," Beatrice said. Knowing this didn't
help. The thought that I had somehow become a daunting chore only
infuriated me. During Beatrice's visit we browsed through a Laramie
antique store, where she picked up a beautiful little carved wooden
box. On the lid she pasted a picture that I had taken on a canoe trip
down the Green River in western Wyoming. The water in the fore-
ground was pale green and so clear that you could see the boulders
underneath, a surface netting of sunlight drifting over them. A slightly
opaque strip of turquoise water mirrored the turquoise on the box's
sides. And the ripples where the water reflected the shoreline glinted
gold, the same color as the metallic paint on the box's rim. The water

had flowed out of the base of Flaming Gorge Dam, so cold I didn't think I could go in at first. But that strip of turquoise had been irresistible. Of course I'd gone in, every time we'd beached the canoe. "Remember who you are," Beatrice seemed to be telling me with that gift.

Another friend, Susan, who'd grown up in Iowa farm country and felt stifled there, told me simply, "He's a settler. You're a seeker. Settlers don't like seekers. They ask too many unsettling questions." She also observed that until I met Ward, I'd centered so much on Jake and work that it was as if I'd forgotten I was a sexual being. Loving Ward had awakened that part of me again, and however painful losing him was, that would be a good thing in the long run.

The wisdom of friends like these—the community I had built up over the years through that forceful urge to connect with the like-minded or like-spirited—would settle in after this crisis in my romantic affairs ended. But the road to acceptance has no shortcuts. I had to walk the distance step by step.

8

IN THE DISTRICT'S NEWSLETTER, THE *WATER TABLE*, I READ THAT OUR BOARD WAS GOING TO HOLD AN ANNUAL MEETING. It would be open to the public, an opportunity to learn how decisions were made. And who knew? I might run into Ward. He warehoused his livestock equipment in Colby. And he sometimes shopped at the grocery store there.

The director greeted me with courteous surprise and ushered me to a row of empty seats reserved for the public along one end of the small conference room. Ten board members, all of them men, sat around the table.

I was forced to sit almost sideways to avoid knocking my knees against the back of a chair occupied by a red-faced cowboy farmer with a handlebar mustache. He was the man who'd once rented our pasture from Bruce. He looked the same today as he had when I'd first met him, at a party Ward had taken me to—Wranglers so crisp and indigo they must have been brand-new, his chest prominent and proud under a starched-white, snap-up shirt. At the party, he made it clear to me that he'd felt hoodwinked when Bruce sold the pasture after getting him to install all new posts and wire. "You owe me," he said, quite seriously. "What are you and your brother going to do with your farm?"

"I don't know. Run it?"

"Really?" he said, holding my eyes with an amused look on his face. "How are you going to do that when that man of yours, Ron, quits?"

"Well, hello, Miss Bair!" he said now, a little jokingly. As the meeting was called to order, he took out a pen and scribbled something on the back of his copy of the agenda. He passed it to me and watched while I read it. *I want to rent your farm.* I gave him a wan smile and nodded mere acknowledgment. After the contentiousness between him and Bruce, there wasn't a chance in hell we'd choose him as a renter.

Ward had told me after that party that I'd rattled his friends by hanging out in the room where the men gathered and striking up my own conversations with them. Men and women normally formed separate clumps at Kansas get-togethers. Now those tables had turned. It was I who felt rattled. Women did not participate in public farm business, I knew. With pad and pen, I pretended to be a journalist, but as a member of a farm family who irrigated, I would normally be thought a partisan. Truth be known—and I believed that some of the men present did intuit this truth—I was a turncoat. They were kind to me anyway. The director introduced me and offered me coffee, and the men smiled and said hello, extending their welcome to the daughter of an old-timer many of them had known.

The cowboy farmer turned in his chair every so often to stare at me unabashedly, like an overconfident suitor undressing the object of his desire. Except his lechery was not sexual. It was fiscal. I thought I could read his mind as he multiplied our acreage times yields and dollars per bushel and estimated our annual Farm Program subsidies.

He knew that heirs usually sought a renter first. Then they sold to him. He and the other board members and their fathers and grandfathers had gotten big this way. Like my own forebears, theirs had made it through the Depression and the droughts, adding sections of land to their holdings as their neighbors either failed or died, leaving nonfarming sons and daughters. Each acquisition reinforced their confidence in their families' special mettle, their plains hardiness, their survivability. I knew that pride well and had basked in it my whole life. This suitor presented no immediate danger, but he clearly smelled opportunity. He traveled in Ward's circle and must have known that we'd broken up. Now that it was certain I would not be coming home, there would be spoils.

The men around the conference table kept stealing glances at me. The looks on their faces seemed to go beyond mere curiosity. Was it suspicion? Guilt? These men were some of the area's biggest irrigation farmers. A few of them grossed more than a million dollars annually and were among the top twenty government-subsidized farmers in their counties. Ron told me that one of the board members had thirty-eight sprinkler systems on his land.

Ron was an opinionated man, and he believed in playing by the rules. Each year he called me with accurate meter readings so we could properly record the amount of water we'd used. He didn't like the fact that most irrigation farmers weren't even required to have meters, whereas we'd had to have them ever since Dad cut a deal with the district allowing us to use water from any of our wells on any of our land. Once, Ron had told Bruce and me that he would run for the board himself, except if he did, and tried to get stronger meter controls passed, he couldn't step outside anymore without wearing a bulletproof vest.

"What if they shot you in the head, Ron?" Bruce had asked. He never missed an opportunity for a joke, although he favored uniformly fair enforcement also.

These big irrigators on the water board tended to be less regulation friendly. They had killed zero depletion and every other attempt to reduce pumping. So now Topeka had enacted a new protocol. The boards were to determine the areas in their districts where drawdown of the Ogallala was most severe. These areas would then become candidates for more aggressive management. It was a plan to plan.

The director suggested that 1996 through 2002 provided a good mix of wet and dry years from which to pull data. But the board members had a lot riding on irrigation continuing unabated, and their biases were showing. "Yeah but we're takin' the last three droughty years that make the thirties look like a walk in the park!" one complained. Of course. If they chose years when it had rained more and farmers had irrigated less, then the drawdown would be minimal, and no one would be asked to cut the amount he pumped.

"We should throw out the dry years," another man blurted. He and several others glanced at me, as if taking the measure of my reaction.

"That's going to skew the whole picture, Max," said the director. "That's not going to be fair." I could see what he was up against. If these were "drunks guarding the liquor store," he was the man hired by the owner, in this case the people of the state of Kansas, to keep them from guzzling every last drop. But how he did this was up to the drunks, who had voting power over their own water rights.

Perhaps to ameliorate them, the director complained about the knee-jerk regulations handed down by the state. "We always tell 'em they won't work, but they go ahead and do them anyway."

"You sound like my wife," said one. "Course I don't know what you're anglin' for." Laughter filled the room like bowling pins toppling after a strike. The cowboy farmer gave me a vulturous leer.

At adjournment, as the men rolled their agendas into their fists, I leaned forward, my hands on the sides of my chair. But the director had one more tidbit to offer. He announced that Harley Owens had called his office wondering why he never received a refund check for his required donation to a cloud-seeding project that had been canceled.

I knew Harley. Because he was thought to be gay, he'd often been the brunt of humor between my father and the men who hung out around the popcorn machine down at the Farmers' Co-Op gas station. Harley's request for a refund seemed reasonable to me because the project had been called off, but laughter resounded once again.

"Probably wanted to buy his wife a present," someone said.

"He doesn't have a wife," announced another, to a general titter.

"Oh, so he doesn't swing that way. I didn't know that."

Almost every eye in the room strayed onto me. I pretended I didn't get the joke.

AFTER IDLING DOWN MAIN AND PAST THE feed stores, I lingered over lunch, my car parked prominently in the strip mall near Ward's warehouse, but no luck. I imagined a barricade across the highway leading out of Colby in the direction of Plum Springs. "Road Ends Here." It was like being in a *Twilight Zone* episode and having a significant part of your past suddenly erased.

I wasn't ready, yet, to drive to Goodland and put on a good face for Mom. Needing some time to absorb the finality of all things Ward related, I decided to explore some countryside I'd never seen before. At first it proved to be an unremarkable drive through horizon-to-horizon corn and wheat stubble. Almost all of it had that telltale drab color indicative of no-till. Only when I saw mist rising from a valley up ahead did I understand what had drawn me this way. The road hit the valley's rim, and the bleak view out my car windows transitioned abruptly into a world of grass.

The Smoky Valley returned me to sanity, to wild land instead of factory land, to the winter-yellow, cougarlike pelt of the Pleistocene instead of the raw-brown, exposed flesh of the Anthropocene. When I reached the bridge, I pulled onto the shoulder, turned off the engine, and stepped into a state of anachronistic grace. The mist stood thicker in the low places, so that the blond grass glowed more brightly on the hills. Through immemorial time, this mixture of native grasses, wild-flowers, shrubs, and trees, and all the creatures that lived in, on, or under them had coexisted in what the renowned plant geneticist and ecologist Wes Jackson called "nature's wisdom," while up above, the gray-brown, sprayed-dead tablelands displayed "man's cleverness."

You didn't have to be a genius to feel the difference. Up above, I'd been depressed, not only by the destructive farming practices but by the conclusion it was taking me so long to reach, that Ward and I indeed "had no future." Down here, this island of hilly terrain, spared only because tractors would topple traversing it, instilled the simplest kind of happiness—the kind the hunter-gatherers must have experienced so much more completely, knowing the grass never ended.

The fog prevented me from seeing the water until I'd walked halfway across the bridge. I hadn't expected to see any this far west, but the Smoky was still alive here, unfurling gray-blue below limestone outcrops, like a forgotten veil snagged on the quivers of yucca poking up beside it. *The valley spirit never dies*, wrote Lao Tzu in the *Tao Te Ching*. What I knew to be happening here belied that assurance. The Smoky was the spirit of this valley, but like almost every other stream on the High Plains all the way from here to Texas, irrigation had so diminished it that it hovered on the verge of extinction.

This was farther west than Ward and I had ever ventured. Could this crossing be the one that Dull Knife and his Cheyenne had used in 1878? Ward always meant to show me where they crossed the Smoky, but somehow he never got around to it. Like so much else we would never get around to now.

The Cheyenne had come north in September, the month of the Plum Moon. The plums I'd planted in our farm's windbreak were descendants of those native plums and, like them, ripened in September. October meant "Moon When the Water Begins to Freeze on the Edge of the Streams." The name had reminded Ward of the cool, musty smell that rose from the valley in the fall. We'd marveled at these surviving touch points—fruit that tasted like a month, frost that smelled like one.

This was December, *Makhikomini*, the month of the Big Freezing Moon. Last year, when I'd spent those nights at Ward's house after Christmas, the moon had not been big. It had been a scythe cradling one star. What had I really loved about him? If he owned a place outside of Laramie and I'd met him one night when my girlfriends and I went dancing at the cowboy bar, I doubted I would have been that interested. Even if I entertained a relationship with him for a while, I would have ended it when I found out how little he cared about wild land. He hadn't even felt a thrill standing on Sheep Mountain and looking over the Laramie Valley. In Willa Cather's Nebraska novels, I read somewhere once, "men changed land." In her southwestern novels, "land changed men." Ward hadn't experienced the desert like I had.

Yet whenever I took the long drive from Wyoming to his house and stepped onto his mud porch and breathed those smells—of dried mud, but also of old house, rolled oats, wool horse blankets, aftershave, hay—it was always as if he'd reentered my cells through the permeable walls of my capillaries. Those were the smells of my childhood. It was Kansas I'd been having sex with, melding with, re-fusing with. My love for him was my love of home.

The Cheyenne had been starving and in tatters when they came through this part of Kansas. So much had been sacrificed for our settlement. And most of those who'd made the sacrifice did not choose to make it. The same was true of the water and all of the animals that depended on it.

It occurred to me that at the board meeting I had failed to advocate for what I loved most. The emotional tone, within me, had been avoidance. And instead of staying after the meeting to mingle and speak my mind, I'd left immediately.

I had definitely been an anomaly, probably the only woman the men had ever seen at a meeting, unless the director's assistant brought coffee or came in to take notes. I sensed that they were flattered by my presence. *Is this little ol' meeting really that newsworthy? Well then, how are we doing? Are we funny? Are we important?* The ordinary things men look into women's faces to discover. But I'd seen more in their looks than ordinary things.

To me, it seemed as if the men knew their water board was a smokescreen, an empty pretense at stewardship. *Is this whole affair as ridiculous as we suspect? Can you see a way out of the compromised predicament we find ourselves in, mining the water while pretending to protect it? Mining it and undermining ourselves, slowly destroying the way of life we were born into and that is supposed to sustain our children and grandchildren?*

For any answers to appear, those questions had to be asked. I was the ideal person to draw them out. I was living with the same disconnect, between what my own family was doing and what I knew needed to be done.

9

HAVING INVESTED SO MUCH HOPE IN PRIVATE SOLUTIONS AND IN A ROMANTIC RELATIONSHIP THAT HAD GOTTEN ME NOWHERE, IT WAS TIME TO FOCUS MY ATTENTION OUTWARD. The need to do this was met when I received an invitation to speak at a symposium in Wichita on the Ogallala. If I was ever going to outgrow my antiquated Kansas reticence and own my true feelings, it had to be now.

The moment I stepped into the crowded room, I saw the director of our farm's water district in the audience. Although this frightened me, I was grateful for the opportunity. I still kicked myself for being so mealymouthed when I'd interviewed him. Instead of pretending to be an objective journalist, I should have told him that even as a member of a farm family who irrigated, I believed what we were doing was wrong.

While listening to the other speakers discuss the technicalities of new sprinkler technology and Kansas water law, my anxiety inched up like barometric pressure on a bruised-blue plains afternoon. No one questioned that pumping at high rates out of a declining aquifer should continue. It would be solely up to me to unleash that storm.

Too soon I found myself standing at the podium with shaky knees. Could others hear my voice quivering over the resonant PA system? But as I announced I was going to offer a more personal take on the

Ogallala, I saw relief on several faces. It had been a morning of PowerPoint presentations and charts.

So I told them my story, of growing up on a sensible farm aligned with the realities of the region's climate and soil. Of the land trade that saw us move to town and begin a life radically different from the one we'd left. Of the erasure of the original farmstead and its replacement by a circle of irrigated field corn. And of how my family still owned a farm although none of us lived there or worked on it anymore. Only my elderly mother still lived in Sherman County.

In this, I told my audience, my family was not unusual. Nearly half of the people who owned farmland in our county didn't live there, and most who did lived in town. Very few were engaged in anything like the way of life that had made farming a noble profession in the past. That life had vanished along with most of the farms. Once there were thirty million farms in America. That number had now dwindled to fewer than two million, many of them very large. The integrated livestock, grain, and haying operations of the 1950s were gone. The plains farms of today were corn, wheat, and soybean factories.

"Each year, the few hundred irrigators in one Kansas county, Finney, pump half again as much water as used by all one million customers of the Denver water utility. How is this conscionable?" I asked. "The news is full of stories of impending national and global water crises. Worldwide, more than eight hundred million people suffer from chronic hunger. Yet we are squandering the majority of our Ogallala water on a crop we feed to cows.

"The farm lobby argues that increasing any regulations on agriculture would hinder farmers' ability to feed the world. But if we really want to feed the world, we should eliminate feedlots and grind the corn into flour for human consumption. The soybeans should be made into tofu and other foods for direct human use. Livestock production is a notorious waste of protein, converting the plant source to a meat source at a ratio of eight to one.

"Regardless of whether we feed corn and soybeans to humans or to animals, we should leave the growing of those crops to midwestern farmers. It rains enough in the I states—Indiana, Illinois, Iowa—and in the eastern parts of Kansas, Nebraska, and the Dakotas to grow them without irrigating. We should return the High Plains to dryland crops and to grass."

I described the many times I'd walked down dry creek beds where past floods had undercut the native sod and saw roots trailing all the way to the ground, "like Rapunzel's hair. You don't have to be a prairie zealot like me to appreciate the nutrient and ecological value of plants rooted that deeply. We should replant as much grass as possible and let it do the job it did throughout all conceivable time before us, sequestering carbon from the atmosphere with its immense root systems and supporting a diverse ecology.

"Let bovines eat the grass, doing the job that bovines have always done, their hooves aerating the soil and their manure fertilizing it. Then eat that meat, instead of going through the convoluted, fuel-intensive process of removing the grass, plying the soil with chemicals, and draining the water out from under it"—I paused to take a breath that came off like panting, and was gratified by my audience's laughter—"to grow crops we then ship to feedlots, where the cattle need antibiotics in order to survive in the cramped conditions and must consume grain that their stomachs were not intended to digest"—pant, pant, laugh—"and then feeding ourselves the resulting 'marbled,' that is, fatty beef that contributes to our nation's diabetes, heart-disease, and cancer epidemics." Some of the audience were still laughing, but many were shaking their heads at the idiocy I'd described. "Oh yes," I added. "Then there's the twenty percent of the corn crop that ends up in processed food, mostly in corn syrup, which also causes health problems.

"To grow these irrigated crops, farmers apply huge amounts of nitrogen fertilizer. Only about one third to one half of the fertilizer is absorbed by the plants. But the rest of it doesn't just vanish. Much of it makes its way into rivers or slowly trickles downward, into the aquifer. Same with pesticides. An Environmental Protection Agency study concluded that farming accounts for seventy percent of the contamination of U.S. rivers and streams."

Was it possible, I asked, to arrest our suicidal course and protect the water that was left? Not, I answered, as long as we cling to our irrational faith in local control.

"People will not buy into policies that are handed down from on high, we are told. They won't vote for legislators who would curtail their property rights. Yet the water of the state of Kansas belongs to all of the people, not just farmers. Meanwhile, the irrigation boards are manned by irrigators. They express views such as this one in our district's newsletter, the *Water Table*: *How is it fair to give up profit now for the benefit of future generations?*

"How is it fair?" I repeated incredulously, careful not to let my gaze stray onto the director's sector of the room. "Better to ask why a hundred years of our now disintegrating and increasingly dismal plains civilization merits draining an aquifer that has supported ten thousand years of humanity before us. We are depriving the next ten thousand years of humans and animals of the water they will need to survive.

"There is something we all need to realize about the predominant mentality of farmers. My father having been a farmer, I know that mentality pretty well. He waged unblinking battles against coyotes with cyanide, drought with irrigation, soil depletion with chemical fertilizers, bugs with pesticides, weeds with herbicides. What he didn't foresee, or understand, was the threat his growing technology posed to the balance of nature, or that there was such a balance in the first place.

"When my brothers and I were children, my father would hold us up to the stars at night. He appreciated stars as much as the next person, probably more. He took great pleasure in pondering them. But if he'd had the wherewithal and it had been profitable and legal, he would have harvested those as readily as he did his wheat. And he would not have stopped until he'd harvested every last one.

"The Ogallala Aquifer seemed as vast as the Milky Way when he first began pumping it. But he went to college. He knew, as did government geologists even back at the turn of the last century, that the water was finite. He understood that it would not last forever. He fully expected that his rights would one day be curtailed by the government, and *he was okay with that*. He didn't want to destroy his land or what was under it, but he didn't believe it was his responsibility to quit and turn his back on those profits either. It was up to the government to protect natural resources.

"In this capitalist society we share, which elevates individual financial success over the common good, we cannot expect farmers to self-regulate any more than we expect other businesspeople to do so. They will work within the law to get rich, and they consider profits their due. They won't change methods until they are required to. And the only one in a position to require them to is a government that governs.

"To govern, according to my dictionary, is 'to exercise a directing or restraining influence over, to guide.' It is also to 'hold in check; to control.' Isn't it ironic, then, that instead of directing, restraining, guiding, holding in check, or controlling the use of the aquifer that makes life here possible, the federal Farm Program encourages and enables the waste and pollution of that aquifer?

"The effect of farm subsidies is circular. The draw of federal dollars drives production up, which, in turn, drives prices down, creating the need for more subsidies. Even if most irrigators don't like the idea of curtailment, they would be far outnumbered by the other citizen owners of the water if only the awareness of those citizens were expanded by open and honest public debate.

"We have to subsidize farms if we want to keep any vitality at all on the rural landscape, but the practices that taxpayers pay for should protect the water, not lay waste to it. Plains farmers, whether real ones or absentee owners like me, should not be subsidized for growing irrigated crops. We should not be able to get government crop insurance for them either. Instead, we should be reimbursed for retiring our water rights, for returning our acreage to dryland crops and to grass, and for adopting nonchemical methods that will protect instead of pollute the aquifer."

LATE THAT EVENING, THE ELEVATOR I WAS riding opened at the same time as the one opposite me. The director and I made brief eye contact, but instead of acknowledging me, he dashed down the hall. I surprised myself by calling his name. He ducked his head and walked faster. I jogged to catch up and called his name again. He stopped, turned, and looked down at me impatiently. "Hello, Julene."

He was a tall man, and I barely reached his shoulders. My sudden courage must have come from the high I was still on. After my talk, several people had come up to me and thanked me for my honesty. Some had told me their own stories—of dried-up creeks and failing irrigation pumps and plowed pastures.

I told the director that I understood how frustrating it must be to do his complex job in the face of criticism like mine.

"Why won't you work within the system?" he asked. "Why don't you run for our board?" He complained about another critic who, instead of doing this, "sneaked around behind our backs and went to the legislature."

It stunned me to think that he might actually see me as a threat. That possibility frightened me, with the onus of the responsibility it implied. If I were to become more politically active, I would have to learn much more than I'd been able to absorb so far—about water law, cropping alternatives, and the gargantuan Farm Program. I reminded him that I didn't live in Sherman County. "I don't think I'd be allowed on the board, would I?"

"Well then," he said, "dryland farmers can serve. A lot of them are opposed to irrigation. For the life of me, I can't understand why they won't get involved."

"Because they don't want to rock boats. They have to live there." Was it possible he really didn't understand this? But I appreciated that my speech had broken through his professional reserve. We were on emotional ground, and he was talking like a human, not a wonk.

"I'm in the middle," he said, "halfway between those who want to go full out and people like you who want no irrigation." He held his hands up to indicate the two extremes.

"In your job I guess you'd have to take a neutral position," I said.

"This is nothing to do with my job. It's how I feel personally. Somehow these two ends have to come together. Is that what you want? Are you arguing this position in order to get us from out here?" He drew his hands together. "To here?"

He held his hands palms up, fingers pointing toward me. His practiced diplomacy made him seem magnanimous. He was giving me an opportunity to be what he considered reasonable. I could feel the pull of harmony, of yes.

What surprised me most was the credence this man seemed to grant me. "No. I'm saying that future generations will need that water."

He nodded respectfully. In minutes, we'd come a long way from his angry avoidance. It hadn't been so hard to look in his eyes and say what I thought after all.

It will take a reversal in state and national policy to protect what water is left. Such a reversal requires a general heightening of consciousness. This is especially difficult when archconservative pundits, probusiness at any cost, falsely pit evangelical Christians and rural populations against scientists and environmentalists. But despite Ward's and my failure to reconcile our political differences in the short time we had together, I must believe that heightening is possible.

You cannot grow up climbing windmills to gaze at sunsets or trekking through pastures rattling grain buckets in pursuit of intractable horses and not see the beauty or regret its passing even if, like my family and me, you've had a hand in the destruction. Honest ideas expressed in the national press seep into local minds like sunlight through gaps in clouds. In Kansas, the gaps are between the way things used to be and the way they are now. Not only did deer and antelope really once play there, but instead of outgassing poison after being infused with ammonia fertilizer, dirt used to smell sweet in the spring. Nights were silent and skies were dark. Water didn't gush from the earth as from a cut artery. And as one Goodlandite told me, "We used to get *snow*. We no more'n get one little finger in the winter, a little blow, and that's about it. It stays too warm." This was a friend of my parents' who, like my father, grew up in a sod house. His wife, a petite dynamo who used to lead the Prairie Dusters, a rodeo drill team I belonged to as a teenager, said, "The weather patterns have changed."

These two were mainly cattle ranchers, although they also farmed and had once run sheep. They always seemed the picture of western glamor to me, she with her cute western bell-bottoms and sexy, lace-fringed western blouses, he a tall, handsome cowboy who wore a big hat and shiny boots. When I'd called and told them I was writing about the Ogallala, they had little choice but to meet with me. I was Harold and Jasmin's daughter. But that didn't mean they had to go along with any liberal claptrap.

The man sat across from me in my mother's living room, his legs folded and his hat hanging off one knee. "Hell, no," he'd answered when I asked him if it saddened him that we'd plowed up much of the prairie. "Baloney to the good ol' days. Outside toilets, freezin' your butt off. Look at you, Julie. You're sittin' in a pretty nice chair, you're not out in a tepee somewhere, weavin' wool."

Now that the conversation had moved on to weather patterns, I could still feel the couple's resistance to my environmental notions, but I was driven to transcend the polarity that, too often, made genuine communication impossible. Did they think changes in the weather were another cycle, I asked, or part of a general trend?

"A cycle," he said. He sounded irritated, ready to go home.

"I think . . . it's . . . a general trend," she said more carefully.

"Is it the greenhouse effect?" I asked.

He stammered, "I don't . . . I don't know if it's the greenhouse . . ." He surprised me then by launching into a spiel that, excepting the diction, might have come out of my own mouth.

"You know, technology's great, but we've gone too far. We can kill bugs, we can kill weeds, we can kill everything, but every time we kill somethin', we kill somethin' else. Just like the wildlife out here. It ain't hard to see we're starvin' the pheasants to death when we spray our stubble after harvest. Spray it clean. Well that's what the chicks lived on, and besides that, when they're pickin', they're pickin' up some of that chemical and they're eatin' it. And I'm not a big environmentalist either. Technology has allowed us to grow lots of crop. But it's also technology that's sendin' us backwards on the other side. Every time you put out fertilizer or chemical, you know it's gonna rain someday and it's gonna run off, it's gonna get into the crick somewhere."

If this conservative friend of my father's knew this, I figure everyone does. It's just that few are as willing to admit to problems with technologies they've always viewed as progress.

Perhaps his willingness was inspired by hard times. A year after we spoke, my mother told me that he and his wife had lost their ranch. I don't know if they ceded it to the bank or sold it, retrieving only meager equity. All I know is that in his seventies, my father's friend had to go to work selling cars for a dealership in town. It was unimaginable to me that the handsome, successful, iconic couple of my childhood had become "all hat and no cattle," as Ward used to say about guys who dressed like cowboys but worked in other occupations.

It was probably unimaginable to them as well, as it would have been to me if someone had told me there would come a day when my family would no longer farm.

IV
KANSANS IN THE
CARIBBEAN

The psychological rule says that when an inner
situation is not made conscious, it happens outside, as
fate. That is to say, when the individual remains
undivided and does not become conscious of his inner
contradictions, the world must perforce act out the
conflict and be torn in opposite halves.

—C. G. JUNG

1

ONE YEAR AFTER WARD AND I BROKE UP, MY BROTHER BRUCE INVITED THE FAMILY ON A CHRISTMAS VACATION TO THE TURKS AND CAICOS ISLANDS, IN THE CARIBBEAN. "The trip will be our present to each other," he said. I couldn't believe such a familial, unironic sentiment was coming out of his mouth. He'd always prided himself on being unsentimental. It would turn out that he did have an ulterior motive.

So here we were descending the portable stairs of a little plane onto wet tarmac in Grand Turk. Dad never would have spent the money it took to fly the family to the Caribbean, and we, coming from that background of thrift, looked as if we'd stepped right out of Kansas in the middle of winter, which most of us had. The majority of us wore some variation of denim. Not Mom, of course. She had on a floral-print blouse and mint-green polyester pants she'd stitched in the middle of the previous century.

Jake still did not adhere to anyone's idea of fashion but his own. He wore a plaid cotton shirt and bright-green polyester pants he'd bought at Goodwill. At the last minute the day before, he'd refused to drive with me down to Denver and stay in a hotel so we could more easily catch our morning flight. He insisted that he needed to spend one more night with his girlfriend in the basement apartment they'd moved into as soon as he graduated from high school. Pounding on his door at four-thirty in the morning, I'd been worried he wouldn't answer.

He hadn't wanted to go anywhere with me since I'd sent him to the wilderness camp in Montana.

I was proud of him, though. For the last two months he'd been getting up early and driving to Cheyenne, where he did the most rugged work imaginable in a Wyoming winter—for a roofing company. And to my great relief, he did answer the door.

"I'm sorry about yesterday," he said as we drove over the mountain pass between Wyoming and Colorado at dawn. He'd been scared to leave, he confessed. He didn't know why. He held out his hand. "Look at me now. I've been shaking all morning."

Was there something he was hooked on? I worried. Something that he wouldn't have access to on a family vacation? But during the long day of traveling and talking, he assured me that his only addiction was to his girlfriend and the emotional safety she provided, apart from me and my corrective input.

And now we made the most of our time together. With and without his cousins we went snorkeling several times, paddled kayaks across turquoise water between islands of white sand, and explored a mangrove swamp. The two of us took turns driving a little rented jeep on the left side of the street, as local law dictated, through pothole minefields and throngs of children, chickens, and stray dogs. We ventured far, over a rough limestone road, to the windward end of the island, where we hiked down a trail carved between cliffs and played in steep waves, leaping them as they broke along the shore. Our daring reminded us both of the outdoor adventures we'd had before his rebellion had put us at odds.

Eighteen was the legal drinking age on the island, and each night Jake and my niece, Abby, would belly up to the poolside bar. After putting Mom to bed, I would join them for a round. I admonished Jake to limit himself to just two. "Sure, Mom! He will! I'll see to it!" Abby would call as I returned to my room. For hours afterward, her laughter would carry on the night breezes through my room's open window. Interspersed among the accented English of their islander mates were bars of Jake's laughter. It had been too long since I'd heard him laugh outside my window. It reminded me of the sound the paddles made knocking against the sides of our kayaks.

But all was not smooth paddling among the Bairs. Baking outdoors in the island's glare, we became hot and temperamental. We made scenes in public and played out our dramas over continental breakfasts, in the lobby and beach stores, and on the boats. We shouted at Mom, using her deafness as an excuse. Josh complained that he couldn't enjoy himself scuba diving because he had to look out for his girlfriend, Lace. She said get used to it, she was always looking out for their daughter, Jess, at home. On several occasions, my sister-in-law, Kris, took care of Jess so that the couple could have some alone time, but when alone together, they fought. Bruce withdrew to his room, where he played his twelve-string guitar and drank six packs and bared his belly to the breeze from the air conditioner. It must have been hard on his nerves, trying to ensure everyone's happiness.

We fulminated over ten-dollar hamburgers but kept slapping down our credit cards, tapping reserves of money stored over years of irrigated grain harvests. What else could we do? We had to eat. Mom surprised us by growing quickly accustomed to the prices. Dad had always said she could pinch a penny so hard it turned into a dime. Now she said, "I may as well enjoy all this money while I still can." What a strange philosophy. Was this the real Jasmin, emerging from the shadow of Harold? If she could change, then were we changing too?

How was it that our family, who had not spent more than a few nights under the same roof since we left the farm, had chosen to be here together? Feeling the strangeness of this, I imagined that the laughter I heard at night was not Jake's, but my brother Clark's, rising through the grate in my farm bedroom's pine floor.

One night, I dreamed that I woke and stumbled out to morning coffee to see Dad sitting across from Mom, wearing the dapper straw hat he reserved for summer trips to town, along with adobe-colored pants and a linen jacket like Pablo Neruda had worn in that movie I saw about his years on Capri.

I woke that morning to roosters crowing. "Listen!" Mom said, from the bed next to mine in the room we shared. "For a minute there I thought we were back on the farm."

THE FARM TURNED OUT TO BE BRUCE'S ulterior motive. Halfway into our weeklong vacation, he asked us all to a group dinner. This was heartening, as we had been straggling off to separate restaurants for our meals.

After we'd devoured the pork, conch, and shrimp dinners he'd paid for, he said, "I gathered you here for a reason."

The rest of us glanced at one another. He gathered us? A reason? Oh God, here it is, I thought, reaching for my beer.

"I will manage the farm for two more years, but I'm giving you my notice. You all will have to decide what to do with it, because I quit." He said he was tired, that the many decisions and responsibilities were beginning to weigh on him. He was almost sixty and he wanted to have his mind back. He wanted to relax and create. He was getting better on the twelve-string and wanted to sit around at bluegrass festivals jamming with his friends. He wanted to travel more in Mexico and Central America.

Abby clapped.

Kris said, "Good for you, Bruce!"

"Yes, good for you," I said.

Mom repeated what she'd said at least twenty times since Dad died. "Harold and I talked about this. He knew we might have to sell it someday. He said that it would be all right." But my father had thoroughly driven into me the commandment that we hang on to our land. I couldn't accept the forgiveness in that final sentiment. *It's not easy to acquire it, so hang on to it, goddamn it. A lot of sacrifice went into getting it and keeping it. Don't fritter it away!*

"Sell it, if that's what you all decide," Bruce now said. "I plan to enjoy my retirement. If the next generation wants to take over the farm from Ron and me, fine. Now's the time to begin learning what you need to know."

I could see a quickening in Josh as his father focused on him. He responded with a treatise more personal than any ever spoken at a Bair table, about how he'd been searching for a purpose in life. He hadn't gone to college because school wasn't really his thing. He knew he wasn't getting anywhere working for the cable company as an installer. This would be a great opportunity for him, he said. "It's what Grandpa would have wanted."

"But you need to do what you want," I said.

"That's right," Kris said.

"I would be really grateful if all of you would give me a chance. I won't let you down."

"Think about it," Bruce said. "You don't have to decide right now. Jake, you deserve a chance at this too."

Jake, who must have felt like young Arthur about to pull Excalibur from the stone, spoke carefully and thoughtfully, as he imagined a man should in the circumstances. "Josh and I could run the farm together. He could manage it and I could do the tractor work. He could learn from you, and I could learn from Ron."

"Ron isn't that keen on teaching you," Bruce warned. "But we do pay his salary. Whatever the rest of you decide, I mean what I've said tonight. I'm quitting. It's up to you."

Given that Bruce once had his own chance to fill Dad's shoes, I understood why he felt he must offer our boys a shot. But I knew Jake and Josh would never take over the farm. They hadn't been hardened into the demands of the life as Clark and Bruce had been. They hadn't spent every summer day in a tractor seat since they'd turned twelve. Hadn't frozen their fingers January nights midwifing sheep or milked the cow each winter morning before getting on the school bus at six-thirty. They hadn't pitched hay, stacked milo, driven wheat trucks, shoveled grain into bins, walked irrigation pipe, dug postholes, strung barbed wire. Nor done the one bit of farm work Bruce still performed, drilling wheat each September for two weeks, twelve incessant hours each day, overcoming bleariness and lack of sleep. They had no idea how lonely it would be, living where the only companionable beings would be their dogs and cats and possibly their girlfriends, although I couldn't imagine

Lace consenting to raising Jess on the farm. No way would Jake's girl-friend, a mountain-camping westerner, want to live there.

THE NEXT MORNING I AWOKE WHEN THE first rooster crowed, before dawn. I grabbed a blanket from my bed and went onto the pool deck, where I lay down in a plastic lounger, watched the last stars fade, and tried to think. With my eyes closed and drifting in and out of sleep, it was easy to imagine this whole foreign escapade as one of those dreams where I hadn't attended class all semester, and now it was time for the test. I was about to be flunked out of my own identity.

Somehow, I'd managed to go on thinking that I was synonymous with my family's land through all the changes, even through my parents' abandonment of the Carlson farm, and my own and my brothers' aban-donments of our father, the man who kept it going in our absences. When I was eighteen and hadn't wanted to settle for being just a wife married to "just" a farmer, I'd depended on Dad to be a farmer. Even as I refused to embrace the unglamorous lifestyle, I took pride in his mastery and success and in the land that empowered him. Through him, it empowered me. I could go make my mark in the world, and the ground of my being would be there waiting for me anytime I wanted to touch in. Now it seemed that I'd been playing hooky for decades. Until Ward came along, I hadn't even realized I'd been absent.

Those tears Dad cried when I wouldn't stay home that summer and farm—they were for me. They were for all of us. He foresaw this day as clearly as if it were tattooed on his hairy forearm.

I rolled over and was startled to see Jake getting a cup of coffee from the urn the waiter had set out for early birds. The sun had only just begun to burnish the tops of the palms. When he lived with me, he never got up without my practically having to throw firecrackers under his bed. I closed my eyes. Maybe he would think I was sleeping.

The legs of a patio chair screeched against the concrete as he dragged it over, making that pretense impossible. "Good morning," I said. "You're up early."

"I didn't sleep much."

"I don't think any of us did."

He leaned his elbows on his knees and cradled his coffee cup between his hands. "So what do you think?"

I knew the vision that danced in Jake's head. He saw himself working side by side with Josh, Ron, and Bruce. Male solidarity. "Jake, it's not realistic. You don't know all you'd have to give up."

He took a gulp of coffee. "You're not going to let me do this, are you?"

"Let you? It's not up to me."

"Don't stand in my way!" he shouted. Somewhat inadvertently but also somewhat purposefully, he tipped over the chair he'd been sitting in, dumped the remainder of his coffee in a bougainvillea bush, and left.

That night I knocked on Bruce's door.

Kris opened it a crack. Her protective instincts had kicked into full gear. Behind her, Bruce sat on the bed, hunched over his guitar. "Come in," he said resignedly, that jagged edge to his voice. Kris opened the door.

"I cannot bear to look upon that which I have wrought," he confessed.

"That which Harold wrought," Kris corrected.

She was right. Dad had placed a guilt bomb in each of us and set it to explode shrapnel in our brains if we ever contemplated selling. Bruce had merely detonated the bomb.

I said, "Our kids aren't equipped for it, Bruce."

"Why not?" he almost shouted. "Maybe Josh will surprise you. Maybe Jake will."

"That's what they think, but we didn't raise them in the life."

"That's exactly why they want it," Bruce said. "Anyway, it's out of my hands." He got up and reached into the room's refrigerator. "Want a Presidente? Bottled right here in the Caribbean."

"No, thanks."

He sat down with a groan, opened his beer, and picked up his guitar.

I returned to my room. Mom had her yellow hairnet on, which matched her yellow nylon nightgown. She looked fragile, but less so than when we'd first arrived. The trip was doing her good. Her back didn't even seem to hunch as much. She had the beginnings of osteoporosis, but was trying to stave it off with the calcium tablets she chewed with every meal. "I think I'll sit up and read a little," she said, getting one of the *Newsweek*s she'd brought from her suitcase. She flicked on the lamp over the corner stuffed chair. "I'm not very tired tonight." Unlike everyone else, she seemed undisturbed by Bruce's news. Not much bothered her anymore. This calm was not solely the product of her habitual repression. She seemed to have entered that state of saintly acceptance achieved by the most gracious of the elderly.

Bruce's Dylan-esque voice reverberated across the stone tile of the hallway. *From this valley they say you are going / We will miss your bright eyes and sweet smile.*

Mom leaned back in the chair and closed her eyes. "My," she said, "isn't Bruce getting good on his guitar?"

He'd probably been anguishing for months over this decision. Kris was right to be protective of him.

ABBY WAS FEELING PROTECTIVE TOO. THAT NIGHT when I joined her at the bar, she said, "The farm was going to kill Dad, and now it's going to kill Josh. I won't stand for that!"

"Oh come on, Abby."

"I mean it, Aunt Julie."

"Your grandfather survived until he was eighty-two."

"But my dad is not Harold. Thank God! And neither is Josh."

"Nor is Jake," I said. Although he'd apologized for his anger earlier, this was the first night he hadn't come out to the bar.

Abby took a drag on her cigarette. "Nor Jake. It will kill them and we can't let that happen!"

"Those are just clove, right?"

She leaned down to reach into her purse, her blouse so tight and low cut that I wanted to suggest she go put on a comfortable T-shirt. "Be natural, be wholesome," I wanted to say. But she was well into her twenties, the man-alluring years. And judging by the stares of the young island men sitting near us, she was succeeding. Their white shirts and loosened ties indicated they were clerks, free for the remainder of the night from their jobs in nearby hotels. She sat up, handing me a cigarette. I said, "I quit again a year ago. But this won't do any harm, right?"

"No, you'll be fine." With a bar match, she lit the slender, delectable, brown cigarette for me. "I could go back there and do it," she said. "I'm smart. I could manage it."

It amazed me how strong the call of farm duty was in the kids. Except for a couple of years when she was little and Bruce was attempting to work for Dad, Abby had never lived on the farm. The complete animaled and peopled Carlson farmstead that Bruce and I had grown up on was ancient history by then. But Dad bought her a goat, Schwanlea, that she loved. Schwanlea and her grandfather's passion had apparently been enough to ensnare her too.

"I would go and do it if only to save Josh," she said. "But who would I ever find to love me there?"

"I can tell you from experience. No one." Ward had been a grass man, not a dirt man, I reminded myself. He had not been the answer to this dilemma. There was no answer except complete personality changes and sacrifices none of us would be willing to make.

"Maybe you could do it, Abby," I said." But you'd have to really want to. You'd be throwing away all hope of a social life, and forget about your real career plans. And you would hate the chemicals and the irrigation as much as I do."

She reared back on her barstool. "Oh the folly!" she shouted at the palm fronds above us. The island men laughed, and I resisted putting my hand on her arm.

"The sheer unadulterated folly! Folly, Aunt Julie—I know you know this—is totally nonclassist and doesn't care which old patriarchal noggin it invades. Whether it's King Lear's or Harold Bair's."

"Let's move over to the pool chairs," I suggested.

Once we were resituated, Abby picked up her theme. "Okay, Jane Smiley keyed in on it too, but it doesn't take a genius to see, if you've read Shakespeare and you ever knew any old farming geezers like Grandpa, that they're all on a power trip."

I felt dizzy, as if I'd downed a barbiturate laced with speed. I looked at the brown wand in my hand. Was there tobacco in it? I'd thought they had only clove in them. Through a gap in the curtains, I could see Jake's profile as he sat watching the TV. I didn't want him to catch me smoking. I remembered the night we'd gone to the *Fellowship of the Ring* with Ward and I'd bought him a pack of Marlboros. Ward had reprimanded me, not for buying them but for complaining about buying them. "Cut it out," he'd said, as if he'd earned the right to interfere. Only later, postbreakup, did Jake's unannounced return to his grandmother's the following morning make sense. How had it made him feel to see the only authority figure he could count on curtly silenced by the cowboy dude she'd gone all ape over? Which was the worse addiction, his to cigarettes or the one we shared to the myths attendant on dads? Which drug had I been pushing to the most ill effect?

I put the cigarette out in the same bougainvillea bush he'd dumped his coffee in. That poor bush.

Like Lear, Abby continued, Harold had been self-deluded about the incomparable value of his domain. "His estate," she said, "meaning everything he had to offer, not just his land. His place in the universe. His mightiness."

"Wow, you're so smart, Abby. How'd you get so smart?" A tobacco high and my second beer induced a sisterly solidarity, along with a euphoric sense of tragedy.

"And of course, you know who played the role of Cordelia."

"Me? That would be the obvious choice since I was the only girl in the family."

"No. Dad did. Bruce. Your brother!"

"Oh right. The falsely judged, least rapacious one of our lot."

"*More sinned against than sinning.* He tried to farm with Grandpa because that's what he loved doing more than anything else, growing things. Look at his gardens. He has ripe tomatoes in June! Not even Grandma has ripe tomatoes in June. But Grandpa treated him like a slave, so he resorted to newspaper work. I'm sorry, Aunt Julie, but you got help from Grandpa. Dad didn't."

It's demoralizing to learn a sibling's opinion of you from his child. How widespread and solidified had this version of 'Julie' become? "Oh Abby. Your father doesn't know how much I hated having to go back home."

"All broke and pregnant?"

I downed my beer. "Exactly how I like to put it."

"And you didn't have a wife to support you," Abby said, conciliatorily. Bruce had lived off Kris's wages for a while after he quit small-town journalism.

I felt around in the bougainvillea pot.

"I'd give you another, but I'm all out," Abby said. As she went to reposition herself on the lounger, her foot shot out and kicked over her beer, breaking the bottle.

"God, Abby, you're drunk. Don't cut yourself."

"I won't. I guess you weren't exactly Regan or Goneril either. And I don't think Clark was, certainly. He didn't take anything, just disappeared honorably, as Cordelia did. Actually, you were all Cordelia. All any of you ever wanted was to make him proud."

"True."

"Me too, Aunt Julie," she pleaded.

"Oh Abby." I reached and she leaned into my hug. A sob escaped her. With one hand, I pushed her long dark-auburn hair behind her ear, dropping its weight onto her back. I rested my hand on the corsetlike blouse she wore. The flesh over her shoulder blades felt cool—soft and foreign. I wished I'd held her more often when she was a child, wished we had all lived closer. I knew how she must have suffered, as we all did, glimpsing displeasure in Dad's glances. She had a brilliant mind but wore a few extra pounds. Dad judged women primarily by their physical characteristics.

Perhaps that's why I'd dreamed of him dressed as Pablo Neruda. I'd always longed for some refinement in him—the understanding of each of our souls that would have come with that.

That night, Abby and I figured everything out for everybody. We would sell the farm. I would invest the proceeds, continuing my role as the family's money manager. The boys, if they wanted to be family heroes, could learn a trade, then we could set them up in business together. We could buy them a house to renovate in the central Kansas town where Bruce lived. He could supervise the first project, and then they'd be on their own.

It all sounded so sane to me then, after two beers and one clove cigarette.

BBY'S AND MY PLANS FOR JAKE AND JOSH NEVER MATERIALIZED. Jake said he wanted to try farming, so I encouraged him to demonstrate his eagerness by moving to Goodland. He could show up on the farm every morning and make himself useful. I would clear the way for him—arrange it with Ron, help him find a house to rent, and then help him move. Understandably, he didn't take me up on that offer. It would have required uncommon determination and self-confidence to go down there and foist himself, a green beginner, on Ron, who could not have hidden his disdain. Those raised in the life don't respect those who weren't.

Josh and Lace broke up, and the cable company he worked for promoted him and transferred him to Corpus Christi, where he could go scuba diving every weekend if he wanted to. He met a woman, married her, and his daughter, Jess, now had a baby brother. Josh's new wife was a showy dresser from the Dominican Republic. She lived in a sea of family who'd immigrated to Corpus Christi. Imagining her in the old farmhouse or in the double-wide, surrounded by fields of corn and wheat, was as absurd as picturing a toucan roosting among the pigeons in our old sheep barn.

The summer after our trip to the Turks and Caicos, I found my own new love. My attraction to Jim, an engineer who lived and worked a two-hour drive south of Laramie, in Colorado, was rooted in my wilderness passions. We swam in mountain lakes, paddled rivers, camped and skied together. Jim also shared my politics, and when we danced, our bodies moved in natural rhythm, like two ocean waves.

On our second date, for a swim in Lake Hattie, I happened to ask Jim if he knew my cousin's ex-husband, who, like Jim, had once worked for Hewlett Packard. I didn't think it likely, as Jim said there had been more than fourteen hundred employees at the Colorado division when he worked there. It turned out that my cousin's husband had once taken Jim pheasant hunting on his mother-in-law's—my aunt Bernice's—land in western Kansas. During the trip they visited a farmstead that had a couple of Quonsets, a barn-shaped house, and a double-wide trailer on it. Jim distinctly remembered meeting an old man on that farm. They'd talked for quite a while. For an atheist who once compared what happens when we die to the fate of a jack rabbit hit by a car—*Bang! When you're dead, you're dead!*—my father sure had an uncanny way of making his presence felt after his own death.

After dating Jim for a little over a year, I sold my beautiful old house and moved to Colorado to live with him. Almost immediately I made new friends, many of them writers whose work inspired my own.

My professional horizons had widened and I was in a committed relationship. So when Bruce e-mailed to say he'd "had about enough"— of farming, that is—and that a real estate agent he'd been flirting with said he had a "hard offer," I believed I was ready to let the farm go as easily as I had Laramie and the beautiful old house.

I thought I understood things so much better now. How lucky I was that I hadn't moved back to Kansas to be with Ward. I recalled the dream I'd had after Clark died. At first I had tried to put a pleasant spin on it, thinking wasn't that nice? Clark was protecting Jake from falling off that seed drill, the same way he used to protect me. But the dream's vibe had been grim, not reassuring. And I knew it had been about all of us, not only Clark and Jake. To be born in Dad's lineage was to be conscripted into subliminal servitude to his passions. When Ward broke up with me, I reasoned, he saved me from a fate worse than my own death—accompanying my father into his. I still believe this. But today I know that you can't cast out your demons with one decisive or, as it would be in Bruce's and my case, indecisive act.

That supposedly hard offer didn't come through, but Ron's emphysema had gotten so bad that he now needed oxygen in order to sleep at night. The "end game," as Bruce called it, was on. We both thought we should sign before what was obviously a national real estate bubble collapsed, but neither of us was ready.

Despite his apparent certainty in the Turks and Caicos, Bruce now wrote in an e-mail that he was *having a lot of problems dealing with the sale of the farm as it has given us all nice lives.* For a man in my family to say he was having a lot of problems with anything was like my saying it was tearing my guts out, which it was.

When we finally signed, the real estate agent succinctly boiled the work of our parents' and grandparents' lifetimes down to thirteen words:

> SHERMAN County
> 21 Quarters irrig., dry land, grass,
> CRP. Nice improvements. 5 wells.

The farm stayed on the market for a year before we had an offer, for a third less than we were asking. "I am not going to give it away," Bruce said.

Another year went by. Then Congress passed a new energy bill upping the percentage of biofuel required in gasoline. The main source of that, given the cropping patterns already established, was ethanol from corn. Ethanol distilleries sprang up in the Midwest and on the Great Plains, and corn prices began to creep higher. It had also begun to rain again.

At night, across the land, along with toad song in the prairie potholes, droned the snores of once sleepless farmers, their dreams overflowing with burgeoning grain bins. The people who'd made the first offer came back with a higher one. Still too low for Bruce, and our accountant warned it would be risky to carry the note for the buyers, who had never farmed on this scale.

Even though I could see it would be a gamble, I argued for accepting their offer. If we were going to commit identity suicide, I wanted to pull the trigger and get it over with. But I needn't have worried, or perhaps I should have, because the revolver's chamber clicked forward and within a week came a third offer, fully loaded. The amount we were asking, in annual installments. It came from three brothers. They were megafarmers headquartered in a little town not far over the Colorado border, where they had a big feedlot. Altogether they owned one hundred sections—one hundred square miles. I didn't like the idea of the farm's being absorbed by such a huge operation and suggested that our other prospect should be granted an opportunity to counter. But the accountant and bank officer who oversaw Dad's trust took comfort from the megafarmers' solid financial statement, assuring us that an operation that size would never renege on the loan. The consensus was that we shouldn't let them slip away.

BEFORE WE COULD REGISTER THE SOUND OF the hammer cocking, Bruce and I found ourselves in Goodland for the final negotiations. We met at Mom's house, although she didn't live there anymore. On one of my visits, she and I had toured Wheat Ridge Acres, the appropriately named local assisted-living place. In the dining room, she ran into some farm neighbors she and Dad used to play pitch with on winter Saturday nights. That comforted her, and in her usual reasonable manner, she had agreed to move. She'd remained reasonable throughout our discussions of the farm sale too, compassionately reiterating that "Harold foresaw this. He said it would be all right."

In advance of this day, I had e-mailed Bruce, suggesting we have lunch together in order to come up with a negotiating strategy. "I'll go," he said now, "but there's no way to wriggle out of this. We signed a good-faith contract with the agent, remember? And he got our asking price for us."

"I didn't say anything about wriggling out of it."

We must have planned to pick up Mom after lunch. That must have been why we took her car. I chose one of Goodland's only bows to the yuppie aesthetic, a restaurant in an old brick building overshadowed by grain elevators on the north end of Main. It had big swaths of plateglass I'd never noticed before, probably because the windows had been heavily draped back when it was home to the Moose lodge.

I'd always been curious about what went on in the town's male hangouts—the pool halls, for instance, that I'd envied Bruce for frequenting as a teenager. Surely, he was having way more fun in them than I would ever be allowed to have in Goodland.

I marveled at the building's splendor, for this town. An embossed-tin ceiling painted a sumptuous chocolate-brown. A new wood floor. Was it ash or birch? A copper countertop. "Where do you want to sit?" I asked.

"I don't care. Anywhere."

A corner table seemed appropriate, given that we had private business to discuss. All week long, ever since I'd heard, I'd been reviewing my reasons. I had no faith in our ability to replace Ron, as I remembered too well the many hired men who had become fired men in our childhoods. Renting would be no less of a gamble. What if the renter didn't work out? Even if we were physically able to farm ourselves, which we weren't, we wouldn't have the equipment anymore to farm with. Equipment depreciated rapidly. You couldn't just let it sit in case you might need it again someday. If we heeded what the climate scientists were saying, the drought might return soon and settle in for decades or longer. And I'd taken Bruce at his word in the Caribbean. He needed to quit, for his happiness and to lower his stress. If he continued, then got sick or died, what would I do then? Even if I had the know-how, I didn't want to run the chemically intensive, water-guzzling farm our place had become.

Bruce flipped open his sandwich, sighed with disgust, and scraped off the feta cheese and dried cranberries. I said, "So I was thinking, we don't have to roll over and take whatever terms they offer. If you have any doubts—"

"I invited Ron to the meeting," Bruce said. "I know he doesn't have a direct role in this financially. But we owe him that. I don't care what you think."

"Of course we owe him. I want him there too." Bruce and Ron had become close over the last ten years of working together, and Bruce had always bent over backward to be fair to him. Ron probably had one of the only profit-sharing agreements in Sherman County. That treatment would have elicited anyone's loyalty, but Ron would have given it to us anyway. He was made that way. Bruce had once told me that he and Ron were alike—a type of plainsmen who hardly existed anymore. Bruce was too original to say "dying breed," but he might as well have. Me too, I had wanted to tell him. I'm one of us too.

He was eating his sandwich as if it were a chore. "The terms are fine," he said, dismissing my whole reason for wanting to talk. Because really, maybe it wasn't too late. All we'd have to do was put up a fuss over a detail. Demand an extra half point of interest perhaps. That's if Bruce wasn't 100 percent on board. There had been that one e-mail when he'd done an about-face in the middle of a discussion of real estate agents and land values and had put forth what must have struck him as a brilliant idea: He would continue managing the farm if I would grant him 51 percent ownership so that I couldn't sell it out from under him when Mom died.

Although I'd been offended at the thought of his having all the say, the idea had appealed to me somewhat because it would have granted me a reprieve. I wasn't sure who I was going to be when this was all over. But the thought of Bruce taking on the farm, given his age and previously stated concerns, didn't inspire much confidence in me.

I said I would make it easy for him to buy my half if that's really what he wanted. He replied that the proposal had been just a backup plan in case we couldn't sell.

What I hadn't understood was the inordinate power that uncertainty cedes to certainty, even if the certainty is just an act.

So here we were. Me with my unfailing appetite. Bruce dutifully chewing.

"We're going to have to find places to put all the money," he said.

"I've been working on it. My financial guy says we can make five percent even if we—"

"Five percent how?" Bruce asked.

"CDs, except—"

"Five isn't that good," he said. "The farm did better than that every year for the last—"

"I wish you wouldn't interrupt me when I'm trying to explain something."

Bruce abruptly shoved his plate aside, then got up. Without saying a word, he walked out the door. I watched through the remarkably large, remarkably clear glass beside me as he tossed the keys through the open window of Mom's LeSabre.

He crossed the street, his back and shoulders hunching as Dad's used to do when he or Clark had done something really stupid, like twist a field implement around a telephone pole or forget to turn off the diesel tank so that all the fuel siphoned out onto the ground.

And they were left just standing there, wondering if they'd lost his love.

IT WAS AS IF WE'D ALREADY TAKEN the step down in stature that our imminent landlessness foretold. The First National Bank's trust officer ushered Mom and me into the staff break room in the basement. Bruce, Ron, the real estate agent, our lawyer, and two accountants were sitting around a table with a Masonite top and folding metal legs like those you see in church basements. The last time we met at the bank, to sign papers shortly after Dad's death, we'd been given the plush conference room. The coffee was made in this room and brought to that one, paneled in mahogany and carpeted in green. To symbolize money, I assumed. On this day the casters of its big cushioned chairs were no doubt straining under the weight of the farm's prospective buyers. The three brothers were as large as linebackers, our real estate agent told us.

Earlier, Bruce had been wearing jeans and a blue Levi's shirt, both faded and baggy. Now he wore white pants and a white jacket over a bold orange-and-green shirt. His Panama hat lay upside down on the chair beside him. Here would be our Pablo Neruda, except he didn't look dapper in summer linen. He looked rumpled and distorted. His beard and hair and eyebrows were all out of hand, as usual. But this seemed preferable today. Any trimming would have left a face and eyes too glaring in their nakedness. I wished he hadn't stomped out earlier. But what had I expected? If we could talk, we probably wouldn't be here.

"Tell 'em we'll throw the wind rights in for free," Bruce said to the real estate agent, then grinned. He was lampooning his own efforts, in the late nineties, to lease our land's wind rights to a Dutch developer, who, during the six-year term of the option to explore, never set up a single wind meter.

Ron, sitting beside Bruce, laughed sarcastically. "He's a firecracker," Dad had often said about Ron. Tightly wound, high-strung, he had the look of a classic cowboy—scrawny bowlegs and nonexistent butt, ruddy skin and face. I'd found out when I'd pastured my horse Henry on the farm for a while that he had no affinity for equines, but that didn't prevent him from wearing shirts that snapped.

The real estate agent had been a popular kid in high school. The banker, also a hometown boy, still called him Butch. When first we asked for a shorter term on the note, then wanted to tie the interest rate to prime, Butch said, "Okay," his voice quaking as if he were afraid to risk the linebackers' wrath. But we hurled him out our room's door and down the hall anyway, like a ball we were working toward our questionable goal.

What would we really be losing? I asked myself. Only some minor conveniences and imagined possibilities. I wouldn't be able to leave my dog on the farm when I traveled anymore. None of us could park our old vehicles in the implement lot as we'd always done, with intentions of rebuilding the engines someday, then watch as, over the decades, they became classics, their book value increasing and their conditions worsening as their tires cracked and hired hands' children shattered the windshields with stones or bullets. When the big flu epidemic or nuclear war hit, we wouldn't be able to reunite on the farm, a cohesive family once again, raising our chickens and watering our vegetable garden with the aid of a windmill.

While we waited for Butch to return from the conference room, one of the accountants said he'd begun investing in Conservation Reserve Program ground, land that the government paid farmers to set aside. Once the contract term ran out, the land could be grazed.

"Lots of farmers in the Texas Panhandle are grazing cattle on their former corn land," I declared, true, as ever, to my obsession over the declining Ogallala. "Only because they have to, of course. They don't have enough water left to raise corn or soybeans. Used it up."

Was it my imagination, or were those scoffing looks on the faces of the men around the table? "We should start doing that here," I added, "before we use up most of our water too. We could sell the beef directly off the grass and just skip the corn-fattening step."

"Oh no!" objected Ron. "We're not going back fifty years."

Fifty years to when no one had ever heard of a feedlot. I didn't want to challenge Ron, whose invitation to this meeting was meant to honor him. The accountant spared me that, saying, "People underestimate the organic and natural-meat markets. The demand has more than doubled over the last several years."

The banker said that his daughter had made the mistake of ordering a sirloin from a grass-finished steer in a fancy city restaurant. Finding it tougher than shoe leather, she had coveted his juicy conventional filet.

"Argentine beef is fed nothing but grass," I said.

"And it's supposed to be the best in the world," added the accountant.

That's not fair, I imagined Bruce saying. Comparing Argentine to American beef is like comparing sun perch to carp, but when I glanced over at him, he didn't even seem aware we'd been talking.

Butch opened the door, but paused with his hand on the knob. Beaming, he cast his gaze slowly around the room. That fetching school-boy smile must have been the cornerstone of his teenage popularity. He gently closed the door.

The gun fired.

"We have a deal," he said.

"Yahoo!" said the accountant.

The banker said, "I'll draw up the acceptance."

Bruce began to speak but interrupted himself. "I can't—" He placed his Panama hat on his balding head and stood. "Send me any-thing you need me to sign," he said, his voice breaking as he rushed from the room.

Had I been twenty years younger, I would have begun to question our accomplishment in that moment, based solely on Bruce's reaction. At fifty-seven, determined to experience my own feelings, I went through a brief elated phase—that of winning a game or concluding any business successfully. I hugged each of the people there, Kansans all, who only hug their moms and spouses.

Mom smiled graciously and thanked everyone as they congratu-lated her. I held her arm to steady her as she eased her walker into the elevator, then helped her into the car so that I could drive her back to Wheat Ridge Acres. Not only had she lost her husband and most of her friends to death, she was now reduced to living in two small rooms. But ownership, the clinging to stuff, she knew on some unarticulated level, was a misplaced passion. She maintained her equanimity by focusing on each moment—that and the immediate future. Her next hair ap-pointment. Or her favorite TV program, *Wheel of Fortune.*

She tilted back her lift chair and pushed the button on her remote control. "Oh good," she said, "It's starting. I didn't miss a thing."

It frustrated me that she seemed to have no misgivings about what we'd done. In me, remorse was setting in. I had closed my eyes and kept them closed until the gun fired. They now opened onto unendurable fact.

"One hundred years," I said to Mom.

She pulled her eyes away from the TV. "What?"

"One hundred years. Your dad traded his Texas land for his Kansas land in 1906."

"That's right. He did. Sight unseen," she said proudly.

"And now it's 2006. Isn't that strange that we'd choose to sell exactly one hundred years after your family arrived?"

"Uh-huh, it is strange," she said, returning her attention to Vanna White's spin of the wheel.

It was like trying to get an emotional reaction out of a turnip, and it was probably wrong to try. What did I want? For her to feel as bad as I did? The one person who did was probably heading down the interstate toward his home. If he'd stayed, he couldn't have hugged me or forgiven me anyway, and if he'd blamed me out loud, I would have cried. Tears in this family were an abomination, as ugly as cutworms, green and squirming in spring soil, and as dangerous to us as the actual worms were to crops. They might cut off our dignity at its roots in our stoicism.

So I did what instinct always told me to do when I was upset in Kansas. I drove out to the farm. The three hundred trees I'd gotten Dad to purchase from the Soil Conservation Service the year Jake turned one were now full grown. The cedars had thickened so much I couldn't see through them to the back row of sandhill plums. "Quit if you want to," Dad had told the hired man, "but she's your boss today." The entitlement I'd felt over that! The ownership.

The old windbreak west of the farmstead, planted God knew how long ago, raised a few rheumatoid fingers against the winter sky. Ron had taken his chainsaw to most of the dead trees. He burned the logs in the double-wide's fireplace, the one I'd ordered with the intention of hanging on to the promising young couple Dad had hired. Not long after that couple quit, Ron and Nila made us all grateful that they had.

Kittens rolled and mewed on the double-wide's front steps. Black, black and white, yellow, gray. Needing a drink of water and to use the bathroom, I knocked, but Ron and Nila must not have come home from town yet. I turned on the step and took in the silence, ubiquitous, like the sun.

In the shop, breathing the scent of dusty grease and oil; in the old house, staring into the living room where Dad and Jake used to take naps together on the couch; in the sheep barn, remembering the joy implicit in so much baaing life; in every inch of the farm, I recalled my father's presence. I drove past the cattle troughs, unused since his death. The hog pens, quiet since my departure in the eighties. If one quality most characterized the place, it was vacancy.

In the old implement lot, I stopped and got out of my car. The grass stretching from there to the first sprinkler-irrigated field was the only flat pastureland for miles around that hadn't been plowed. Sitting on the iron seat of an ancient, rusted wheat drill, I floated for a few final moments on the quietude.

A red-tailed hawk was perched on a fence post opposite me, watching the ground for mice. At dusk the coyotes would be yodeling over their conquests and yearnings. When spring came and the grass greened, the satiny ribbons of the meadowlarks' calls would wind through the sky, as absent in its blueness as my absence would be. I would never again hear those calls winding around me in that particular place, tying me to it with their gentle, melodious bonds.

Sliding to the ground, I ran my palm over the grass. The blades were curled and tawny, many of them streaked in red and burgundy. It comforted me knowing that at least this one patch of mild, short-grass prairie would outlast me. Each evening of every season in the years to come, it would swallow the setting sun, as it had always done. I wished that, rather than burying Clark and Dad in the Goodland cemetery, we had cremated them and spread their ashes here.

Then the one thing I hadn't considered hit me.

"No!" I yelled into the deafness surrounding me. "What have I done?" The linebackers would not have any use for grass.

V
THE OGALLALA ROAD

*Now, on the road to freedom, I was pausing for a
moment near Temuco and could hear the voice of
the water that had taught me to sing.*

—PABLO NERUDA

1

I SAT IN THE HALLWAY OF AN OLD DORMITORY, ON A CAMPUS THAT WAS ONCE A SEMINARY, IN CAÑON CITY, COLORADO. It was 2008, two years after we'd sold the farm. The organizers of the Buddhist retreat had placed wooden chairs outside three doors. Behind the doors, the teachers were granting private interviews. I was next in line for Terry. I'd chosen her because she was the only female teacher and because, when students asked questions after dharma talks, waves of empathetic emotion crossed her face, like the shadows of clouds sailing over the prairie.

I expected Terry to be in the lotus posture she had amazingly held throughout the previous day and a half of the retreat. But now she sat like a normal sixty-year-old, in a stuffed vinyl chair. She had long gray-blond hair and a welcoming presence.

How was the retreat going for me? Did I have any problems meditating for long periods, she asked.

No, other than I tended to get sleepy.

"That's not uncommon," Terry said. "Go take a nap if you need to. Sometimes people come here from working nonstop."

"That's me," I said. "I've been writing a book for what seems like forever."

"What is your book about?"

"At first it was about the Ogallala Aquifer, the water under the Great Plains. But it turned out it was about more than that. My family.

And this man I fell in love with who lived back there. Except he broke up with me, and then we sold our family farm. And I discovered that's what I'd been writing about all along."

"Selling the farm?"

"Yes. It was up to my brother and me to save it. I mean, this has nothing to do with the dharma or anything, but that's what I've been thinking about when I'm supposed to be meditating."

"Is your father still living?"

She does have a way, I thought. "He died . . . ten, no, eleven years ago now. I haven't quite come to terms with selling his farm. It's all he ever did. The retreat is helping, though. So thank you."

I was prepared to leave, but Terry's eyes kept me pinned. "I know it's just attachment and ego," I added, in an effort to be a good meditation student.

"It's okay to feel the pain," Terry said. "You're grieving a loss."

A warm sheet of tears filled my eyes. "It's hard to, I mean—"

Terry probed on. "Do you feel as if you sold your father when you sold the farm?"

A tsunami rose in my chest.

"Forgive yourself," Terry said.

The tsunami broke. I hadn't let myself cry this openly in front of anyone since Clark died—my face contorted, mouth open, lips down-stretched.

"Would he want you to feel bad?" Terry asked.

I could barely breathe, let alone answer. I grabbed a tissue from the strategically located box.

"He just wanted to share all he had with you," Terry said. "He wanted you to have his connection to the land."

Dabbing my eyes with the tissue, I said, "I'm not so sure about that part."

"No? Do you want to meditate on it for a minute?"

I sat up straight, assumed the posture, shoulders straight, feet planted parallel, hands on thighs.

Connected to the land. I tried that phrase out on the dad in memory, the dad who presided perennially in my psyche. His face turned red and he smirked with embarrassment and disdain, his hypertuned schmaltz detector going off.

No, we kids weren't supposed to hang on to our land because we were connected to it. We were supposed to hang on to it because it was *real* estate. It was real. The price might go up. It might go down. But it would always be there.

Cash would slip through our fingers. Stocks would crash. We would end up like Uncle Leonard in his decrepit trailer house with its weather-warped plywood porch on the edge of Goodland; or Aunt Ruth in her purple-and-yellow basement house; or Uncle Johnny, who had to come home and work for Dad because he lost all of his money investing in city real estate; or Uncle Raymond, who was ending his days in a VA home in South Dakota.

Broke, struggling for the rest of our lives to make ends meet.

Dad's parents and Mom's parents had managed to hold on through the thirties drought. Some said that the fifties drought had been even worse. And then along came Bruce and I, who sold in a wet year.

Then the other shoe dropped, as Dad liked to say. The government mandate on ethanol had caused the price of corn to triple. Land values tracked grain prices like a bird dog tracks scents. If we'd waited until now to sell, we could have gotten more than two times what we'd sold for. I imagined the three linebackers smirking. They had foreseen this.

At closing, they had sat across from Mom and me in the bank's green-carpeted room, three hulks who'd probably grown up on tractors and who'd given their dad what he wanted most, sons who farmed. And farmed. And farmed. I asked them flat out. "Are you going to plow that grass in the west pasture?"

The oldest one, the Harold in their clan, answered. "We paid dry cropland prices for it, so yes, we're going to farm it." Hell, yes, we are, he probably thought. Who does she think she is even asking? They didn't graze cattle themselves, apparently. They bought cattle off other people's grass and finished them in their feedlot.

They'd even planted all of the wheat ground to corn, Bruce said. Plus all of the irrigation circles. They must be using our water rights to the hilt. They must—

Terry touched my knee.

"I'm sorry," I said.

"Did you have any insights?"

"It was the connection to the land thing. Dad would never have used a phrase like that."

I watched her absorb this. She said, "He did have a connection, though."

I nodded. "Yes, but he didn't know it."

"So do you. You just have it in a different way."

"I guess," I said. "I'm not so sure anymore."

AFTER THE SALE, I BECAME A LOST soul without a construct. There were actually two constructs, and they'd always been in opposition—the conscious one of ourselves as landowners and our unconscious connection to the land.

On the Carlson farm, we'd all been part of a tapestry, a weave. There were animals and grains, vegetables and prairie, trees and people, play and work, mud and stars, the scents of manure and of flowers. I choose these things at random and it doesn't matter what order I list them in. A specific list of the "ten thousand things," to use a phrase from the *Tao Te Ching*, would fill many pages. They were all entangled, of a piece.

But when we traded that farm and moved to town, then when I left Kansas altogether, I became a lone thread. While I was trying to weave myself back into the natural world, in the mountains and deserts of California, my family's relationship with our land back home was continuing to unravel. Dad drove to it every day. He didn't live on it. Its meaning had shifted from the seat of our family's life to solely a source of revenue. Dad's success growing crops still affirmed and satisfied him, but his land had become more of a thing to him, and to us. It had become a financial asset, not who we were. It is no mistake that we use the same word in English to denote both financial worth and a moral principle we hold dear. In one line of reasoning, I actually obeyed my father's value system by violating his first precept. I thought selling was the best financial decision.

Today, farmland prices have tripled, a greater rise than my father saw in his lifetime. Would I sell again at triple the price? If I didn't share ownership and the decision were entirely up to me? Would I sell? Even if I knew the grass would be plowed and more of the water would be used? What bothers me more, the profits I missed out on or how our land is now being farmed? Could I have found a way to farm it sustainably that wouldn't have led to financial disaster and without having to give up the rest of my life? Should I have given up the rest of my life?

THERE ARE PEOPLE FOR WHOM CHOOSING TO farm is not a choice between doing right by the land and giving up the rest of their lives. For these people farming is their life. If it had been that way for me, then I never could have brought myself to sell.

My search for a way to meaningfully contribute, now that I no longer owned land, brought me to a book called *Inquiries into the Nature of Slow Money: Investing as if Farms, Food, and Fertility Matter.* The book's author, Woody Tasch, suggested that instead of chasing fast "hockey stick" growth of their assets, investors might want to emulate earthworms, and put their money to work aerating and providing nutrients to the soil of the new food economy. *We don't have to keep sending our money into distant, invisible portfolios, while wondering why Main Street is dying, our food is irradiated, and geneticists in China are breeding square apples.* After underlining that and much else, I closed the book thinking, That's what I want to be! An earthworm investor.

I finagled a press pass to a national Slow Money gathering in San Francisco, where I attended pitches by farmers, growers of grass-fed beef, innovative distributors of organic and locally grown food, and dozens of inspiring entrepreneurs. These ranged from the owner of a

Point Reyes, California, compost company that recycles manure from dairies, "closing the loop on poop," to a pair of young Seattle women who are repurposing shipping containers into grocery stores for "food deserts," those neighborhoods where you couldn't buy a carrot if your life depended on it. Which it might, the only option in those places being a steady diet of McDonald's or other brands of fat.

On returning home, I joined with some Coloradans I'd met at the conference to form our own Slow Money investment club. We have made two loans so far, one to a distributor of locally grown, mostly organic food and another to a company that grows vegetables in space-saving, aeroponic towers, which use water rather than soil to transfer nutrients to the plants. The company harvests the vegetables when they are still seedlings. Microgreens, they are called.

This type of investment does not come without risk. Last year the two community activists who spearheaded the investment club asked me to join with a few others in the group to help the region's largest organic farm stay in business. The farm had sold five thousand CSA, or community-supported agriculture, shares. In this arrangement, members help finance crops by paying in advance for weekly deliveries later, during the growing season. The vegetables and fruits had always come reliably in the past, March to November, rhubarb to rutabaga. But due to poor recent management, the farm was now on the verge of bankruptcy. They needed a large one-year loan in order to ensure delivery to those customers and to the many supermarkets that had added organics thanks to the reliability of this particular supplier. An investment partnership had been formed and a new experienced agricultural manager was now in charge, but no one could promise we would get our money back.

Woody Tasch argues that in order to build a saner food system, we will have to become "return agnostics" for a while. We've seen recent proof that the stock market is not that dependable either. And just think about the environmentally harmful and inhumane ways many stock-market profits are generated. That investment model originated and evolved when we had not become aware of planetary limits.

Hmm. No or little gain, possibly even a complete loss, helping a local organic farm stay in business versus investing in further environmental and social collapse. If I made this decision the way my father had farmed, with my focus solely on the bottom line, I would follow his tractor up and over that dream hill, ever the slave to his will and vision.

We lent them the money. At the end of the year the company entered bankruptcy proceedings and the investment partners had to take over farming operations, so we all had little choice but to re-up. I may never recoup my investment. But I don't feel nearly as bad about the decision to make that loan as I did about land values tripling after selling the farm. Because this time, instead of selling out of what I could no longer stand behind, I had bought into what I believed.

2

I DON'T KNOW WHY I HAVE TO DO THIS EACH TIME I COME HERE. After driving around for half an hour, leaving tracks in the snow up and down the cemetery, I spot them, and almost wish I hadn't. So . . . stonelike in their finality. BAIR. BAIR. No other words on this, the grave side of the stones, except at the bottom of Mom and Dad's, it says *Parents of Clark - Bruce - Julene*. On Clark's, Mom went all out, having his picture etched into the granite. He's doing what he'll be doing for the next however many hundreds of years, until some future civilization decides it wants the stone for another purpose. Dressed in his lab coat, he's pouring liquid from one test tube into another. The photo was taken when he still had a beard and most of his hair.

The surnames on the surrounding stones are the old family names, most of them associated with a section or more of land someplace in the county. The map that hangs in the registrar of deeds office over at the courthouse still has our name on it, but only because Bruce and I held back from the sale a half section of Conservation Reserve Program land that was too hilly to farm.

Our disappearance, by and large, from that map doesn't bother me as much as it has over the six years since the sale because on this visit home I've seen some heartening things. On a farm about halfway between Goodland and what was once our farm, I met Sherman County's largest organic farmer. Just having to use the superlative form of the adjective, alone, is amazing. There is more than one!

Yesterday, I sat in Stan and Becky Purvis's kitchen and heard Stan's story of growing up on the farm with one brother. They both wanted to come back, but their parents didn't have enough land to support three, or even two, families. Stan tried to farm anyway, but in the early nineties, after his dad called him an "environmental wacko" for experimenting with organic grains, he bought a truck and began a career hauling grain for others. Ten years later he was hauling a load of wheat to a Front Range mill for some Mennonites from the county south of ours when a number on the computer screen inside the scale house caught his eye. "Is that what you're paying for this wheat?" he asked. The guy inside said yes. Stan knew what he was going to be doing from then on.

It seemed fitting that he got his start in organic farming by following the Mennonites' lead. Kansas's early Mennonite settlers brought winter wheat to this country in the first place. They emigrated from the Russian steppes, where the climate and soils were very similar, and the wheat thrived here. Hard, red winter wheat. I'd heard the phrase since earliest childhood, when the market grain announcers on the radio spoke so fast the words blurred together. *Kansas City barley upapenny at three-twunny-three, sorghum's holding steady at two-eight-dee-nine. Hardredwinterwheat offanickel.* The Mennonites never stopped raising it the old way, without chemicals.

Stan's uncle helped him purchase some family land that his great-grandfather had homesteaded in 1886. He now received two to three times the price conventional growers did for not only his wheat but also everything from white corn to millet. The profits had made a convert even out of his dad, who let him take over his land when he retired. Stan now farmed fifteen hundred acres organically.

This was a lot for an organic operation, but not by plains conventional standards.

"Conventional agriculture is all about bigger equaling better," he said. "That has cost a lot of young farmers the ability to get in the game." For him, going with organics and not expanding beyond his ability to keep up with the crops, which do demand more cultivation and time, had been a way to stay on the farm. That was as philosophical as Stan got. He wasn't like the young farmers I've met along the Front Range who want to grow healthier food while building the soil, although when I mentioned earthworms—the real kind, not investors—he did affirm that his neighbors' soil probably had next to none, while he had plenty. And he was proud of that.

The wind blows stinging snow at my face, making me glad that I'm wearing my sunglasses. I usually want to rip them off here, to enjoy the colors in their pure form. I am bundled in my down coat and wool mittens over wool gloves, but my bottom half is cold already. On the back side of the stone, Clark is still doing his triathlete thing—swimming, biking, running.

And Dad still has his stalk of wheat. Mom has an iris.

What are you doing out here on a day like this?

Coming to see you, Mom. What'd you think?

Why didn't you wait for a nicer day?

I couldn't, Mom. Remember? I don't live here anymore.

Oh. Well, I still think you're crazy. I wouldn't be caught dead going out on a day like this.

There are many things I want to tell her. But it's too friggin' cold out. *Look, Mom, I brought you some flowers. Daffodils.*

It's crazy putting flowers out in this weather.

They're fake, Mom.

Well I know that.

I wanted to buy something better suited for winter, but there wasn't much choice at Walmart. I've been in town two days and already I've had to go out there three times. A whole town under a metal roof. There's Twila's, I think as I walk past the fabric section. There're four clothing stores. There's the shoe store. There're all three groceries—Safeway, Bogarts, and the IGA.

When the snow melts, Mom, it will be spring and yours will be the first ones. Bright yellow when no one else has even a bud showing.

I insert the first of the four bouquets into the vase on her side of the stone but see from the way the wind catches it that it won't stay long. I forgot to bring newspaper. I always stuff some down in the bottom, to hold the flowers in place—the way she used to do when we visited family graves together.

I'll come again tomorrow, Mom. Right now I'm going to go sit in the truck. I'll talk to you from there.

Okay. But you really don't have to go to all that trouble with the flowers.

THE DAY AFTER MEETING WITH STAN, I went to Atwood, in the county northeast of Sherman. Much of the land around that small town is rugged and hilly, dotted in soap weed, the local word for yucca. To me, the hills are beautiful, and I suspect that beauty has a lot to do with why I've never met anyone from that little town who didn't love it. If they no longer live there, they want to move back. Chris Sramek, the guy I went there to see, had made it his life's work to help people do exactly that. He graduated from high school in the mideighties, a very difficult time for farmers and farm communities, and was told that he would have to leave home to find a good job. But he stayed in touch with his classmates, many of whom felt the same way he did about Atwood. Over the years, a dozen or so, like him, had managed to return.

I wanted to talk to him because he directed the High Plains Food Co-op, a group of farm families who raised everything from free-range chickens to yaks and sold their food products in cities along the Front Range. The co-op seemed to be only one of about a thousand ways that Chris and his friends were revitalizing their community. But for me it was the most interesting because here were people who had grown up on farms like ours and who'd left, as I had, but unlike me, they hadn't dismissed or rejected the place when they were young.

Chris told me stories of returning farmers' children who were starting over from the ground up, with egg farms and roving chicken-processing businesses and free-range turkeys. I learned from him and others I spoke to that this type of thing was happening all over the area. One of Sherman County's own county commissioners raised grass-fed bison and cattle and sold the meat both locally and nationally.

I asked Chris what motivated his involvement in organic and natural foods. He said, "Health, health, health." He said it three times because he wasn't talking only about human physical health but the health of the community and the land. He thought of the High Plains, all the way from western North Dakota to the Texas Panhandle, as a single bioregion, the Ogallala Commons. He'd been influenced in this thinking by a nonprofit group of that name, led by a friend of his, Darryl Birkenfeld, also a friend of mine. That's how I'd found out about Chris.

Darryl was a former Catholic priest, educator, and sustainable ag apostle who devoted himself to helping High Plains communities survive. He and his board of directors—Darryl's "five foot soldiers," as Chris called them—advocated taking common responsibility for the "commonwealths," including water. The group's literature featured a map of the Ogallala Aquifer. During the opening ceremony at one conference, which took place, fittingly, in Ogallala, Nebraska, two performing artists held up jars of Ogallala water and called it sacred. The leaders of that organization knew the names of the plants and animals that thrived on the High Plains, whether in the past or present. They knew which tribes had been evicted for their great-grandparents' settlement and the names of those tribes' leaders. They had a sense of history and a conscience. If I were a young person and had encountered thinking like that when I still lived at home, I might never have left.

"Darryl and his five foot soldiers came through here scattering their seeds," said Chris, "and they've been growing ever since." With their help, Chris had organized an entrepreneurs' fair in Atwood ten years ago, and still staged it annually.

A winter storm had been forecast, but after leaving Atwood, I entered the Beaver Valley on the east end and began angling toward Sherman County. It would be perhaps forty miles of back roads in advancing inclement weather, but I wanted to see the Collier spring once again. It was instinct, a form of touching home or paying my respects, not unlike stopping at the cemetery to see Mom, Dad, and Clark, although the spring, I hoped, would still be alive.

On the way I had a stop to make, at the Beaver Creek Lodge, a pheasant-hunting lodge owned by a woman named Alice Hill and her husband, Jeff. Alice was one of these powerhouse foodie entrepreneurs I would expect to meet at a national forum on Slow Food, but never in my own home territory on the Kansas plains. She and Jeff had turned their old stone house, which sat on a grassy ledge beside the creek, into a gorgeous showplace. Like the farmers in the High Plains Food Co-op, they drew on clientele from the Front Range.

Alice, who had always been an avid reader, had learned much about organic gardening and animal husbandry from magazines and books. She grew almost all of the ingredients in the home-cooked meals she served her lodgers. And she had recently gotten a grant to build an agroponics demonstration project, which would add fish and lettuce to her menus year round.

Like Chris, she proved to be openly environmentally minded. "Look at what we've gone to," she said. "Almost all of the land around here is on chemical fallow now and one hundred percent petrochemical inputs." Chemical fallow is one of the forms of no-till agriculture that is getting all the hype. It means fallowing ground to conserve moisture, as we always did, but spraying it instead of tilling it after harvest to kill weeds. The inputs Alice referred to are petroleum-based fertilizer and pesticides plus all of the diesel fuel it takes to run the equipment. As to outputs, those are the crops themselves. Food. "Inputs and outputs." Everyone uses the lingo in farm country, even if, like Alice, they don't buy into the mentality of industrial farming. The same type of thinking views those who purchase the outputs as consumers instead of simply people.

"You see the airplanes spraying crops or you see the spray rigs going back and forth across all of the fields, and you know those chemicals permeate everything," Alice said.

I'd observed one of the giant rigs spraying a field the day before. It had a cab on big wheels and two long wings sticking out, like a giant robotic dragonfly, except it had no tail and there had been nothing beautiful about it. It crossed the field at a faster clip than I'd ever seen a farm implement travel. On the plains you are constantly aware that you are on a planet, but in witnessing an operation like that, with endless miles of farmed land as a backdrop, I felt as if I were on a planet in a science-fiction movie, one that had been completely colonized by aliens.

"It's going to be the next big environmental disaster," Alice said. The resulting cancers and other health harms, she believed, were already catastrophic.

Like Stan, Alice and her husband grew organic wheat. The first year they harvested it and got eighteen dollars a bushel, three times the price of conventional wheat at the time, they paid off debts they'd been carrying for more than twenty years. But she'd been warned at a recent meeting of organic growers that China was beginning to export organic wheat and other cereal grains to the United States. Stan also warned that if everyone grew organic crops, the price would come down. But most important, he, Alice, and other farmers like them are proving that grain grown without chemicals can match yields in their neighbors' conventional fields. Alice suggested that flour milled from U.S. grain should be labeled that way, so that consumers could make a choice. A lot, Alice pointed out, is up to consumers—make that people, us. The more we demand healthy food, the more of it farmers will grow.

I could see that Stan, Chris, Alice, and others like them were making inroads. The changes might not look like much yet, but this type of talking and thinking and doing had never happened before, not in my Kansas. All farming used to be organic, but that was before farmers had any choice. When they chose to go with groundwater pumping and chemicals, they thought of the changes as progress. Now a few people were finally questioning that approach. If there were a few, there would be more.

That morning at breakfast, I'd overheard two older men talking in the restaurant. They sat alone at a table for ten. One of them, glancing at the door every so often, wondered out loud why the usual Sunday-morning crowd hadn't shown up yet. They'd run out of things to talk about. The other one said, "It sure got awful boring yesterday. Inside all day and nothing to do. And nothing good on TV." He followed this with an attempt at a laugh.

I'd seen plenty of people in Goodland who look bored with their lives. But Alice spoke about how, during her years as a school nurse in Atwood, she always loved her involvement with kids because she got to share her life philosophy with them and she didn't have to give them grades. "I told them to look for something to do that inspires you. I told them what that word means. The root means breath or spirit. Choose something that fills your spirit." She said she didn't have time for TV, and I suspected that even when she got old, she would be too active to spare time for it. I hope to be like that too.

Alice pointed out some wild turkeys on the front lawn. I turned to look. Their feathers were copper, black, and tan, with white bars on the wings. "They are beautiful."

"They are," Alice said. "So many colors."

They were also comical, she pointed out. Red wattles dangled from their long, naked necks, and they stopped after each step to gawk in all directions, open beaked. Looking at them, I noticed that the sky was getting grayer and the wind had picked up.

Quickly, Alice gave me a tour of her agroponics project, contained in a brand-new building with a cutting-edge heating system under the floor and special insulating wall panels and blue-plastic tanks for the tilapia and other bigger tanks for the lettuce that she would grow in water enriched by effluent from the fish. Dashing upwind, we entered a shed where she'd already started her broccoli and cauliflower plants and where she grew microgreens in trays and oat grass so that her chickens always had fresh greens in their diet. Wow! I thought. She grows greens for her chickens. We raced past the Dutch Belted milk cow that she'd driven to Wisconsin to pick up and which delivered seven gallons of milk each summer day, and the two sweet and friendly hogs, also an obscure heritage breed. She pointed at the coops where her chickens were spending their day—too cold out for anything but hunkering down.

With the wind sweeping me toward my pickup, and Alice toward the shelter of her house, she shouted that it had been the Laura Ingalls Wilder books that had first inspired her, as a child. "They used *everything.* They relied on themselves. Nothing went to waste. I mean *nothing.*"

That had been Mom's philosophy too. All of us plains kids were raised that way.

3

I TURNED RIGHT INSTEAD OF LEFT OUT OF ALICE'S DRIVE, ALTHOUGH LEFT WOULD HAVE BEEN THE SANER CHOICE. If I die out here today, I'll deserve to, I thought. What plainsperson didn't know the dangers presented by a blizzard on any road, let alone one that would be abandoned by everyone else on a day like this? I could end up in a ditch with engine damage and no way to run the heater and wouldn't be discovered until morning, when some rancher came along to check on his cattle.

But I wanted to follow the water home. Chris had a mission. So did Darryl, his mentor. So did Alice. The Ogallala was mine. I wanted to, needed to, see it. It was the same thing I'd been doing in 2001, when I'd found my first spring on the Little Beaver and met Ward.

I thought the creek would be running low, if at all, but the ponds at Alice's place had been full. I'd never seen them in late winter, I reflected, when the ground began to thaw. Perhaps they normally overflowed this time of year.

Because drought had returned, and it was bad, more than half the counties in the United States had been designated natural disaster areas in 2012. Among them, Sherman County had only 9.59 inches of precipitation, the third driest year since 1895, when records were first kept. Less than ten inches defines a place as desert. Sherman's dryland wheat yields had been good despite the drought because wheat can survive on stored ground moisture. But all of that had been used up now. The winter wheat farmers had planted in September had failed to grow. They expected little if any crop this year.

Irrigation farmers make up for low rainfall by pumping more. In Texas, aquifer levels had dropped more last year than in the previous twenty-five. In southwest Kansas, levels had dropped more than four feet the year before last and three feet last year. In our district, 2012 declines had exceeded two feet. As if drought stressing the aquifer were not enough, the number of corn acres in the nation had expanded almost 20 percent since the ethanol boom had begun. Of the corn crop, 40 percent was now going into ethanol, spurred on by a government mandate requiring that fifteen billion gallons of it be mixed with the nation's gasoline by 2015.

Ethanol is not an efficient replacement for gasoline. Cars don't go as far on gas mixed with it as they do on gas alone; almost as much fossil fuel is required to make ethanol as it is supposed to replace; and at a time when drought is driving down yields on food crops, growing corn for fuel robs even more mouths of food than even growing corn for cows does. At least some lucky people get to eat the cows.

Hardly anyone thinks the ethanol policy is a good idea anymore—other than segments of the ag and ethanol industries, and all corn farmers supposedly. But I'd talked to many farmers who knew they had to stop using so much water.

Just that morning over breakfast a farmer told me that in some parts of the county, irrigation was already in trouble. "At the end of the season, they have to change the nozzles on their sprinklers just to get the water to go all the way out to the ends of 'em." He knew people who lived near Stan, the organic farmer I'd interviewed, whose house water pressure went down when the well engines were running.

Stan hadn't mentioned this. But even though he does irrigate some of his crops, he said, "I know we need to do something about the water. We're using too much of it, and it's going to be gone." The Smoky Hill River, which used to run through his place, once had ponds in it large enough for his father to swim in when he was a kid, but now it was completely dry on his farm. I told him I'd been appalled when Ward and I visited the Sherman State Fishing Lake and discovered it was empty. Stan said that as teenagers, he and his brother had waded into that lake as it was going down in order to rescue as many channel catfish as they could. They'd moved them into the ponds all the irrigation farmers had back then to catch the runoff from their irrigated fields—like the one I'd tried to swim in back in the eighties.

Meanwhile, nearby cities are also running out of water. Within fifty years, the Bureau of Reclamation predicts that demands on the Colorado River, which brings water not only to southwestern cities but also to Colorado's Front Range, will exceed supply by 3.2 to 8.0 million acre feet.

"Don't think Denver doesn't have an eye on our water," said my father's old friend when I'd met with him and his wife years before, in my mother's living room. "The legislators in the cities want water for their people. They ain't gonna much worry about us out here gettin' a little water or not. They're gonna try to tie up all the water they can."

The Ogallala Aquifer is a mastodon in the room, being driven to extinction on the plains east of Denver. It isn't talked about much in public because farmers have senior rights to the water. But a question begs to be asked, and it will be very soon: Why are a few thousand plains farmers allowed to pump nineteen million acre feet out of the aquifer each year? That is more than half again as much as the annual flow of the Colorado River, which brings water to thirty million people.

When I told the farmer over breakfast what I'd discovered in my research, with special emphasis on that one statistic that never failed to shock people—nineteen million acre feet out of the aquifer each year, more than half again as much water as flows down the Colorado River in that same amount of time—he said, "It's not going to stop until ethanol stops."

"And the Farm Program subsidies for irrigated crops," I said.

"Those too," he concurred.

But no large environmental organization is fighting this fight. Maybe because you can't see the aquifer, and it's in a low-density population area where to call someone an environmentalist is an insult. A Republican governor did recently get the law changed in Kansas. You don't have to "use or lose" your water rights anymore, and Kansas now requires flow meters on all irrigation wells.

In Texas, the High Plains Water District passed a fifty-fifty rule mandating reductions meant to ensure that at least 50 percent of what the aquifer held in 2010 will still be available for irrigation in 2060. But as myopic as that rule is—what about enough water to *live on* in 2060 and beyond?—enforcement of it will be hampered by irrigators' resistance. And large parts of that North Texas district, like many other pockets throughout the Plains, have already run out of water.

Water-quality issues are also beginning to proliferate. In a 2009 study, 14 percent of Ogallala wells tested by the U.S. Geological Survey contained one or more pesticide. Most common was atrazine. This weed killer has been used on cornfields everywhere over the years even though it is a known endocrine disrupter, suspected of interfering with the human reproductive system and of retarding fetal development. In 5 percent of the wells, nitrate levels either equaled or exceeded EPA safety standards. High concentrations of nitrates in infants' drinking water deprive their blood of oxygen, causing a condition known as blue-baby syndrome, a serious threat to lifelong health and fatal if left untreated. During the coming decades, contaminant levels will continue creeping down into the Ogallala and up the charts as more wells exceed levels safe for human consumption.

Most of the focus, however, has been on declines. "The water-level decline of the Ogallala Aquifer is the largest single water-management concern in the U.S.," says Mario Sophocleous, a senior Kansas Geological Survey scientist and one of the leading experts on the aquifer. The nation depends on the aquifer for 30 percent of its irrigated crops. As that water vanishes, farmers will suffer, but so will everyone else. Food prices will escalate. The economy will be forced to absorb the inflationary costs at the same time that grain exports diminish.

But the economy will be the least of our problems if we continue to waste water at this rate. At current usage levels, and if efficiency gains are not made, world water demands are likely to exceed supplies by 40 percent within twenty years. This conclusion was reached not by an environmental organization, but in a study funded by the World Bank and by companies such as Coca-Cola, Nestlé, and Syngenta AG. There is really no polite way to put it: Now is not the time to be pissing away the nation's largest aquifer.

So I HAD PLENTY OF THINGS TO be bummed about concerning the Ogallala, and I was duly bummed. But I had also been talking with people who were passionate about topics that I'd seldom heard discussed in Kansas. My relationships here were expanding just when I thought they were over forever. Those relationships weren't only with people.

As I continued my drive through the Beaver Valley, my pickup kept veering toward the ditch, my wheels catching in the gravel just as Dad's used to do when he got absorbed by neighbors' crops. What I got absorbed by was the beauty in the rare places that remained like this, where there were no crops. To my eye, the buffalo grass on the hills was beautiful even in the winter, although it was more like a carpet than grass this year. There hadn't been much growth due to the drought, but the subtle and surprising colors were as enchanting as ever.

During my lifetime, I've tried to duplicate the plains palette when painting the walls of houses I've lived in. But no sky-blue ever looked like real sky, and no pale green ever came close to evoking a buffalo grass pasture. Although predominantly grayish-brown with only a hint of green this late in the winter, the grass also had patches of salmon, and even strips of neon yellow. No single or solid color anywhere—everything complex, everything variegated, like the human eye and human consciousness. That is why coming upon a patch of wild prairie affirms me so much. Wild life recognizes wild life. All life is wild at its center. We need the natural world to know ourselves.

The sky was low for a change, and droplets were beginning to splatter my windshield. I was in a race with the storm and knew I should turn south toward the interstate and the safety of Goodland, but there was a lot of water in the Beaver, way more than I expected. I had to keep stopping to roll my window down and breathe the cold, moist air and gaze at the marshes—large pools of water shimmering silver-black, surrounded by tall, russet valley grasses. In the middle of one large pond paddled a black and white duck. I vowed to look it up on the Internet when I got back to the little guesthouse where I was staying.

The Ogallala was all right today, there in that meadow. Seeing it that way, I felt as I had when Mom was in the nursing home and I would go in and find her bright and chipper and having a good day. The nearer she drew to the end, the more it meant to see her and be in her presence. Being in that relationship wasn't a choice. We simply were in a relationship. It meant helping her fight for her life, advocating with the doctors, making sure she was getting the physical therapy and medicines she needed, and sleeping on the floor by her bed when the nurse began administering morphine.

Same with the aquifer. I'd been on this Ogallala road since birth, just as I'd been on the road with my mother since birth. I'd grown up slaking my thirst with Ogallala water and bathing in it. I'd gotten much of my financial support from Ogallala crops. And ever since I was a young woman and had knocked open the pipe gates myself, I'd been thinking Ogallala thoughts. Like my mother, the Ogallala had sacrificed a lot on my behalf. I wasn't going to get off that road anytime soon, and I didn't want to.

Even if it did mean abandoning it in the here and now so I could get back to Goodland alive. I didn't even reach Sherman County before I had to give up. The sky was closing in, not only visually, but palpably.

The water in the corners of my windshield had turned to ice. I got to town just as the storm hit, and the blinding force and fury of it caused me to shake my head at my bottomless imprudence when in nature's thrall and my infinite good luck.

I watched the storm from the window of a pleasant little cottage belonging to a new Goodland friend. I first stayed there when I gave a book talk at the Goodland library a couple of years before. In thanking the woman, I confided that I had feared what it would be like to stay in a motel in my own hometown. "You will never have to stay in a motel here," she'd told me. "Our guesthouse will be your home away from home."

It had been a long drought, and then a long winter, but new life was setting in. Nestled securely as the snow flew, I logged onto my hostess's Web server and discovered that my duck had likely been a male common goldeneye.

4

AND NOW I AM SITTING IN THE GRAVEYARD, STARING AT TWO HEAD-STONES, AND FEELING GOOD AND BAD AT THE SAME TIME. The way we do when our own lives continue to unfold, but the lives that gave us life and others that gave our lives meaning have ended. Finished, *fini*, supposedly. Except Mom and I are still talking, and I complained most of my adult life that we couldn't talk at all.

You have a new great-grandson, Mom. His name is Indy.

Indy? What kind of name is that?

I know. It's not traditional, but it's what they chose. I didn't like it either at first, but I'm getting used to it. Not just used to it. I like it. He's the greatest little boy, Mom. So smart and cute, and his heart is full of love.

It is? Mom says. I can hear the joy in her voice, although the only empirical evidence of my mother's existence in this place is a block of very cold, almost-black granite.

Yes, and Jake is doing fine, Mom. He's a certified nursing assistant, and Kate wants to be a hairdresser. They're getting a late start because they were busy trying to reinvent society more to their liking.

Kind of like someone else I know.

There's one thing I need to tell you, Mom. I should be telling this to Dad, but I mainly want to talk to Mom now because it's her voice I hear. *I need to tell you about the farm.*

Everywhere I drove in Sherman County, I found that any land that had less than a thirty-degree incline had now been farmed. Lots and lots of corn. More than ever. Lots of thick wheat stubble too, "sprayed clean" as my father's old friend had said, leaving nothing alive. But when I came to our farm, I discovered only corn stubble from one end to the other. Both dryland and irrigated. All corn right up through what had been the last of our pasture.

Before going to Goodland, I'd braced myself for this by visiting the Kansas Geological Survey Web site. The blue line representing our observation well confirmed my fears. The line's angle of decline had indeed steepened. I studied the related numbers for an inordinate hour or more. The annual drops in water levels weren't really that much worse than when we owned the place, I rationalized. And at least part of the decline would have been due to returning and intensifying drought. But seeing all of this corn now, I knew that the linebackers had to be placing much greater demands on the wells than we had even during those drought years that had helped persuade me to sell.

The farmstead was still there, although they'd torn down the house Mom and Dad lived in when they were first married and that Jake and I had once lived in. The sheep barn had burned down a year after we sold. Someone had been welding and a spark had lodged in the old timber unnoticed. Or so we'd been told. Maybe they'd just wanted to get rid of the barn so there could be more corn. They'd even taken out three rows of the windbreak we'd planted. Only the cedars were left, with corn right up to them. It couldn't be good for the ground to have corn on it year after year. Corn is a big plant and must have space to grow. So its stubble leaves lots of bare ground to erode in wind or heavy rains, whereas wheat stubble is thick and protects the ground much better. We had always rotated corn with soybeans, a legume that fixed nitrogen in the soil. But forget natural systems. As Alice Hill had said, it was all petrochemical inputs now.

"You don't know what you let in here," one neighbor, who was a pallbearer at Mom's funeral, told me afterward. "They're already buying other quarters."

And Stan had said, "My place won't ever go to somethin' like that. They're like a vacuum cleaner. They've been buying land up in Rawlins County, where Becky is from too."

It doesn't help much knowing that ours is a common story or that what happened to us is happening everywhere on the Great Plains and in the Midwest. I know that we also brought it on ourselves. I sit in my truck, an ant steamrolled by my own confused and confusing interests as much as by history, and try to imagine what it will be like if there really is an afterlife, as Mom thought, and I have to explain this to Dad. In ag school he learned all about soil conservation and protecting his land from erosion using contours, and rotating crops, and browsing livestock in his stubble fields. He was gradually abandoning all that too and moving in this direction, but he never would have gone this far.

What would Dad say if he knew, Mom?

It's all right. We talked about it. He said it would be all right.

Of course she isn't going to tell me anything new. Just the same old things are replaying in my head. But that's okay. They are the things I need to hear. And maybe I hear them in a new way.

Bruce and I didn't heed Mom much whenever he and I were in the same room together. Even when she wasn't repeating herself, her voice got lost in our eagerness to impress each other. At least that's what it always felt like to me. It took me a long time as an adult to understand that he'd seen me as a rival in childhood. There was always that competitive charge between us. Then after Clark died, we were the only ones left, the only contemporaries. We needed to understand each other, were perhaps more capable of understanding each other than anyone because we shared a family and a past, but we never took it far enough into actual understanding. Meanwhile, the treasure that gave us content to talk about as we discussed its disposition to grain bins or banks was Mom's, earned through a lifetime of garden growing, chicken tending, cow milking, bum lamb feeding, meal making, housecleaning, husband tending, and kid rearing. And she just kept repeating herself, being ignored. I am so grateful she repeated herself now.

Forgive yourself, Terry also said. Her words had forgiveness in them. That's why I cried on hearing them. Taking a more tender view of my own fallibility really helps.

The one other forgiving thing is the land itself. The high point of this trip was seeing the half section of Conservation Reserve Program land we'd withheld from the sale. Bruce had bid it into the government program because it had been too hilly to farm in the first place, but Dad had gotten greedy at some point and broken it out. That type of greediness is rampant now, and many farmers have abandoned their contracts, plowed their CRP land and planted it back to corn or wheat. More than nine and a half million acres have been returned to cropland since the ethanol boom began. That would have happened to our CRP land too if we'd sold it, but we kept it in reserve partly as a retirement plan for Ron. We signed over the remaining proceeds of the contract to him.

After driving through our corn-blighted farm, I turned onto the track along the fence line, hoping for respite, and that's what I found. Respite in beauty. A hill rose in the center of the field, so when I switched off the engine and got out, it blocked my view of the road. As was customary with CRP contracts, Ron had planted the field with a mixture of grasses that were more native to places east of us. They were bunch grasses, meaning they didn't form a turf and grew in clumps. The tallest was little bluestem. I never understood why it was called that, because its most distinctive trait seemed to be how red it turned in the fall and winter. It liked the low, moist spots best. On the hill, blond clumps of another type of grass—some kind of fescue?—formed a bumpy silhouette against the sky. The pasture that Bruce had traded off years ago adjoined this land, so I could stand as I had in the old

Carlson farm's canyon pasture and imagine grass going on forever in every direction.

I was once a purist and didn't like the way CRP grasses looked compared with the locally indigenous buffalo grass, but the plow's incursion over the last few years made me grateful for what I could get. Most people would think the bunch grasses were more beautiful, and they were definitely more dramatic. Besides, if it was buffalo grass I wanted, I could find it there too, in small patches that would most likely spread and replace the others eventually because it was the true native.

An awareness of the land's health coursed through me, whereas on the flat part of the farm, I had been painfully aware that the land was being enslaved and abused. Standing there proved to me that it could all be put back someday. That would be the one advantage to running out of well water or of drought. If grain crops couldn't be grown here anymore, there would be horrible consequences for the world's people, especially the poor, but the land would return to grass and it would heal. Ever since I was a child, I'd been thrilled to imagine the world "pre-us." I wasn't exactly thrilled to imagine it "post-us," but I did take some comfort knowing that it might recover from our brief and injurious tenure.

I noticed a large object in the distance. Rectangular and gray, it lay in the crook of the valley. I wended my way through waist-high bluestem and the brittle branches of large wildflowers. I would have to wait for summer to see them in bloom and find out what they were. As I drew nearer the object, I began to notice animal trails. I stopped to photograph one particularly clear paw print, which might have been that of a kit fox, or possibly a bobcat because I didn't see any claw marks. I'd always heard that was how you could tell between canine and feline prints, because cats can retract their claws. What a joy it was to imagine either of those animals alive and well here!

Arrival at the object confirmed my suspicion that it was a wildlife waterer, installed by Ron as part of the CRP contract. It had a corrugated tin roof built low to the ground and at a slant to collect rainwater, which flowed into gutters and down into a plastic holding tank. The tank had a hole cut in the top large enough for animals to reach in and get a drink. That afternoon, the tank was a quarter full and had ice floating on top. I scooped out the mud that had collected in the rain gutter, wiped my hands on my jeans, stood up, and gloried in the survival of the animals that had made those trails.

Looking around the budding grassland, I understood what I love most about this place. It is the sun. The plains are high and bright, wide and exhilarating. To be outside here is to be on top of the world, lifted up and exposed to sun from all directions. Yes, the sun more than anything. Knowing it the way I do, it knowing me, so intimately and in every aging crease, many of which it caused to form, and being comfortable with so much light and openness tells me I am native here.

I AM ESPECIALLY AWARE OF THE SUN now as I follow my shadow across the snow in the cemetery, carrying flowers and a newspaper I bought from the machine at the diner. And always this shadow traveling with you everywhere. It brings a certain level of self-awareness. You know you exist and that you exist in relation to the sun and to the world. It makes you aware of the imprint you are making on the land.

I don't have to worry about walking on their graves, because beside them are a couple of empty plots Mom and Dad purchased for Bruce and me. But my remaining brother and I won't be buried anywhere, not if our wishes are obeyed. He wants to have his ashes scattered on a certain bend of a river he loves, and Jake is to divide my ashes between the canyon pasture on the old Carlson farm and the rock-house hill, in the Mojave. It troubles me imagining how difficult it will be for him to arrange a ceremony, because neither of us lives where he grew up anymore. Even if we'd stayed in Laramie, he would have had to think it through. Nothing ever has to be thought through in Goodland. You just make arrangements with the church your relative belonged to, and the pastor and the funeral-home director walk you through it, the way they walked Bruce and me through it with Mom.

To have deep roots in a place means having dead buried there. It is almost that literal, the dead forming your bond to the earth and to the others whose dead lie buried there. I always had that bond whether I knew it or not. Whether I bemoaned the loss of it or failed to have the meaningful conversations I wanted to have or couldn't get back in by way of a man. After this trip, I am more sure of that than ever.

Daffodils for each of you. See, Mom?

In this weather and with a newspaper you had to pay good money for? It's a bunch of dumned foolishness if you ask me.

The stones look beautiful with the flowers beside them. I always used to think that decorating graves was pointless, but I don't think that anymore. I have two sets of grandparents, several aunts and uncles, and one cousin buried in this cemetery, but it would take me all day to find them. *I'm sorry, Mom. I don't have time.*

That's okay. You should be getting home to Jim.

Mom, Dad, Clark. How is it possible that they live so fully in my mind yet they aren't here anymore? That no matter how much I imagine conversing with them, the responses are only memories? I turn to leave but change my mind. I need to say a fitting good-bye, so I kneel, knees in the snow. I put my hands together. I say "Dear God," because the word, however inadequate, acknowledges agency in the universe and I want there to be agency. "Help me accept the loss of these people who gave me everything and asked for so little. Thank you, Mom. Thank you, Dad. Thank you, Clark. I love you. Amen."

I follow my shadow back to the truck.

ACKNOWLEDGMENTS

"Perhaps the soil of your narrative needs to be turned once again," said visual artist Joan Waltemath at the Jentel artists' residency I attended in Wyoming. Earlier that evening, I had read aloud from what I thought was a finished chapter of this book. I have been grateful to Joan ever since for voicing then what would become my operant metaphor throughout the many years and drafts that followed.

My sincere thanks to the members of my writing group, who nurtured me through those plow-ups and replantings: Elisabeth Hyde, Lisa Jones, Marilyn Krysl, and Gail Storey. Many thanks to others I unwittingly called upon to explain how much work yet awaited me. Abby Bair, Marian Clark, Mary Galle, Janis Hallowell, Joy Harris, Kathy Kaiser, Vicki Lindner, Laura Pritchett, and Jessica Tauber read and commented on entire drafts. Jody Berman, Chavawn Kelley, John Price, Priscilla Stuckey, and Elizabeth Wrenn read portions.

I am grateful to David Chernikoff, who helped me come to terms with the sale of the farm and convey that understanding onto the page and to Terry Ray for her wise counsel in that matter. Thank you Stephen Collector, for the head shots; Joy and Dick Hayden, for your hospitality in Goodland; Tony Hoch, for the use of your cabin on Lake Hattie; Sharon Palmquist, for forwarding me articles on the Ogallala; Lee Rentz, for the cover photo; and Steve Sutter, for loaning me your library card.

To those whom I've interviewed or consulted over the years, thanks for your patience and honest sharing. Among these were Kim Barker, Darryl Birkenfeld, Scott Bontz, Wayne Bossert, Rex Buchanan, Robert Buddemeier, Beulah Cress, Alice Hill, Bob Hooper, Charles Howe, Doug Irvin, Mark Jones, Joan Kenny, David Kromm, Freddie Lamm, David Leonard, Bob Mailander, Tom Potter, Becky and Stan Purvis, Marios Sophocleous, Chris Sramek, Donald Worster, and Tobe Zweygardt.

Thanks to Peter Barnes, Katie Christensen, Sharon Dynak, Mary Jane Edwards, Neltje, Raymond Plank, and all the others who directed or provided refuges where it was safe for creative energy to flow. At Jentel, I discovered and found the courage to begin the first of many rewrites. At Ucross, I remember with special fondness my fellow resident Susan Gordon Lydon, who, although she was terminally ill, kept me laughing while convincing me it was okay to write honestly about sex. At Mesa Refuge I received encouragement from coresidents Jane Juska and Dan Nickerson. At Brush Creek, I was given a womblike cottage where what really was, at long last, a final draft found its way onto the page.

Here at home, the Boulder Media Women provided me with a warmly supportive professional community. I also received generous advice and referrals from Joe Blair, John Calderazzo, Rosemary Carstens, Lisa Hamilton, Celeste Labadie, and Florence Williams. Thanks to Elizabeth Howard and Julie Heins for your assistance.

I regret that I was not able to do full justice to the story of the plainspeople whose lives ours supplanted. For any who wish to learn more, I recommend Donald J. Berthrong's *The Southern Cheyennes*, William Chalfant's *Cheyennes and Horse Soldiers*, Stan Hoig's *The Sand Creek Massacre*, George Hyde's *Life of George Bent*, John Monnett's *Massacre at Cheyenne Hole*, and all of the seminal histories on the Cheyenne by George Bird Grinnell.

Thank you, Jo Ann Beard, for your inspired craft advice and much needed encouragement and advocacy. Thank you, Emma Sweeney, for your passionate representation. Had you not championed this book, I might have given up and plowed it back to dust. I am also grateful to Noah Ballard, who helped me publish related essays. I have been blessed by the counsel of a discerning, insightful, and accomplished editor, Carole DeSanti. Thank you, Carole, for believing in the story and working tirelessly to help me perfect it. Thanks also to Chris Russell, who smoothed the publishing process, and to the entire Viking Penguin team. Your professionalism, generosity, and flexibility exceeded even my optimistic expectations.

For enduring my version of our shared truths, thanks to my beloved son, Jake; my brother, Bruce; and all others whose partial stories landed in these pages. And thank you, Jim, for your insights, and for believing in me and my work.